Physical Education Futures

Can we imagine a future in which physical education in schools no longer exists?

In this controversial and powerful meditation on physical education, David Kirk argues that a number of different futures are possible. Kirk argues that multi-activity, sport-based forms of physical education have been dominant in schools since the mid-twentieth century and that they have been highly resistant to change. The practice of physical education has focused on the transmission of decontextualised sport-techniques to large classes of children who possess a range of interests and abilities, where learning rarely moves beyond introductory levels. Meanwhile, the academicisation of physical education teacher education since the 1970s has left teachers less well prepared to teach this programme than they were previously, suggesting that the futures of school physical education and physical education teacher education are intertwined.

Kirk explores three future scenarios for physical education, arguing that the most likely short-term future is 'more of the same'. He makes an impassioned call for radical reform in the longer term, arguing that without it physical education faces extinction. No other book makes such bold use of history to interrogate the present and future configurations of the discipline, nor offers such a wide-ranging critique of physical culture and school physical education. This book is essential reading for all serious students and scholars of physical education and the history and theory of education.

David Kirk is Alexander Chair in Physical Education and Sport at the University of Bedfordshire. This book was written while he was Dean of the Carnegie Faculty of Sport and Education at Leeds Metropolitan University. He is editor of the Routledge journal *Physical Education and Sport Pedagogy*.

Physical Education Futures

David Kirk

Routledge
Taylor & Francis Group

LONDON AND NEW YORK

First published 2010
by Routledge
2 Park Square, Milton Park, Abingdon, Oxon, OX14 4RN

Simultaneously published in the USA and Canada
by Routledge
711 Third Avenue, New York, NY 10017

Routledge is an imprint of the Taylor & Francis Group, an informa business

First issued in paperback 2011

© 2010 David Kirk

Typeset in Goudy by
Taylor & Francis Books

British Library Cataloguing in Publication Data
A catalogue record for this book is available from the British Library

Library of Congress Cataloging in Publication Data
Kirk, David, 1958-
Physical education futures / David Kirk.
    p. cm.
  Includes bibliographical references.
  1. Physical education and training. I. Title.
  GV341.K565 2010
  613.7—dc22
                          2009003841

ISBN10: 0-415-54993-0 (hbk)
ISBN10: 0-415-67736-X (pbk)
ISBN10: 0-203-87462-5 (ebk)

ISBN13: 978-0-415-54993-6 (hbk)
ISBN13: 978-0-415-67736-3 (pbk)
ISBN13: 978-0-203-87462-2 (ebk)

Contents

And I? How can I not be product of my times? Look to Mr Bligh's bad language, I say, and all that that may mean. Our lives are a double helix of past and present. We are the language of our representations. We are caught in our webs of significance.

(Greg Dening, 1993, *Mr Bligh's Bad Language*, p. 9)

Preface

> Although people differ in their assessments of the value of school physical education, both while they are students and later as adults, a significant number report having learned to dislike physically active play, to disrespect physical education teachers, and to devalue their own capacity to learn movement skills. Given the ostensible purposes of most programs, that constitutes a fair indication that the conventional offering is a failure. Nobody needs to be blamed. We have a programmatic lemon. It is made so by design flaws, the limitations placed on teachers by workplace conditions, changes in youth culture, and the inexorable forces of history. There are no villains. It's just that making lemonade with what we have is beyond most of us, and it probably wouldn't yield the product we really want in any case.
>
> (Locke, 1992: 363)

This book is about physical education futures. The plural is important, since I will argue that there is more than one possible future for physical education. In order to arrive at a position of proposing what those futures might be, there are several other tasks I need to undertake that are contained in the statement by Locke. He claims that the design flaws in our currently dominant version of school physical education are so serious that our subject in this form is beyond rescue. We have, in his colourful prose, a 'programmatic lemon'. I believe, with some considerable regret, that Locke is correct in this assessment, and so one of my tasks in this book is to assist you, the reader, to confront this unpalatable truth by carefully assessing and compiling the evidence on where we are now. For anyone committed to a healthy and sustainable future for physical education in schools, this may make uncomfortable reading. But along with Locke, I believe that unless we first of all face up to and fully acknowledge the extreme seriousness of our current situation, until we grasp the nature of the problem, we cannot begin to contemplate a positive future.

Having established precisely the nature of the design faults in the currently dominant form of physical education, my next task will be to spell out in detail 'the inexorable forces of history' that have led us to where we are.

Without a historical analysis, we can know only part of our 'webs of significance', as Dening (1993) puts it. If our lives are, as he claims, 'a double helix of past and present', then ignorance of the past means we are trapped in and transfixed by the immediate present. Preoccupation with the here and now might create an impression of being 'up with the pace' in a manner consistent with so much of the frenzied 'innovation' in physical education over the past two decades. A wealth of research literature has revealed, however, that this preoccupation has not brought about real, sustainable or desirable change. Moreover, when we get too close up to something, we are apt to miss the bigger picture. A key task of this book is to map out that bigger picture, not just in terms of a version of the past, but also in relation to the world outside the school. It is only then that we can see why Locke might mention changes in culture as another force to be accounted for in shaping the contours of our current predicament.

It is only then, too, that we can appreciate the insightfulness of Locke's claim that no-one needs to be blamed for the current state of affairs, that there are no villains. Indeed, a study of the modern history of physical education shows we are where we are mainly as an unintended consequence of a fierce struggle by our predecessors over many decades for respect within the academy of higher education and a place in the school curriculum just like other subjects. Indeed, the book will show that we are where we are now because they were so successful in this struggle. So there are no villains, there is no-one to blame. But at the same time this does not exonerate us from a responsibility to understand the current state of affairs and, once the problem is grasped, from the need to act.

Of course, we can act only with due consideration of the constraints working on us at any point in time. Locke notes the 'limitations placed on teachers by workplace conditions' as a real constraint on their ability to 'make lemonade' from the resources and opportunities available to them. I will argue that making lemonade with what resources they have has been increasingly difficult for teachers as a result not just of their workplace conditions fashioned by the school as an institution but also by their training programmes in higher education. Another task of this book then is to consider, after we have identified possible futures for physical education, who can do what to create conditions for change towards desired, culturally relevant and educationally defensible futures.

This book is not about predicting the future of physical education. Nor does it argue for any particular future over another, though it does attempt to assess the probability of particular future scenarios. As other futures writers who appear at various points in this study have been at pains to point out, the task of futures research is not about getting predictions right. It is, instead, about preparing ourselves as best we can to meet whatever challenges arise by having a sense of what those challenges might be. Being well prepared to meet the challenges of an uncertain future requires a disposition to imagine beyond the present. This is possible only for individuals who understand something of how the double helix of past and present intertwines. Currently, I believe that the physical education community knows little of its past and thus often misunderstands what should be the urgent priorities of the present. We are then arguably poorly prepared collectively for physical education futures. It is this situation that this book seeks to make a small contribution to redressing.

I don't expect all readers, or even most, to agree with my selection and interpretation of the evidence and the arguments I will claim this evidence supports. Why should they since we come to topics such as this with quite different histories of personal and professional experience? What is more important to me than agreement with my point of view is that others shape their own positions with at least the care and consideration with which I have tried to construct mine. If we could, as a professional community of physical educators, achieve at least this, we would move some considerable distance to a form of scholarly practice that I do believe is essential for a sustainable and healthy future.

The arguments of this book took only a few months to put together. They have, however, taken considerably longer to formulate. This specific project was conceived as I was preparing my inaugural professorial lecture at Leeds Metropolitan University (as it was, Leeds Carnegie University as it is now) in the first half of 2006. Too many colleagues have contributed to my work on the social construction of physical education over the years to name individually here, but I would like to offer thanks in particular to everyone who contributed to the Physical Education Futures conference held in Leeds in June 2006 which in so many ways has informed my thinking on this topic. Others have also contributed in less direct ways, and I thank them too for being a supportive community of colleague-scholars, rich in ideas and sincere in their commitment to the physical education of young people. The book was written in the second half of 2008 while on sabbatical leave from Leeds Metropolitan University, and for providing the opportunity for this leave and for the leadership that inspired me to take this study forward, I thank Professor Simon Lee.

David Kirk, January 2009

1 The social construction of physical education

Present, past and future

Subject fields or disciplines have been invented; they are socially constructed and constituted by humans.

(Lawson, 1991: 286)

We will always be in the middle of the story of our society, and thus judgement of the significance and value of what has already happened is inseparable from judgement of the present, and of the feasibility and desirability of possible futures.

(Chanan and Gilchrist, 1974: 62)

The act of defining physical education goes somewhat beyond the statement of beliefs, values and aspirations, important though these statements may be. Physical education is defined by what is said, done and written in its name, as are all other school subjects and university disciplines. It is, in the words of Ivor Goodson (1997) and of Hal Lawson (1991), socially constructed. So when some physical educators bemoan a lack of consensus among their peers about the nature of their subject, when a number of apparently competing written definitions of physical education vie for their attention, and when they point to a proliferation of titles for university departments, they overlook the enduring commonalities of physical education practice, particularly in terms of what people say and do in the subject's name. This practice conforms to a concept of physical education – what I will in this book refer to as 'the idea of the idea of physical education'[1] or the id[2] – that has remained more or less intact since around the middle of the last century, transcends the national borders of economically advanced countries and other nations that have had some formal association with these countries, and that has been highly resistant to change.

I use the expressions 'more or less' and 'around' because each country, each region, each state and each city can demonstrate differences in terms of key events and moments, outstanding leaders, local forces and particular circumstances. For instance, Britain resisted the overt influence of militarism in favour of a more therapeutic form of physical training in the early 1900s when it adopted the Swedish system of gymnastics as its preference for elementary schools while in the same period Australia located its elementary school physical training squarely within a national scheme of compulsory military cadet training. Or, more precisely, and to make my point, the neonate Australian states of Victoria and Queensland, the two main sources of evidence for *Schooling Bodies* (Kirk, 1998a), adopted the cadet scheme, though each in its own, inimitable, way. Regardless of where we look and with only a few exceptions, we will find histories of physical education dating from the late 1800s to the present that show differences in nuanced detail. But the differences are for the most part less significant than the similarities.[2]

Physical educators, perhaps more than educators in other subjects and disciplines, have a history of passionate advocacy for their specialism. Indeed, this characteristic would be one of the things that they have in common, across nations, cultures, gender and time. Why this is so we can only speculate; perhaps it has been something to do with living in a marginal role, as Leo Hendry (1976) put it, as the pre-eminently most embodied subject of an otherwise mostly cerebral curriculum. Whatever the reason for their passion, physical educators have typically held strong opinions about their subject and have felt compelled to express these, sometimes forcefully, to whomever might listen. This characteristic in itself has been partly responsible for the enduring but misleading idea that physical education is a field riven by difference, where disputatious individuals and groups offer rival philosophies of their subject. At least, the idea has been misleading since around the 1970s onwards, when the current id^2 of physical education was consolidated in secondary schools and teacher-education colleges. Prior to the 1970s, as a shift from gymnastics to sport-techniques was bedding down, the field was indeed riven by noisy disputes, as I pointed out in *Defining Physical Education* (Kirk, 1992a). Since that time, a proliferation of definitions of physical education allied to a rapid expansion of programme content and considerable variance between schools in terms of what is offered as physical education have together combined to create the impression of a field that is amorphous (Proctor, 1984), an impression that succeeds in masking the commonality of practice within the id^2 of physical education-as-sport-techniques. I suggest too that at a more philosophical level, many (though not all) disputatious physical educators have misunderstood the object of their disagreements (Locke, 1998: 248); as one example, those physical educators who insist that 'physical education' and 'sport' are such different phenomena that no definition of physical education should even refer to sport, as is the case with the National Curriculum Physical Education in England and Wales (see Green, 1998; Penney and Chandler, 2000: 74), when in fact, as I aim to show, the currently dominant id^2 of physical education has been grounded in a particular version of sport from at least the 1950s.

So what is the practice of physical education that informs far and wide this id^2 and that is apparently so enduring and resistant to change?

Penney and Chandler (2000) claim, in their paper 'Physical education: What future(s)?', that the enduring and resistant characteristic of physical education is its focus on 'activities', by which they mean physical activity. In making this claim they are I think on the right track. But it is not just the fact of its practical nature that constructs and constitutes the id[2] of physical education. Indeed, I see this fact as far less problematic for physical education futures than they. The nub of the matter is what people *do* with these physical activities, that is, *how* they are practised. What teachers and pupils mainly do in the name of physical education is teaching and repetitious practice of the techniques of a wide range of individual and team games, aquatic activities such as swimming, gymnastics, athletics, exercise for fitness, and various forms of dance.[3]

In games such as basketball, to take a typical case that illustrates the situation in many other games, pupils practice various forms of passing the ball such as chest pass and bounce pass, various forms of shooting such as the set shot and lay up, how to dribble the ball, and perhaps some techniques for guarding players. In swimming, they learn the techniques of the main strokes and water safety. In gymnastics, they practise movements on the floor such as rolls, cartwheels and balances, and possibly some apparatus work. And so on. The key point to note about this teaching and learning of techniques is that these practices are typically abstracted from the whole activity; they are typically decontextualised practices. Indeed, the concept of skill acquisition this approach embodies is sometimes called 'whole/part/ whole' learning, although I am suggesting here that the 'whole' is often omitted or offered instead in a form similar to Carl Bereiter's (1990) 'schoolwork module', a version that has lost its original authenticity and is imbued with the school's own institutional imperatives (see Kirk et al., 2000).

For the most part (though there will undoubtedly be exceptions) secondary-school physical education classes, where most of the specialist teaching takes place, may be populated by up to 30 or more pupils, typically taught by one teacher. The larger the class, the more compelling the perceived need to use a teaching style Mosston described as 'command' or 'directive' (Mosston and Ashworth, 1994), in which the teacher makes the decisions about what is to be taught and learned, in what sequence, provides verbal direction and possible visual demonstration either personally or through a pupil, seeks to ensure all pupils engage in the set tasks as required, and provides feedback on behaviour and performance. Lessons are rarely timetabled for longer than 40 or 50 minutes, and this includes changing time and, where appropriate, either setting out equipment or walking or running to the playing field. Occasionally, pupils might actually play a game of basketball in a physical education lesson, though often only towards the end of a unit of work and for only part of a lesson.[4] Similarly, a sequence of gymnastics movements on the floor might form the basis for an end-of-unit assessment task. Again, typically, there is little vertical progression in the development of these techniques; in other words, it would be unusual to see pupils year after year being introduced to progressively more advanced techniques in each of these categories of activities, although this is, I would agree with Underwood (1983: 11) among many others, the intention. As Daryl Siedentop (2002a: 372) put it, the same introductory unit gets taught 'again, and again and again'.

If this seems like a gross caricature then so much the worse for physical education. Because I am convinced after more than 30 years work in the field that this is the unfortunate reality of much of what is practised in the name of the subject, a claim that I will evidence in the course of this book. Yes, there is also evidence of innovative teachers in schools who teach games, for example, using a 'teaching games for understanding' (TGfU) approach. There are teachers who use reciprocal, guided-discovery and problem-solving teaching styles to good effect. There are very sophisticated forms of physical education in the senior high school curriculum of regions such as Queensland, Australia. There are teachers who do genuinely manage to progress some of their pupils' learning. There are others who, despite this caricatured practice of physical education, still manage to inspire love of physical activity in some of their pupils because of the qualities they themselves possess.

Indeed, it could be argued that many physical education teachers perform beyond all reasonable expectation, given the dominance of this form of practice and the very limited educational benefits that can be derived from it (see Hoffman 1987: 128 and in Chapter 3). Many become skilful operators of a hidden curriculum that uses the technique practices merely as a vehicle to communicate the values and joys of physical activity, or to facilitate for students the practice of responsibility for self and respect for others. And this is not to say, in any case, that physical educators have been somehow unaware of this practice I am calling here the id[2] of physical education-as-sport-techniques. How could they not have been aware, given the unquestionable intellectual quality of many recruits into physical education teaching? Many have attempted resistance. Some have failed and left teaching. Some have found a vocation in a related field such as sports coaching. A few may have simply submitted to the regime and sought to make the best of a bad lot, or resigned themselves to the inevitable and retired on the job.

There have, of course, also been reformers, some of whom we will meet later in the pages of this book, who have championed new pedagogical models such as TGfU, Sport education, personal and social responsibility, sport for peace, girl-friendly physical education, health-related exercise, outdoor adventure activities and so on, and alternative notions of physical education requiring study and integration of theoretical subject matter with practical physical activities in courses that lead to high-stakes examinations, such Queensland's Senior Physical Education, and Advanced ('A') Level Physical Education in England and Wales. There are other reformers who have presented visions for particular futures for physical education where they have dreamed im/possible dreams of decline or triumph of physical education. But there have also been advocates for this technique-based approach, in one form or another, such as those who claim, as we will see in Chapter 4, that there are 'fundamental motor skills' that must be acquired before children can engage in the fully fledged form of a game or athletic activity.

The id^2 of physical education that is generated from, and then in circular fashion informs and legitimates, this practice, I will, as I have already indicated, call 'physical education-as-sport-techniques'. My words are chosen carefully. Prior to the 1950s (in Britain and Australia, earlier in the USA and later, for example, in Sweden), the practice of physical education had also been largely concerned with learning and performing techniques, but almost exclusively in relation to one or other system of gymnastics. Even though sport in the modern form with which we are familiar had been by then in existence for around 100 years, generated initially in the private schools of Britain's social elites and spreading rapidly through class structures and nation-states and regions from that time forward, it played very little part in either the professional preparation of teachers of physical education or in the physical education provided in state elementary schools. So the inclusion of *sport-techniques* into the core of the practice of physical education was in its time a revolution for the subject.

Indeed, we could argue, and in fact I will in the course of this book, that the introduction of sport-techniques into the practice of physical education was the outcome of a momentous reorientation of the id^2 from its original modern form, which we will name 'physical education-as-gymnastics'. It is noteworthy that the shift was not to an id^2 of physical education-as-*sport*, although this might seem to be an altogether more obvious descriptor. But the nuance here is important, and this is a point that some physical educators in Britain in particular seem consistently to misunderstand. If the practice of physical education had been to play sport, that is, to form teams, to arrange competition and participation around seasons, to coach players in training sessions, to develop fitness to improve performance, to study and practise tactics, to learn about and practice the etiquette of sport including fair play, to include roles additional to player such as captain, equipment officer, statistician and referee, to celebrate the climaxes of sporting achievements through festivity, then we might more accurately have described the shift from an id^2 of physical education-as-gymnastics to physical education-as-sport. But, in fact, for the majority of everyday physical education lessons, few if any of these features apply.[5]

The practice of extra-curricular sport is a separate matter. There is no question that since the beginning of the twentieth century in countries such as Australia, Britain and the United States, school sport has been highly organised, mimicking the adult structures of leagues, cup competitions and championship events. There are some physical educators and others who would argue that extra-curricular sport, which has many of the features listed in the previous paragraph, is an extension of curricular physical education. Indeed, the Munn Report on years three and four of the secondary school in Scotland did exactly that (Scottish Education Department/Consultative

Committee on the Curriculum, 1977). Others still might point out that extra-curricular sport in Australia and Britain is run mainly by physical education teachers, many of whom consider coaching school sports teams to be more enjoyable and fulfilling than teaching curricular physical education. Be that as it may, I suggest that it is not particularly persuasive to argue that extra-curricular sport could be considered as an extension of or even as a part of physical education. For one thing, as I noted in *Defining Physical Education* (Kirk, 1992a), the uproar around teachers' pay in mid-1980s Britain caused considerable and lasting damage to their willingness to work beyond the formal school day, in evenings and on weekends. That local circumstance aside, extra-curricular sport is in most cases exclusive to a relatively small minority of pupils whom teachers consider excel in particular sports. So not only are the majority of pupils excluded, but the range of sports offered by any one school is usually far from comprehensive, depending heavily on teacher interest and the availability of facilities. If extra-curricular sport was a requirement of pupils, as it is in some private schools, the argument that it could be a form of practice best described by the id^2 of physical education-as-sport would perhaps have some validity.

The issue of extra-curricular sport aside, this broadening of physical education beyond gymnastics to include a wide range of sports whose techniques could be practised abstracted from and occasionally located within the whole sport (or 'schoolwork' versions of it) was a matter of momentous occasion around the 1950s, so much so that the whole concept of physical education, the idea of the idea, shifted fundamentally. Precisely what I mean by this id^2 I will explain in the next chapter since this explanation will lead us into the sustained consideration of the kinds of issue we need to grapple with in order to begin to glimpse the possible futures that may be available to physical education. But first, we might conclude these preliminary remarks by highlighting one further historical trend of considerable importance to physical education futures.

This historical trend relates to physical education teacher education, and it is intimately wrapped up in the shift in the id^2 of physical education around the 1950s and the consolidation of physical education-as-sport-techniques since. About the same time as the 'sportification' of school physical education was taking place, physical education teacher education also embarked on a process of 'academicisation'. The 1960s and 1970s were (roughly, slightly earlier in some places, later in others) the decades in which the basic qualification to become a physical education teacher changed from sub-degree (certificate or diploma) to degree level. Even though courses increased in length, from one or two to three or four years, the need to add 'theoretical' material to make courses degree worthy put pressure on the time available for engagement with practical physical activities, that is, the subject matter teachers would be required to teach in schools.

The 1970s and 1980s were also degree decades,[6] but in this case the degrees were not in physical education teaching but in 'human movement studies', 'leisure studies' and later 'sport and exercise science', 'kinesiology', and so on. As this process of academicisation developed, space on the timetable for practical experience of physical activities became increasingly pressured, understandably so perhaps in courses such as sport and exercise science but less justifiably in physical education teacher education. By the end of the 1980s, Daryl Siedentop (2002a), commenting on the situation in the USA, was moved to say that

> We have arrived at a point in our history where we can now prepare teachers who are pedagogically more skillful than ever, but who, in many cases, are so unprepared in the content area that they would be described as 'ignorant' if the content area were a purely cognitive knowledge field.
>
> (Siedentop, 2002a: 369)

The 'content area' for Siedentop is sport, though however we characterise it the message is clear. The academicisation of the physical activity field in higher education from around the 1960s to the present led to a situation where teachers of physical education in many countries and regions now gain degree level qualifications. But the cost of this progress has been two-fold. First, rather than being the sole focus of the field in higher education as it was prior to the 1970s (more or less), physical education teacher education from that time forward has been a 'sub-discipline' of the broader field, treated at best with parity by biological and social scientists of sport, leisure and exercise but more often as a less academic and so a marginal member of university departments, schools and faculties, as we will see in Chapter 4. And second, physical education teachers increasingly gained less and less experience of the subject matter that they would be expected to have mastered so that they could teach it in schools, a matter we consider in Chapter 5.

I want to suggest in this book, along with Lawson (2009), that the durability of physical education-as-sport-techniques and this widespread trend in physical education teacher education are inter-related. Indeed, ironically, physical education-as-sport-techniques may have survived as long as it has because it requires relatively little depth of knowledge from its practitioners. The late Alan Guy of Loughborough University was interviewed for an infamous *Panorama* documentary in 1987, which features in the opening chapter of *Defining Physical Education* (Kirk, 1992a). In the interview, he commented that the ever-expanding physical education curriculum and the academicisation of teacher education ran the risk of developing expertise in teachers that is, as he put it, 'a mile wide and an inch deep'. Asked by the interviewer if he felt this undesirable situation now applied, he answered 'no'. It gives me no pleasure to say that I think he was wrong.

Some could argue that the durability and universality of physical education-as-sport-techniques is a good thing. To endure when all else seems to be changing is surely a sign of quality, and so physical educators should vigorously conserve and protect this approach. Unfortunately for the advocates of this position, there is an important relationship between forms of school knowledge and wider cultural referents that they should take into account (see Williams, 1985; Lawson, 2009). The world has changed profoundly since the 1940s and 1950s when the id² of physical education was shifting from gymnastics to sport-techniques. Toffler (1970) argues that it was about this time that we entered a third wave of civilisation, shifting to a post-industrial, digital society. The school as an institution rests, however, on the processes generated by industrial society, such as standardisation, centralisation, specialisation and bureaucratisation. Contemporary schools remain, in Lawson's (2009) terms, 'industrial age schools'. Given the exponential growth in the supply of information and new means of delivering it, the role of the school in the early twenty-first century has thus become highly problematic, particularly in relation to the transfer of learning beyond the school, and the processes of cultural transmission and renewal more broadly.

More particularly, the physical culture of economically advanced societies has changed since the middle of the twentieth century. Sport is considerably more globalised, professionalised, commercialised and commodified now than it was then. The growth of high performance elite sports raises questions about how we define excellence and ability. Representations of the body, of sport, exercise and active leisure are powerfully constructed through electronic, televisual media in a manner that could scarcely have been imagined even by the most insightful science fiction writer of the mid-twentieth century. On the one hand they provided physical culture with a reach into people's everyday lives that was not possible in the mid-1900s, and on the other, with an accessibility that has to some extent removed or at least reduced barriers constructed by social class (Roberts, 1996). The beliefs and values about embodiment expressed in and through contemporary physical culture arguably bear little resemblance to the beliefs and values in the 1940s and 1950s. A constituent part of this change in beliefs and values, for better or worse, is that science has advanced our understanding of the relationships between organised physical activities, health and psychophysiological processes.

So those specialised aspects of culture that act to legitimate forms of school knowledge, in the case of physical education the wider *physical culture* of society, have changed profoundly. In these circumstances, it seems hardly credible that a particular concept and associated practice of physical education could remain relevant, educationally, while the wider culture has changed profoundly. What we are led to suspect is that change-resistant physical education-as-sport-techniques may already be, and seems increasingly likely to become, culturally obsolete.

Beyond the more general concerns this suspicion raises, other questions might be asked. Are children benefiting educationally from school physical education programmes? Is the cost to taxpayers of teachers' salaries, expensive facilities and equipment, and the salaries of teacher educators and the expensive facilities and equipment of universities required to train them, good value for money? Add to this the inconvenient truth that more and more is expected of physical education. In Britain, the government has invested in the past five years more than £1.5 billion in its physical education and school sport strategy with the intention of increasing the numbers of winning international sports performers, reducing the numbers of obese children and adults, and ensuring the good behaviour and citizenship of all members of society. These three ambitious aspirations are being set, albeit in different forms and in different ways, in other countries around the world (Puhse and Gerber, 2005). How might a school subject that continues to be practised in a form that was considered to be cutting edge over 60 years ago fulfil such ambitions? Quite clearly, according to this line of argument, it cannot.

So change seems inevitable. But what futures might be possible for physical education? Can physical educators themselves bring about the changes that seem to be needed? Or will change be forced upon them by governments' growing impatience with lack of progress? Indeed, does physical education as we know it have a future?

2 Defining physical education and the possibility of the id²

> Cultural and historical judgement cannot be left to 'the past' alone, since the particular picture of the past which is invoked is the one selected by these very judgements.
>
> (Chanan and Gilchrist, 1974: 62)

I have already made reference in Chapter 1 to 'the idea of the idea' of physical education which, for the sake of brevity, we will call the id². This notion is pivotal to the argument of the book and so requires some explanation. The id² builds on earlier historical work published in *Defining Physical Education* (Kirk, 1992a) and *Schooling Bodies* (Kirk, 1998a). In these studies I argued that physical education is socially constructed in the sense that it is a human invention rather than an occurrence in nature. More than this, and following Goodson's (1997) lead, I proposed that this process of social construction involves struggles over resources between vying groups. Building on insights from 'new directions' sociology of education (Young, 1971; Evans, 1986), which was itself a reaction to a particular approach to the philosophy of education fashionable in the 1960s and 1970s, this work sought to show the importance of human action within particular local and, increasingly, global contexts in determining the form and content of physical education.

Demonstrating that physical education was socially constructed, however, admitted the possibility of relativism. In contrast to one version of analytical philosophy of education in which key concepts were considered to possess essential, transcendental characteristics, or to be constituent of 'the rational mind', relativism suggests instead that concepts have multiple meanings that are context bound. As Chanan and Gilchrist (1974) note, construction of 'the past' is a selection from possible other 'pasts' and is thus value laden. In an extreme form of relativism, there is no basis on which to differentiate among this multiplicity of meaning. If knowledge is socially constructed, physical education can be whatever I decide. No-one's definition is better than anyone else's; in other words, anything goes (Whitty, 1985).

While a social constructionist perspective on physical education may admit to the possibility of relativism, it does not endorse this extreme perspective as inevitable or desirable. It does create a challenge for social epistemology, though, a challenge that needs to be acknowledged and wrestled with, if not completely resolved. If, as I will argue in this chapter, physical education has no essential, transcendental characteristics since the historical record shows it has changed over time, how then are we to avoid the position at the other extreme, that it has no meaning at all or, at least, only the meaning we arbitrarily select and choose to give it? From a social epistemological perspective, we might point out that something called 'physical education' is practised in particular locales at specific times. What physical education 'means' is embedded in and expressed through the interactions of the participants; the teachers and students, the designers of lessons and programmes, the builders of facilities, and the creators and suppliers of equipment, just to name a few. If physical education has no essence, no features which transcend time and space, how can we recognise its occurrence in these context-bound instantiations of interactions of teachers and students around subject matter, using equipment in spaces such as gyms and playing fields?

This is the question this chapter seeks to answer, at least to a level that can satisfactorily permit this study of physical education futures to be undertaken. The purpose of this chapter is to outline how the id² is to be deployed in this study, how it is intended to be understood, as a means of dealing with the tension between essentialist and relativist perspectives. An obvious issue that needs to be examined first of all is why the statement of a definition of physical education does not seem to resolve the matter of what physical education means, particularly when, according to Laker (2003), Penney and Chandler (2000), Locke (1992) among many others, definitions abound. I then go on to provide a context within social epistemology and curriculum history to develop the id² from the work of Rothblatt (1997), with support from Bernstein's (2000) theory of the social construction of pedagogic discourse. The chapter concludes with a short discussion of four relational issues for the id² of physical education, each of which is developed more fully in Chapter 6.

Definitions of physical education

The most common and straightforward approach to defining physical education is, simply, to state a definition of physical education. Defining physical education has been something of a preoccupation of physical educators, pre-dating the emergence of the term itself in modern usage, with A.D. Munrow (1963) devoting a whole chapter of his book *Pure and Applied Gymnastics*, first published in 1955, to the question 'What is gymnastics?'. There are many definitions of physical education in existence today which vary in specificity, explicitness and scope. Some make links between learning in the physical domain and a range of related outcomes concerned with physical and social skills, moral values, health, spirituality and intellectual ability. Penney and Chandler (2000) express concern that, while physical educators seem to be agreed on what physical education is *not*, the matter of what the core aims of the subject *are* remains far less clear and a source of apparent tension. Claims about the contribution of the subject to children's development, later lives and to society are multiple and diverse, ... (we) ... question the degree to which physical education can legitimately continue to make varied claims and pursue multiple agendas.

(Penney and Chandler, 2000: 74–75)

I noted in Chapter 1 that these claims for physical education and the defini- tions they either explicitly or implicitly announce provide an impression that the field is conflict ridden, that it is indeed a good example of extreme rela- tivism with its 'varied and multiple agendas'. While it may be accurate to say this in a very specific sense which I will develop in the course of this book, my comment in Chapter 1 was that much (though not all) of this apparent dissent misses the point, since it has done little to seriously challenge the dominant id^2 of physical education-as-sport-techniques. I argued, moreover, that the differences in the practice of physical education in economically advanced countries and regions are for the most part less significant than the similarities.

For these reasons, an exhaustive examination of the many definitions that abound is unnecessary because they give a misleading impression that there is more diversity of practice than in fact exists. It may be helpful, none- theless, to gain some sense of the kinds of definition that have been offered for physical education if only to appreciate why this is the least satisfactory means of defining physical education.

Writing in 1951 in the USA, Brownell and Hagman helpfully offered a definition of a definition by reasoning that 'a definition should explain the meaning or properties of a word or phrase that show its distinguishing fea- tures and point out its relationships to other things of an associated nature' (Brownell and Hagman, 1951: 17). They acknowledge that definitions should reflect the purposes of the writer, and since writers may vary in their pur- poses for physical education, for example one emphasising physical fitness while another stresses recreational outcomes, their definitions may also vary. Brownell and Hagman's own definition of physical education was intended to contribute to the goals of education more generally while identifying physical education's unique contribution. Thus, 'physical education is the accumulation of wholesome experiences through participation in large- muscle activities that promote optimum growth and development' (Brownell and Hagman, 1951: 17).

This is a relatively broad definition that identifies some properties of physical education such as 'wholesome experiences' and 'large-muscle activ- ities', while leaving much scope for what learning experiences and subject matter in particular might be selected to construct a programme. We can compare it to a definition provided by English physical educator Martin Randall, also writing originally in the early 1950s but still current in a third edition of his book in the late 1960s. Randall argued that the ultimate aim of physical education was to contribute to the overall education of young people. In this context, 'physical education ... covers the whole field of physical activity, all sports and pastimes, in and out of doors, of a competitive or recreational character involving either team cooperation or individual effort. Its variety is infinite' (Randall, 1967: 32). Randall is rather more substantive and content specific than Brownell and Hagman, making explicit reference to sport, recreation and other pastimes indoors and out, though no mention is made of outcomes such as health or fitness implied in the American 'optimum growth and development', while the inclusion of only 'wholesome' activities is no doubt assumed.

A somewhat more sophisticated definition is offered by Morgan (1973) in a sustained argument in his book *Concerns and Values in Physical Education*. After careful consideration of a number of possibilities, Morgan (1973: 9) chooses as his preferred definition that physical education is 'education through athletic forms of activity'. The characterisation of forms of activity as 'athletic' was intended by Morgan to provide a means of linking the riskily disparate categories of physical activities such as sport, gymnastics and dance. Like Randall, Morgan expressed the view that physical education must contribute to the broader aims of education. In order to do so, he suggested that the concerns and values that identified physical education's contribution to education were enjoyment and satisfaction, skill, beauty, fitness and health, and mind and character.

More recently, the definition of physical education that will guide physical educators in schools in England and Wales from 2008 can be found in *The National Curriculum for England: Physical Education*:

> A high-quality physical eduction curriculum enables all pupils to enjoy and succeed in many kinds of physical activity. They develop a wide range of skills and the ability to use tactics, strategies and compositional ideas to perform successfully. When they are performing, they think about what they are doing, analyse the situation and make decisions. They also reflect on their own and others' performances and find ways to improve them. As a result, they develop the confidence to take part in different physical activities and learn about the value of healthy, active lifestyles. Discovering what they like to do, what their aptitudes are at school, and how and where to get involved in physical activity helps them make informed choices about lifelong physical activity. Physical education helps pupils develop personally and socially. They work as individuals, in groups and in teams, developing concepts of fairness and of personal and social responsibility. They take on different roles and responsibilities, including leadership, coaching and officiating. Through the range of experiences that physical education offers, they learn how to be effective in competitive, creative and challenging situations.
>
> (Qualifications and Curriculum Authority, 2007)

We can see some commonality between these definitions, but only at a relatively abstract level. All mention 'physical', 'athletic' or 'large-muscle' activities. Three mention or imply health as an outcome. Two others mention competition. The Qualifications and Curriculum Authority (QCA) and Morgan definitions mention cognitive processes such as confidence, attitudes and learning to think, though only Morgan's and Randall's mention sport explicitly. Insofar as they together map out the field or define the subject, these links may be judged to be somewhat tenuous at a written level. Far more problematic is the large variability in the kinds of programme that might result from these definitions in practice. This variability should at least challenge our thinking about what practices might count as 'physical education', the issue that is the central concern of this chapter.

As definitions go, the QCA version is very carefully worded. It provides enough information about the content of the subject to differentiate it from other subjects, but at the same time allows us to imagine how links to other subjects might be made. It also contains information on outcomes, in terms of what pupils should be able to do, and so is in this sense aspirational. In technical terms, as a piece of curriculum writing, it could be viewed as a 'good' definition. But why should we accept this definition over the many other just as well written definitions that are available, particularly since it rather bizarrely, and for most people (I imagine) unexpectedly, fails to mention sport explicitly? In this sense, far from stating what physical education is *definitively*, it could be argued that the act of stating definitions such as this in fact contributes to relativism instead, to the idea that there can be a proliferation of definitions. To be sure, as Brownell and Hagman note, definitions will reflect individual purposes. But, as Penney and Chandler protest, how many purposes can physical educators be permitted to pursue while describing what they do as physical education? This in turn creates a problem of credibility. For example, how can an organisation such as the QCA offer a definition that omits to mention sport while the teaching of sport-techniques has been the substance of the subject since at least the 1950s? What kind of subject is it that cannot agree on its 'essential' character?

The mere statement of a definition, no matter how well crafted, is of limited assistance in defining physical education. The proliferation of definitions may in any case be counterproductive to gaining a better understanding of physical education past, present and future. Rather than capture the 'essence' of physical education, the sheer quantity and dissimilarity of definitions may encourage an extreme relativist attitude instead, where one definition is as good as any other and, thus, anything goes.

Analytical philosophy of education, social epistemology and curriculum history

Epistemology is the study of the nature of knowledge. For scholars of education, it is a field of study of central importance. Since the beginning of formally organised school education funded by governments, limited resources have forced educational policy-makers to confront epistemological questions such as which knowledge is of most worth, and related questions such as which knowledge should children be required to study or, in other words, what should be its 'core', what should be optional, and how should the school curriculum be organised.[1] In the late 1950s through to the 1970s, analytical philosophers of education grappled with these epistemological questions, developing an approach that involved the analysis of concepts such as education.

The work of English philosopher Richard Peters was particularly influential. Peters (1966) argued that education involved initiation into worthwhile activities. An educationally worthwhile activity, according to Peters, is of value for its own sake. We can recognise such activities, claimed Peters, since they will be 'serious' in the sense that they will inform other areas of life, they will offer a cognitive perspective on the world with wide-ranging cognitive content, they have the capacity to enrich and change a person's view of the world, and they will illuminate the truth. Furthermore, worthwhile activities are transcendental in the sense that they are forever and always worthwhile, regardless of time and place.

Peters and others (White, 1973; Hirst, 1974) were taken seriously by educational policy-makers and their advisers (e.g. Lawton, 1993; Skilbeck, 1984). While they did not necessarily agree with all of the detail, the curriculum makers accepted the main implications, such as the possibility of distinguishing between what knowledge should be in the school curriculum and what should not. This philosophising may have seemed some distance removed from the 'real world' of schools but it had very serious potential consequences for the perceived educational status of activities such as physical education, which predictably failed to make the philosophers' list of essential subjects. Interestingly, wherever the core curriculum idea was applied, for example in mid-1970s Scotland (Scottish Education Department/ Consultative Committee on the Curriculum, 1977) and in Australia in the 1990s (National Professional Development Program Health and Physical Education Project, 1997), physical education managed to retain a place as an area that pupils were required to study in secondary schools, though typically with less time than most other core subjects, but nevertheless suggesting that this approach to epistemology had limited impact in the longer term. This analytical approach is at the same time important to our task here, as we will see momentarily.

As the popularity and influence of analytical philosophy of education reached its height around the early 1970s, a challenge presented itself in the form 'new directions' sociology of education. Research in the sociology of school knowledge, particularly as it began to take shape in the work of writers such as M.F.D. Young, Basil Bernstein, Pierre Bourdieu and Geoff Esland (see Young, 1971), put forward the radical proposition that the school curriculum is an example of the social organisation of knowledge.

This proposition suggested that rather than school knowledge possessing an intrinsic worth that transcends societies and historical epochs, as the analytical philosophers had it, the knowledge that constructs and constitutes the school curriculum is the product of a range of social forces, involving the exercise of power and embodying particular values and beliefs.

The full significance of this insight was brought out in the work of school curriculum historians such as Kliebard (1986) and Goodson (1985), and university curriculum researchers such as Rothblatt (1997) and Becher and Trowler (2001). Goodson proposed that school subjects and university disciplines follow trajectories of popularity and perceived importance over time through struggles between vying groups and individuals who actively contested each others' values and sought to establish their own preferences for particular versions of school knowledge. The message of this social epistemological approach was that, if we wish to define a field or subject such as physical education (or geography or mathematics), we must, as Becher and Trowler (2001) proposed, study what people do in the name of that subject.

Curriculum history research seemed to support an anti-essentialist position by demonstrating empirically that not only did the fortunes of subjects wax and wane, but that their form and substance also changed over time. A social epistemological approach to the curriculum is left with a problem to deal with nevertheless. While this approach suggests there is no enduring 'essence' of physical education, there must still remain some means of recognising when a practice is physical education and when it is something else, say, active leisure or sports coaching. So while there can be no unchanging, immutable, transcendental, essential physical education, a practice needs to have some distinguishing physical educationness in order to be recognised as physical education. Sheldon Rothblatt's attempt to confront this difficulty in his historical research on the university provides us with a possible means of grappling with this challenge.

The idea of the idea of the university

The id² of physical education owes a debt to Rothblatt (1997) and his book *The Modern University and Its Discontents*. Rothblatt (1997: 36) noted that for centuries universities have been in the habit of reinventing themselves in order to remain current and to garner prestige. In these circumstances of regular reinvention, what is it, he asks, that allows us to recognise an educational institution as a 'university'? In order to answer this question, Rothblatt turns to the famous definition of the university provided by John Henry (later Cardinal) Newman in his book, *The Idea of a University*, written in the 1850s. The university, stated Newman, is a place for teaching universal knowledge. 'Such is a University in its essence.' Rothblatt shows that Newman's definition had strong resonance with the Oxford of Newman's undergraduate days some 30 years earlier and as such the teaching was focused on the cultivation of character rather than the mere acquisition of expertise. But by the time of writing *The Idea*, this notion, that the university was primarily concerned with teaching, was already under threat at Oxford as research grew in importance. Moreover, by the 1850s, there were other, rival notions of the university emanating from Germany, the USA, Ireland and from neighbouring Scotland.

Newman's legacy was not then his actual definition of the university, since there existed in the 1850s and exist now many examples that do not match this precise definition. According to Rothblatt, the importance of Newman's contribution to the history of the university is *the idea of* the idea of the university. While there is in fact no essence that distinguishes universities from other kinds of educational institution and educational institutions from factories, since universities and other educational institutions and factories are regularly changing, the idea of the idea presents the possibility that there could be an essence. In other words, the idea of the idea is a kind of *as if* proposition, that imagines the possibility of some essential characteristics that make universities recognisable as universities without locking them forever into a definition that states unequivocally 'the university is a place for teaching universal knowledge'.

Rothblatt resists the suggestion that this 'idea of the idea' is merely a discursive device. It is instead an organising principle, a means of making some sense of situations in which there is great diversity and complexity. The idea of the idea is contingent rather than transcendental, a work in progress rather than a timeless, immutable and finished product. Universities are notoriously diverse and complex, and yet we need to be able to imagine the possibility that different institutions have, as Wittgenstein put it, some 'family resemblance'. For, Rothblatt asks, what use is the alternative? If we cannot imagine the possibility of what it is that marks a university *as a* university, then perhaps, as we noted earlier with the extreme relativist position, anything goes? In this scenario, any educational institution can be a university if I choose to say it is. Faced with this prospect, even Rothblatt's discontents who are sceptical of essences might want to argue, as he himself does, that the idea of the idea of the university is useful. Without it, he suggests, 'a university is utterly shapeless and possesses no means of distinguishing itself from any other kind of educational institution' (Rothblatt, 1997: 43).

The possibility of the idea of the idea of physical education

It is in this same sense of an organising principle, as an *as if* proposition, that I will write about the idea of the idea of physical education, in a shorthand form as the id². In using this notion of the id² of physical education we accept that there is no transcendent, immutable and finished physical education; there is no primary Platonic form behind the shadow-world of everyday life. But in order to make sense of a diverse and complex set of practices, we can, in applying the id² of physical education, imagine the possibility of some family resemblance among practices that allows us to recognise them as physical education or, conversely, to disallow them this description or, in the basic sense recognised by the philosopher John Wilson (2003), at the very least to allow us to have a conversation in which we can sensibly dispute each others' views.

Wilson (2003) has proposed that it is not possible to have a meaningful conversation about the nature of education, for example, without agreeing what the concept of education might or might not mean. He insists that there are two ways in which the word concept might be used, and suggests that in analytical philosophy of education both senses were sometimes used, though it was rarely explicitly acknowledged which. One is a context-bound sense in which we might speak of, for example, the Victorian concept of laissez-faire in the context of the Industrial Revolution; in this example, use of the word 'concept' is attached to what Wilson calls 'empirical facts'. Another is a more rarefied sense in which we identify the meaning of a concept, which exists for Wilson 'in a purely logical space'. It is this second sense that Wilson claims analytical philosophers sought to conduct their inquiries, though they did not always explicitly say so.

There is also a hierarchical order between these two senses of the word concept, whereby 'we can distinguish an enquiry into the nature of things from an enquiry into the meanings of words' (Wilson, 2003: 102). Wilson assumes then that an inquiry into the meaning of words in a purely logical space must come *before* an empirical inquiry into the nature of things or otherwise, he asks, how are we to know what we are talking about? From a social epistemological perspective, however, the questions that might be asked of Wilson are 'for whom is a concept meaningful, for what purposes, and in what contexts is the question being asked?'. In other words, a social epistemology would invert the order of Wilson's process by arguing that concepts of education or physical education are meaningful only in relation to the practices that take place in their name. In addition, the purely logical space Wilson envisages needs to be viewed as a context in itself, populated by philosophers like himself. At the same time, the notion of the id^2 fulfils a similar if not identical function as his sense of concept relating to the meaning of words insofar as it provides an organising principle, conceptualising practice. In other words, the id^2 is empirically informed or practice referenced (in Wilson's context-bound use of the word concept) and to an extent serves the function of the concept concerned with meaning, but always qualified by meaning for whom, for what purposes, in what socio-historical contexts.

The id^2 of physical education is not, then, simply a broad definition. It is not a statement of what we wish physical education might be, but of how we make sense of the range of practices that go on in the name of physical education. As I will elaborate in more detail in Chapter 6, the id^2 of physical education is an outcome of the embedding of school physical education in physical culture, a process defined technically within Bernstein's (2000) theory of the social construction of pedagogical discourse as the embedding of instructional discourse in regulative discourse. It is well suited to a social epistemological approach to the curriculum that recognises that subjects are defined by what people do and say, rather than only by the logical word games played by analytical philosophers or definitions constructed by policy-makers and authors of books. At the same time, these word games of philosophers, policy-makers' and authors writing definitions, aims and sylla-buses are also empirical activities that go on in the name of physical educa-tion and so contribute to our understanding of the diversity and complexity of practice.

I argued earlier that one id^2 of physical education dominates con-temporary physical education practice. This id^2 of physical education-as-sport-techniques is the organising principle of contemporary practice that goes on in the name of physical education. Rather perversely, give the thesis of curriculum history that institutions and school subjects regularly reinvent themselves, I argued in Chapter 1 that this id^2 of physical education has endured for about 60 years and has all the appearance of immutability. In Chapter 4 I will explore the evidence to support this claim before going on in Chapter 5 to recount the circumstances that lead to the emergence of this id^2, contributed to its longevity and which may also lead to its demise. Before doing so, we need to complete this account of the id^2 by considering four important relational issues for institutionalised educational practices of all kinds.

Relational issues for the id^2 of physical education

In chapters that follow we will see that there have been a number of rival ideas of physical education, such as Swedish versus educational gymnastics and a motor-skills approach to games versus teaching games for under-standing. Disputes between physical educators, insofar as they exist, are often at this level, contesting one idea of physical education against another. I will argue that much, though not all,[2] of this argumentation literally misses the 'bigger picture', the broader organising principle of the dominant form of physical education at any given time or, in other words, the id^2. In order to more fully comprehend the nature of the id^2, I suggest there are four relational issues that all institutionalised forms of educational practice must take into account.

These are, first, the wider field of knowledge which gives the institutional form of knowledge (e.g. 'the school subject') its legitimacy and currency, in Bernstein's (2000) terms the regulative discourse produced in the field of the production of pedagogic discourse in which instructional discourse is embedded. Second, all forms of instructional discourse in schools and uni-versities must confront the issue of transfer of learning, and the relationship of learning in educational institutions to work, play and life in general beyond the institutions (Lave, 1997). Thirdly, as social practices in the sense intended by MacIntyre (1985), school and university subjects and in particular their value within and beyond the academy will be determined by how they define standards of excellence and, therefore, notions of 'ability'. Fourth, all institutionalised educational practices will be shaped by those aspects of the valued culture and heritage of societies they seek to transmit to new generations, and their role in cultural critique and renewal (Chanan and Gilchrist, 1974; Friere, 1973; Giroux, 1981).

In physical education, these issues take on a specific form. For the id² of physical education, we need to ask questions of the relationship of school physical education to physical culture; transfer of learning beyond the school; how excellence is defined and how it in turn defines 'ability'; and the ways in which physical education is active in cultural transmission, reproduction and renewal. I introduce each issue briefly in the context of this account of the id² and then will devote a chapter to a discussion of these issues later in the book.

Physical culture

As I will use the notion here, physical culture is a specialised form of corporeal discourse concerned with meaning making centred on the bodily practices which constitute organised and institutionalised activities such as sport, exercise and active leisure (Kirk, 1999).[3] The purposefully moving body is of particular importance within physical culture. Corporeal discourse in turn is a broader concept referring to all meaning-making activity centred on the body and includes the operation of corporeal power. Corporeal discourse consists of a vast array of what the anthropologist Marcel Mauss (1973) called 'techniques of the body' and is produced in what Bernstein (2000) named 'the field of production of pedagogic discourse'. Both corporeal discourse and physical culture are the non-pedagogical raw materials, the regulative discourse, out of which the instructional discourse of school physical education is constructed; the id² of physical education, its 'pedagogic discourse' in Bernstein's terms, is the conjoining of specific forms of school physical education and selected aspects of physical culture.

As they emerged in government schools for the industrial age in Australia, Britain, the USA and elsewhere towards the end of the nineteenth century, forms of school physical training were practices that had the explicit, though often unstated, purpose of regulating and normalising working-class children's bodies through precise formal exercises carried out in unison within large groups or classes. A primary purpose of corporeal regulation through schooling was the creation of a population of productive but compliant workers and citizens. Elsewhere (Kirk, 1998a) I have argued that as the id² of physical education shifted from gymnastics to sport-techniques, so too did the operation of corporeal power, moving from what Foucault (1977) more generally referred to as a shift from a 'heavy, ponderous and meticulous' form of corporeal power to a 'looser form of power over the body'.

In order to consider physical education futures, we need to understand how physical culture is changing, its shifting relationship to corporeal practices more broadly, and how new forms of corporeal power emerge. We need to ask what kinds of body are constructed by and for physical culture and whether these are forms of embodiment we value and desire (Penney and Chandler, 2000). How might various forms of physical education socially construct bodies in ways that best equip our children for useful, fulfilling and productive lives?

Transfer of learning

The school as an institution is not a neutral relay of physical cultural and other knowledge and values. The ways in which schools are structured as institutions and, indeed, have continued to be structured since the late 1800s, around manipulations of time and space through the timetable and classroom, the gym, the laboratory and the assembly hall, set parameters for what might be learned in physical education. We must ask two specific questions here. First, how does the learning that occurs within the school relate to the life beyond the school gates? We need to recognise that it is the same child who plays soccer in physical education class and soccer for the local community club, or who supports a particular professional soccer team. In what sense might school learning and learning in other settings be meaningful to young people, and how does each setting relate to the other? Second, how does school physical education during childhood and adolescence relate to the needs of adulthood? For example, is it merely preparation for an active lifestyle? What, in short, and echoing Chanan's and Gilchrist's (1974) question of the school more broadly, is physical education *for*? How, specifically, might learning in school physical education transfer beyond the school?

Standards of excellence and ability

Standards of excellence feature prominently in educational institutions because education systems place a high value on testing, assessment and examinations. In this context, physical educators have struggled with the question 'What is ability in physical education?' (Evans, 2004), and their inability to agree an answer to this question may have contributed to their often-cited marginal role in the academy. As we will see in Chapter 6, agreement on how to formulate standards of excellence in physical education has been a massive challenge for physical education-as-sport-techniques, and represents a significant impediment to its survival in schools.

Cultural transmission, reproduction and renewal

An increasing volume of research in physical education over the past 20 years has recognised that physical education reproduces valued aspects of the cultural heritage of society such as sports and games (e.g. Siedentop,

1994). In so doing, physical education has also reproduced social inequalities concerning gender (Flintoff and Scraton, 2001), ethnicity (Benn, 2005), social class (Evans and Davies, 2008) and disability (Fitzgerald, 2009). As physical education's role in social and cultural reproduction has been increasingly recognised, it has also been claimed that physical education could offer opportunities for cultural renewal, for example, for new ways to understand the social construction of the body (Evans et al., 2004).

The relationship between forms of school physical education and physical culture is the primary matter for consideration, since the nature of this relationship determines the possibility and contents of transfer of learning, the activities that contain standards of excellence, and the specific form of cultural transmission and renewal. Indeed, as I already suggested in this chapter, it is this conjoining of forms of school physical education and aspects of physical culture that creates the id² of physical education; in Bernstein's (2000) terms, the instructional discourse of school physical education is embedded in the regulative discourse of physical culture to produce the pedagogic discourse of the id² of physical education. The id² of physical education-as-sport-techniques is produced by the juxtapositioning of a particular version of physical culture with a particular form of physical education strongly shaped by the school as an institution. These four relational issues are, then, of fundamental importance to understanding the notion of the id² of physical education.

Conclusion

The purpose of this chapter has been to outline how within a social epistemological approach to defining physical education the construct of the id² of physical education might be deployed as an organising principle and a means of conceptualising practice. Rather than defining physical education through conceptual analysis in a 'purely logical space', the id² offers a means of identifying practices *as* physical education in different places and at different times in history without resort to seeking transcendental features or essences. It is, following Rothblatt's lead, an *as if* principle; this principle considers the possibility of 'the idea of the idea' without making a commitment to seeking the essence of physical education. The id² of physical education accepts the social constructionist perspective that the school curriculum is the product of a range of social forces, involving the exercise of power and the selection of particular values and beliefs, and that the curriculum changes through struggles between vying groups, without accepting a position of extreme relativism that such a perspective could entail, that is, that anything goes. Instead, the id² of physical education allows us to identify clusters of common institutionalised practices that, taken together, amount to a recognisable and particular configuration of knowledge, with a specific relation to physical culture, a view of transfer of learning, a notion of excellence, and a mission for social and cultural transmission and renewal.

I hope that as this study progresses it will become increasingly obvious why it has been necessary to manufacture this *as if* principle of the id². When physical educators in the USA engaged in the so-called 'battle of the systems' in the late 1800s (Ennis, 2006), as did the female gymnasts in Britain in the 1940s (Fletcher, 1984), the disputes were merely between rival ideas of physical education, between versions of the same configuration of knowledge. When the practice of physical education swung away from gymnastics towards sport-techniques sometime between 1920 and 1960, the struggle was indeed at the level of the id². I will suggest in the course of this book that the biggest and single most significant barrier to renewing physical education has been the failure to understand the id² of physical education and to mistake it instead as simply one of a number of rival ideas of physical education.

This is not to say that all analysts of physical education, particularly those concerned with change and the future, have missed this point. As we will see in the next chapter as we investigate futures talk in physical education, the nature of the problem has been plain to a considerable number of researchers. Or, at least, they have recognised the effects of the id². But rarely have they named the id² fully, in all its complexity, in any thoroughgoing contemporary and historical study. There has been no shortage of good ideas for reforming physical education. But they have fallen short because they have mostly failed to confront the id² squarely, explicitly, and to have insisted on the kinds of radical change to practice that are required to overcome the currently dominant id² of physical education-as-sport-techniques.

3   Futures talk in physical education

Imagine a future 20 years from now where physical education programs are all in a valley of despair. In fact, physical education programs have largely been eliminated from schools, because they failed the test of accountability. Children were not learning in physical education. ... Now imagine a future 20 years from now where physical education programs take center stage in the school. Every child has quality instruction provided daily by a specialist and physical activity is centrally important to children, teachers and parents. ... Either future is possible.

(Sanders and McCrum, 1999: 3–4)

John Charles in his 2005 Delphine Hanna lecture to the National Association for Kinesiology and Physical Education in Higher Education (NAKPEHE) in the USA observed that there has been little systematic study of physical education futures, though there nevertheless has been some interest in futures research periodically and there exists a slender volume of writing. The Delphine Hanna lecture series, Charles noted, has often contributed to futures talk, and the NAKPEHE sees itself as a 'future-oriented professional organisation' with a specialist Future Directions Committee. While Charles welcomed this role for the NAKPEHE, he acknowledged that its futures research had yet to match John Massengale's (1987: 2) vision of 'a group of professionals associated with the general field of physical education who have the ability to conduct advanced research with some creativity' in the style, if not on the scale, of the RAND Corporation, the Institute for the Future, the Hudson Institute and others.

The book edited by Massengale, *Trends Toward the Future in Physical Education*, was an explicit attempt to initiate the creation of such a group of professionals, though by itself it did not generate the momentum needed for systematic futures research that could tackle the problems facing physical education at the time, where 'for years physical education has lacked the ability to predict, control or determine its own destiny' (Massengale, 1987: ix). According to Massengale, physical education instead has been the testing ground for short-lived fads and the whims of sectional interests. The main motivation for carrying out futures research, clearly evident in Massengale's introduction to *Trends Toward the Future* and in most other futures talk, is to gain some degree of control over the fate of the field, either in schools or higher education or both. Most futures writers, like Charles (2005: 272), readily agree that 'looking ahead is a risky business', and that the process of prediction cannot overrule complexity, uncertainty and chance. Futures talk in physical education is nevertheless on the whole optimistic and aspirational. Speakers typically deplore feelings of helplessness and hopelessness; what they fear most is having no control over or responsibility for their own future.

Most futures talk acknowledges the importance of history as a beginning point for understanding the present and the future. W.L. Steel (1965: 19) in his 'Twenty years on' paper to Carnegie students and alumni quoted Churchill, who reputedly said 'the further you look back the further you can look forward'. George Sage (2003) took the opportunity of providing the foreword to the book edited by Laker, *The Future of Physical Education*, to provide a brief historical context for the chapters that followed. Charles (2005: 269), like many others, talks about learning the lessons of the past; 'even as we drive forward toward the distant horizon, we should keep the rear view mirror in our peripheral vision'. Yet despite this widespread acknowledgement of the importance of history for futures talk, few futures writers use history in any depth,[1] and not all who do base their analyses of the future in history make coherent connections between present, past and future.

But as Charles, Massengale and others acknowledge, there is more to futures talk than understanding the past. Analysis of trends in physical education, both in schools and universities, and of broader social and cultural trends, is also important.[2] Seeing the 'big picture' (Charles, 2005: 285), increasingly in global terms while making connections to the local, is part of the intellectual and creative work that analysts of the future need to undertake. In the best futures talk in physical education, we see most though rarely all of these elements.

In this chapter, we listen in on a selected sample of futures talk to find out what physical educators have predicted, aspired towards and hoped for as a means of framing the analysis to come in the rest of this book. We are interested in what they have had to say about physical education futures, but not only this. Each prediction emerges from an analysis, if not of the past, then, at least, of the present (Dening, 1993). The questions we choose to ask about the past and the language we use to frame these inquiries tell us much about the inquirer's current preoccupations, concerns and values. We might add that any prediction about the future is also a comment on the present, on how the present is understood, and on those aspects of the present that we feel may be deficient and in need of remedy.

In the first two sections of this chapter I investigate the futures talk about school physical education. In the first section the talk is about the 'decline and fall' of physical education, about its demise and eventual disappearance from schools. In the second section, the talk is more positive and is focused on the 'rise and triumph' of physical education or, at least, on new forms of physical education which are more successful than those currently practised. In the final section we listen in on futures talk in the higher education field and find there a 40-year old and, at times, fractious and acrimonious debate about the proper name for the field and its characterisation as a profession or a discipline. What becomes clear from all of this futures talk is that the future fate of school physical education and the forms of the subject in higher education are, as Lawson (2009) understands, intimately intertwined.

The decline and fall of physical education

At least two kinds of future generally feature in the physical education literature, one which predicts the demise of school physical education and its higher education counterpart or its replacement with something inferior, and another that advocates for a different, new but desirable form of physical education. Both scenarios feature in Sanders' and McCrum's (1999) account in a special issue of *Teaching Elementary Physical Education*, which they edited. Physical education in the USA, they claimed, features both 'peaks of excellence' and 'valleys of despair'. While their hope is that the former prevails, where all children receive the high quality physical education enjoyed only by a minority currently, they feared that unless urgent action is taken it is more likely to be the latter that becomes commonplace. Stier, Kleinman and Milchrist (1994) posed the question 'The future of physical education – survival or extinction?' and offered three alternatives. Taking a conservative line, Stier et al. suggested all is well with physical education and that only occasional fine-tuning will be needed to maintain quality programmes. Milchrist disagreed and argued that physical education should survive, but that radical reform is required. Klienman predicted the just demise of a subject that is, as he saw it, elitist, scientised and obsessed with technical minutiae.

Along with Klienman, several prominent researchers in the USA had been predicting the demise of secondary school physical education from at least the early 1980s (Dodds and Locke, 1984; Siedentop, 1981). They were somewhat dismayed to have to report by the late 1990s that the same flawed programmes remained in place despite clear evidence that they were failing to meet their own aspirations to produce skilful, lifelong participants in physical activity (Siedentop and Locke, 1997). For Locke, the problem was the 'dominant model' of physical education.

> The dominant program model includes (a) required attendance without choice of activity or instructor; (b) class assignment without the use of student needs or achievement; (c) short classes with time eroded by management rituals and low ALT [academic learning time]; (d) short

units with only brief introductory level instruction; (e) evaluation based on rule-compliance, participation, and demeanour; and (f) program content based on instructor interest and convenience.

(Locke, 1992: 361)

We will learn more about Locke's 'dominant model' in Chapter 4, since it fairly accurately captures some of the main features of the id^2 of physical education-as-sport-techniques. According to Locke, nothing short of replacing this model completely could ensure physical education with a future in secondary schools at the beginning of the twenty-first century. As with much of the writing about the future of physical education, Locke is concerned only indirectly with predicting the future and more substantively with the process of change and how to make it happen. Examining this process in some detail, he came to the conclusion that no matter how difficult it may be, and how resistant to change are schools as institutions and teachers as people, genuine and radical change is the only route available for the survival of secondary school physical education. Echoing the work of Lawson (1983) on the occupational socialisation of teachers, Locke concluded that teachers hold the key to bringing about genuine change.

> The possibilities for significant change in secondary school physical education in the United States will be determined, in large measure, by the kinds of people who have been attracted to careers there. Their professional and interpersonal skills, and what they believe about themselves, adolescents, the subject matter, and education will make change easier or more difficult.
>
> (Locke, 1992: 369)

His estimation of the possibility of teachers voting to bring about radical change, even when they recognised the need for it, was not optimistic, in small part due to teachers' abilities to envision different programmes for physical education, and in larger part due to their disinclination to live with the disruption to the routines of everyday working life change inevitably creates, a judgement to which I return in Chapter 7.

Siedentop, in the company of his colleagues O'Sullivan and Tannehill, concluded in similar fashion to Locke that physical education's resistance to all efforts to reform its failing practices was due to its deep institutionalisation in schools.

> High school physical education is trapped in what might be described as the dysfunctional 'family' of the American high school. ... Dysfunctionality is most often a two-way street in the sense that there is a co-dependence, in this case between the teacher and the institution. If the high school ecology marginalizes physical education and makes it difficult to change, certainly the manner in which physical education

teachers and programs succumb to those contingencies makes it difficult for high school change agents to get physical education moving.

(O'Sullivan, Siedentop and Tannehill, 1994: 426)

Siedentop's wide-ranging analysis of the ills besetting secondary school physical education included the failure of teacher education programmes to provide student teachers with the subject-matter knowledge they needed to teach beyond introductory lessons (Siedentop, 2002a). In his account of the deficiencies that need to be remedied, Siedentop, like Locke, points to the dominant form of physical education and, in the case of the following observation, its approach to sport.

> Skills are taught in isolation rather than as part of the natural context of executing strategy in game-like situations. The rituals, values and traditions of a sport that give it meaning are seldom even mentioned, let alone taught in ways that students can experience them. The affiliation with a team or group that provides the context for personal growth and responsibility in sport is noticeably absent in physical education. The ebb and flow of a sport season is seldom captured in a short-term sport instruction unit; ... physical education teaches only isolated sport skills and less-than-meaningful games.
>
> (Siedentop, 1994: 7–8)

Siedentop's response to these deficiencies and his own vision of one future for physical education, in the form of the Sport Education model, we will return to in Chapter 7.

Writing more explicitly about the future of physical education in primary and secondary schools and in higher education, Shirl Hoffman's (1987) satirical contribution to the Massengale collection predicts a grim decline and fall. In 'dreaming the impossible dream', Hoffman tells the tale of the last elementary school physical education programme in the USA to be closed, in fictional 'Murrysville' in the year 2020, five years before the disappearance of secondary physical education. In its place, self-directed play (SDP) was supervised by lowly qualified managers. Students received the break from academic study that physical education used to offer, but at a fraction of the cost. Inter-school sport remained in the secondary schools but was provided by a company called Pedasport Inc., which saw that in both the secondary and elementary schools there was profit to be made by running instructional programmes as well. Pedasport's profitability was underpinned by the pay-for-play plan or P^3, in which parents who could afford to paid for their children's participation, while others who couldn't went without. As for the inter-school sport programme, any remaining vestige of educational value disappeared as competition increasingly resembled professional adult sport. Rubbing salt into the readers' wounds, Hoffman has it that only a few of the redundant physical education teachers were deemed to be employable by

Pedasport, since students chose their teacher and teachers were paid only if they were in demand. Meanwhile, Hoffman reflected concerns about infighting within higher education in the USA (a matter we come to later in this chapter), as the sport and exercise scientists of kinesiology sell out their teacher education colleagues only, in an act of grim justice, to be excluded themselves from taking over a role in children's physical education.

His biting satire identified a number of concerns with the physical education of Hoffman's present, in the mid-1980s. Physical education was expensive, but physical educators seemed unable to demonstrate that they were effective in achieving any of their loftily stated goals such as preparing children for an active lifestyle. The things they *could* do well, such as giving children a break from academic study, could be delivered much more cheaply by lowly qualified play supervisors. Hoffman recognised that there was money to be made from school sport programmes, if approached with a business-like attitude. When compared to subject experts such as sports coaches, physical educators appeared to be 'specialists in generalism'; 'if physical education teachers had any talent at all, it seemed to be the ability to teach a broad range of skills at an introductory level in environments that promised little hope of success' (Hoffman, 1987: 128). In any case, teacher education programmes were too theoretical and physical education teacher educators too preoccupied with fighting their corner in an increasingly hostile academy. Behind all these problems, as Hoffman saw it, was physical educators' failure to agree on just about anything concerning their subject which made them vulnerable and unable to see off other interest groups who had designs on their territory, which included children, schools and physical activity.

Hoffman's futuristic satire was the inspiration for another dream experience, Tinning's (1992) 'On speeches, dreams and realities', his predictions for Australian physical education by 2001. In Tinning's future, physical education had also disappeared and had been replaced by programmes of skills, fitness and sport run by commercial organisations such as 'SportEd Inc.'. Moreover, the interests of elite sport had come to dominate university sports science programmes which no longer hosted teacher education programmes (see also Maguire, 2004), a configuration of the field that Tinning (2002) had elsewhere dubbed 'performance pedagogy'. Sport Education instructors were, in similar fashion to Hoffman's scenario, trained in sub-university, low-status institutions. Emphasising the processes of commercialisation and commodification, Tinning has it that SportEd Inc. itself was sponsored by McDonald's, Coke and Pizza Hut. Tinning's dream included a long list of concerns expressed by physical educators about the shortcomings of their subject, ranging from inadequate teaching in primary schools and entrenched practices in secondary schools that were resistant to reform, to ineffective teacher education programmes and lack of organised political influence to shape government policy.

In similar fashion to Hoffman's futures scenario, Tinning awoke from his nightmare to discover that some aspects of the future were already at work in the present. While wideawake Hoffman had carelessly thrown away a leaflet advertising Pedasport Inc., the reality for Tinning was that the privatisation and commercialisation of physical education was already well advanced in the form of a company called Tri-Skills, which offered P³ programmes to children in South Australian schools and employed up to 30 physical education teachers.

Tinning (2001) returned to his task of thinking about the future with a second paper some ten years later where he created a scenario for Australian physical education in 2012. He commented that many of his predictions for 2001 had not come to pass. Nevertheless, the trend towards commercialisation has continued, with many new companies emerging to follow the lead of Tri-skills which has itself continued to expand. In the UK, for example, the magazine *Future Fitness* (November, 2008), received by all members of the Association for Physical Education (AfPE), carries advertising for the companies Zig Zag, TriXter, Freddy Fit and Fit For Sport which offer schools, families and community groups ready-made programmes and equipment, at a price. For Tinning, the importance of creating scenarios for the future is less about getting predictions right and more about providing new perspectives on the present. On this point, in terms of thinking about the present, there is considerable consistency in the critiques of those authors who have imagined the decline and fall of physical education. The problems range across the board are deep seated and resist change.

The rise and triumph of physical education

Other authors have engaged in talk that imagines rather more optimistic futures for physical education than those predicted by Kleinman, Locke, Siedentop, Hoffman and Tinning. As with the pessimistic predictions, these more hopeful authors' identification of shortcomings in the present can clearly be seen in their advocacy for the future. Writing in the same volume as Hoffman, Hellison (1987) dreams 'the possible dream' for the 'rise and triumph of physical education'. For Hellison, the underpinning problem was that physical education in higher education had moved away from its applied or service mission, which was to work with practitioners in all settings. Consequently, research no longer benefited practice, practitioners lacked support to further their professional development, and increasing specialisation meant that physical education was fragmenting as health education and recreation education took their own paths towards the future. This view of the need for an applied mission for higher education to address these issues was, of course, very much a reflection of Hellison's own teaching and research programme centred on personal and social responsibility (Hellison, 1995), a matter he readily acknowledged. He also acknowledged, however, that all the trends he identified as problematic seemed to be moving physical education away from the future he would hope to see.

Penney and Chandler's (2000) 'Physical education: What future(s)?' also took an optimistic view that physical education could change for the better.

Building on Michael F.D. Young's (1998) book *The Curriculum of the Future*, they echoed Hellison's concern to connect with and impact on social issues by considering future physical education as a 'connective specialism'. Their vision is shaped by questions about the type of citizen physical education can nurture, and how the subject can become more connected across its own subject matter, across the school curriculum, and to society beyond the school. Their analysis of the barrier to creating physical education as a connective specialism is the current activity-based structure of physical education programmes which emphasise *difference* rather than connection, or, in Bernstein's (1971) language, the strong 'classification' of physical education. On this analysis, anticipated by Lawson and Morford (1979) for 'kinesiology and sports studies' at university level some twenty years earlier:

> We see a need for a *thematically oriented, rather than activity-based curriculum*, and a framework that openly privileges what we may term 'themes' or 'strands of learning'. Such an approach would emphasise the way in which *collectively* various activities (or areas of activity) may facilitate and further particular learning. It would provide a direct challenge to the current insulation and strong classification inherent in physical education curricula and specifically, in the statutory texts of the National Curriculum Physical Education.
>
> (Penney and Chandler, 2000: 77)

They proposed four themes for their preferred physical education of the future: movement and physical literacy; physical activity, health and fitness; competition and cooperation; and challenge. Penney and Chandler recognised that to allow physical education to retain its current form would provide the opportunity for current organisational practices to persist and in so doing undermine attempts to reform. They argued that a close up view of pedagogy is essential, and that a more student-centred approach to learning is required in which relevance to each individual is important. In a follow up paper, Penney et al. (2002) questioned whether Sport Education has the potential to connect in the ways they outline, to which they reply with a qualified 'perhaps'.

Sport Education is also the topic of Hastie's (2003) chapter in the collection edited by Laker, *The Future of Physical Education: Building a New Pedagogy*. Sport Education is a response, for Hastie, to three major concerns about what he described as 'traditional physical education': lack of content mastery, discriminatory and abusive practices, and boring and irrelevant content. Hastie asked whether Sport Education could address these and other problems associated with institutionalised sport. His response was also qualified but rather more emphatic and optimistic than Penney et al.'s, in so far as he recognised that the potential of Sport Education will not be realised without explicit and deliberate efforts by teachers and schools, but that the extensive research that has focused on this pedagogical model (see Kinchin,

2006; Wallhead and O'Sullivan, 2005) has shown that it can offer an alternative future for at least one aspect of physical education, which is sport.

Of the rest of the collection edited by Laker, only two chapters were expressly concerned with the future of physical education, his own contribution and that of Fernandez-Balboa. The other chapters provided, variously, a postmodern justification for physical education based on the oral, particular, local and the timely (Estes); sports culture; citizenship (both chapters by Laker); teaching for social responsibility (Morris); the possibility of teacher reflective practice (Macdonald and Tinning); skill learning (Silverman); and as we have just noted, the chapter by Hastie. Laker added a short editorial note before Fernandez-Balboa's and his own chapters, which appear at the end of the book, to state that Fernandez-Balboa's future for physical education may seem to be somewhat radical to readers, while he (Laker) advocates 'evolution' rather than 'revolution'.

It comes as no surprise to discover, once forewarned by the editor and author himself, that Laker's vision for the future of physical education is much like the physical education of the present. At least, his proposals arguably fall some way short of the 'new pedagogy' this book seeks to build. The theoretical underpinnings of the new pedagogy are based on Jewett et al.'s (1995) five value orientations of discipline mastery, self-actualisation, social reconstruction, learning process and ecological integration. Laker proposed that all five in combination provide a sound and balanced basis for curriculum construction. Laker's future physical education has three 'progressive phases', roughly corresponding to the early, middle and later years of schooling and matching foundation, development and advanced levels of learning. In the first phase the emphasis is on skill development, dance, and self and other responsibilities; in the second, on Sport Education, health-related exercise, and outdoor pursuits; and in the last, recreational physical activities in which choice would feature prominently, social critique of the body and an emphasis on extended social responsibility.

Laker's scheme contains some genuinely radical and 'progressive' elements, such as the Personal and Social Responsibility, TGfU, Sport Education and health-related exercise pedagogical models, a cultural studies approach to popular physical culture, and a theoretical framework provided by the various value orientations. It rests somewhat heavily, however, on the other connotation of 'progression' in a traditional sense, in which, increasingly, advanced movement competencies and social awareness are added on to foundational skills and foundational attitudes. As I will argue in Chapter 4, this is very much the kind of linear thinking that informs the id^2 of physical education-as-sport-techniques. At the same time, Laker may well be right to argue that a genuinely new form of physical education will *evolve* from current practice rather than from a more radical break with the present that, for example, Locke (1992) and Penney and Chandler (2000) predict.

Fernandez-Balboa framed his futures talk within Toffler's three waves of civilisation. He pointed out that current practices in schools, including physical education, have as their reference point the processes associated with the second wave of large-scale industrialisation, including standardisation, specialisation, centralisation and bureaucratisation. The third wave, which has created a post-industrial digital society, emerged in the middle of the twentieth century in economically advanced countries and regions. Fernandez-Balboa speculated on the changes this latest wave has brought to education, including the increasing privatisation and commercialisation of educational services, home schooling, and pressure on government-funded schools and teachers to begin to align themselves to the processes that constitute a digital society. In contrast to Hellison (1987: 151) who wished rather forlornly 'a future without computers', Fernandez-Balboa predicted that in a digital age physical education programmes would be delivered remotely, for example, university study in football coaching undertaken from the comfort of the student's living room, and, echoing Hoffman and Tinning, an increasing privatisation of educational programmes in which the profit motive dominates. He recognised that any changes to physical education arising from digital society will need to contend with stiff resistance from conservative physical educators. Nothing less than a radically new kind of physical education teacher education would be required, argued Fernandez-Balboa, to harness both the empowering and the oppressive double edge of new digital society, producing teachers who have a deep and mature commitment to equity in an increasingly inequitable world.

Futures talk that predicts either a decline and fall or a rise and triumph shares a view of the present, at least at one level. This view of current physical education programmes is that they are failing to achieve the goals they have set for themselves in terms of producing skilful, lifelong participants in physical activity. Producers of these programmes recognise, at various levels of depth of analysis, that the world beyond physical education is changing, and that the institution in which physical education is practised is also facing new, increasingly demanding, challenges. In most of this slender volume of futures writing it is noted that teachers play a critical role in making change happen, though few writers are confident that teachers will embrace change if and when the opportunity is offered. Some of this futures talk has also understood, consistent with the theory of curriculum historians such as Goodson (1987), that the fate of school physical education is intimately related to the future of the field in higher education (see also Lawson, 2009). While we explore historical developments in higher education in some detail in Chapter 5, in the next section of this chapter we consider what researchers have had to say about possible futures for the university version of the field.

Murder or suicide? 'Physical education' or 'kinesiology'? Profession versus discipline?

As with school physical education, there has been very little explicit futures talk as such in relation to the field in higher education and even less empirical research. There has been an ongoing debate since at least the 1960s, however, some of it highly charged and acrimonious, emanating principally from the USA, over the proper name for the field of study. Struggles over the name of the field have also been struggles over its sub-stance in terms of the knowledge base of the field and whether it should properly be described as a profession or a discipline. This debate has gener-ated a considerable literature, much of it appearing in *Quest*, the journal of the NAKPEHE, and in the Academy Papers of the American Academy for Kinesiology and Physical Education (AAKPE) which are published annually in a special issue of *Quest*.

While the majority of these papers don't necessarily attempt to predict futures for the university field, many are keenly aware of the implications of their analyses for possible futures. This is because the debate has been far from merely academic. It has taken place amid the closure of academic pro-grammes and, in some universities, of whole departments in the USA (Rikli, 2006; Wilmore, 1998). Little wonder then that words associated with life and death such as 'survival', 'extinction', 'murder' and 'suicide' feature regularly in this literature. Any debate that concerns life and death has an inevitable and unavoidable future orientation.

At the same time, as Lawson (2007: 27) notes, the 'name-game' and its associated configurations of the field are not restricted to the USA and have 'gone global'. It is somewhat surprising then that there do not appear to have been similar debates in other parts of the world, though some voices have been raised, for example, Crum (2001), Maguire (2004), Tinning (2000), Kirk (1992a, 2000) and Macdonald et al. (1999). The fact that the USA has fora in the form of the NAKPEHE and the AAKPE and a conduit in *Quest* to facilitate discussion about the configuration of the field in higher education may explain in part why the conversations have been concentrated there. It may also be of some consequence that the trend towards academicisation and disciplinarity was initiated in the USA. And physical education was firmly established in the university sector in the USA long before it found a place in universities in Britain and Australia. The important point to note from this, however, is that the issues debated predominantly in the USA are indeed global, with again similarities more prominent than local differences.

Most of the contributors to the name-game and profession-discipline debates agree that the publication of Franklin Henry's (1964) paper 'Physical education: An academic discipline' marked the beginning of explicit advo-cacies for changes to the field in higher education that in little less than 40 years have brought about a fundamental reconfiguration. As Lawson (2007) among others have pointed out, Henry's paper may have captured the mood of the times in physical education, but it was also an act of enlightened self-interest. In the face of new legislation[3] that questioned the credentials of physical education as a university field, Henry and other advocates for dis-ciplinarity sought out a means of convincing university authorities that phy-sical education was theoretical enough to be a serious subject of scholarship, actions that Rikli (2006) claims may at the time have saved physical education from extinction. However, the particular configuration of the new academic discipline of physical education, based on a sub-discipline model, very quickly propelled the field towards ever-increasing specialisation and fragmentation (Lawson, 1991).

In addition, the new discipline of physical education created serious problems for physical education-the-profession. If the biomechanics, physiology and psychology of physical activity or human movement were the knowledge base of physical education, where would teachers study the games, sports, exercise and other movement forms they were required to teach in schools? Indeed, as undergraduate degree-level study based on the sub-discipline model of the field came to consolidate itself through the 1970s and into the 1980s, the time available for the study of practical physical activities was decreasing, a point noted by prominent advocates for physical education-the-profession such as Daryl Siedentop (2002a).

According to Siedentop, not only had the discipline reduced or eradicated the experience of physical activity from programmes of study, but the Franklin Henry model was itself based on 'faulty logic'. Siedentop cited Larry Locke, another vocal advocate for the profession of physical education, who pointed out that if Henry's model of the discipline of physical education was applied to mathematics, students would study the sociology of mathematics, the history of mathematics, and so on, but very little or no mathematics. In drawing out the absurdity of this position, Siedentop (2002a) went on to show how other practical and professional fields of university study such as dance, for example, engaged students in the study of dance which included the practical activity of dancing for much of their programmes. If the same notion of a discipline was applied correctly to physical education, Siedentop and Locke both argued that students would study, through first-hand practical experience, sport, exercise and other forms of physical activity.

At the heart of the debates that ensued around the academicisation of physical education in higher education from the 1960s on, Lawson (2007) suggests there have been at least three areas of conflict. The first is the notion of a discipline versus a profession. The second is what should be the proper name for the field. And the third is the sub-discipline model organisational framework. Each of these issues has had a projected future in the literature.

On the first point of conflict, Bressan (1979) predicted that by 2001 it would be possible to proclaim that 'the profession is dead'; but dead by whose hand? Was it murder or suicide? In her first scenario, the possibility of murder by the disciplinarians was explored. In this scenario, she predicted that an increasing number of new staff would be recruited through the 1980s and 1990s who had been trained in a sub-discipline and who had no affiliation with physical education teaching – once the common experience of all academics in the field. The professionals who were left by the 1990s would be held in low esteem because they would not be able to contribute to research, to generating grant income or to producing publications. Eventually they would be exiled to schools of education where they would immediately come under attack, and challenged to prove they were worth their expensive salaries, facilities and precious programme credits. Bressan concluded that in this scenario we have a clear case of murder. But in the absence of 'a smoking gun', she entertains a second scenario in which the possibility of suicide is explored. Here, through a dogmatic refusal to even acknowledge that they might need to respond to the challenge presented by the academicisation of the field, the old guard professionals bring extinction upon themselves.

In painting her futuristic scenarios, Bressan clearly understood the interdependent relationship between the configuration of the field in higher education and its form and substance in schools. In this she provided support for curriculum historian Goodson's (1987) studies (based in geography and environmental studies), in which he claimed that the survival of a school subject depended very much on the development of a university discipline in which future school teachers can be educated. Goodson's work showed that without the anchor of a corresponding university discipline, school subjects struggled for legitimacy and survival. This is because their teachers' material conditions, in terms of salaries, promotion and tenure, depend on the status of their subject. For Bressan, the irony of the murder scenario is that, ultimately, the profession of physical education would not be able to supply teachers to schools, leading to the elimination of school physical education which in turn would, according to her analysis, starve the university discipline of students, leading to its own eventual demise. Clearly, she hadn't reckoned on the possibility that the school subject might begin to resemble the university discipline form, as it now does in the UK, Australia and New Zealand in senior high schools, a development that lends further support to Goodson's thesis.

Hoffman (1987) came to a similar ironic conclusion to Bressan in his futuristic satire, in which the exercise scientists in biokinetics at the university close to Murrysville not only had a hand in the demise of physical education in local schools, but were also to suffer a similar fate as their specialisms were taken on by more prestigious fields such as medicine and physical therapy. As they desperately sought out alternative employment, they strove to replace the traditional physical educators by training teachers of 'lifestyle education', only to be trumped by university departments of home economics who could produce lifestyle teachers with a broader education. In all the debate about the future of profession versus discipline, this theme of conflict over territory and resources is repeated.

Much of the discussion through the 1980s and into the 1990s only thinly disguised this theme by focusing on Lawson's (2007) second and third sources of conflict: the proper name for the field and its curriculum model. Newell's (1990) so-called 'epic' (Struna, 1991) intervention through the pages of *Quest* was intended to bring 'order to chaos' and to make a definitive argument not only for the proper name for the field in higher education as 'kinesiology' (which according to Lawson, 1991, had been agreed for the USA by the American Academy of Physical Education in the late 1980s), but also to provide a new curriculum model based on inter-disciplinarity,[4] with a clear focus on physical activity. Newell's proposals were well received by some writers (e.g. Kretchmar, 1990; Spirduso, 1990; Wade, 1991). Advocates for physical education-the-profession such as Siedentop (1990) and Locke (1990), however, saw Newell's intervention as a blatant attempt to justify what they considered to be the already serious damage done to the professional preparation of physical education teachers by physical education-the-discipline, damage which Newell openly acknowledged.

Writing in Newell's defence, Wade (1991: 208) stated that 'the undergraduate program in kinesiology should relate to, but not be driven by, the certification requirements of the professional fields that logically connect to the disciplined study of physical activity'. This comment seems reasonable enough but unfortunately misses the point, simply repeating the faulty logic of Henry's original proposal. The nub of the issue is the nature of the discipline, its subject matter and configuration. Indeed, as if to rub salt in the wounds of the advocates for the profession, Wade (1991: 207) claimed that 'the reputation of physical education is poor and ... deficient', apparently failing to see any connection between the preparation of teachers derelict of direct and in-depth experience of actual physical activities and the sub-discipline knowledge-dominated teacher education programmes.

The Newell epic generated much heat but also some light. Two points in particular stood out. First, and in tune with Locke (1992) and Lawson (1983, 1984, 1988), Hellison (1992: 399) commented that 'to really understand what is valued, we must look to those areas that control the socialization process – where the stakes are high and conformity is most important'. Stakes were high because resources were always scarce. At root, all the debate over the future configuration of the field in higher education is, as Goodson and other curriculum historians have shown, based in the pursuit of material interests, interests that are moreover always unevenly distributed and accessed. As we will see in Chapter 4 and elsewhere in this book, Hellison's point about the importance of socialisation, of the shaping of the next generation of teachers and scholars, a point also noted by Bressan (1979) and others, is fundamental to the future configuration of a field. Second, Lawson's programme of scholarly writing provided further support for this proposition that occupational socialisation holds a key to understanding the development of fields of educational knowledge. Rather than something to be avoided, he claimed that specialisation and fragmentation are 'endemic' features of fields (Lawson, 1991). He predicted that growing interest in society in all aspects of sport and exercise was likely to promote only 'the continuous formation of paradigmatic communities and the kinds of fragmentation and specialization they auger' (Lawson, 1991: 291). The trick, according to Lawson, is not to seek to eliminate specialisation and fragmentation but to find ways of controlling the process. He also suggested, as we will learn shortly, that these processes may have some positive dimensions.

Further futures talk followed the Newell epic, most of it continuing to work over the three areas of conflict proposed by Lawson.[5] Krahenbuhl's (1998) contribution very valuably reminded the debaters that they must take account of the changes in the higher-education sector and the new challenges facing universities deriving not just from economic pressures but also from government policies and community expectations. Prefiguring Tinning's (2000) exploration of how universities might fare in 'new' postmodern times, he also expressed his concern with and disapproval of the coming of the virtual campus. No university field was above these challenges, as Park (1998) made clear in her analysis of the crisis confronting the once seemingly impregnable field of medicine. Thomas (1998) reinforced both Krahenbuhl's and Park's points by reminding Academy members that, when academic units were threatened with extinction, local reputation within the home institution counted for much more than reputation abroad.

Siedentop (1998), writing from the point of view of a university administrator, argued that universities, once held in high esteem by the general public, had fallen from grace and needed to regain public trust. Quoting Lawson (1997), he argued that 'society has needs and problems; universities have disciplines and departments' (Siedentop, 1998: 173). Lawson (1998) himself noted that in an era of burgeoning interest in all aspects of physical activity, the field in universities was paradoxically in decline, and set himself the task of answering the question 'why?'. By taking a macro-level view of the university as an institution, Lawson noted that other fields face the same challenges as kinesiology/physical education. He identified the characteristics of 'runaway fields' as displaying signs of 'disconnection, incoherence, splintering, narrow self-interest and fragmentation' (p. 226) and concluded that as a runaway field in danger of becoming a disappearing field, kinesiology/physical education must act responsibly or else 'get what they deserve and deserve what they get' (p. 226).

Locke's (1998) elegant synthesis of the conference proceedings left Academy members with two challenges for the future and a dire warning. These challenges were to reform school physical education and to reform physical education teacher education, both of which were, in Locke's view, failing. Locke charged that the responsibility of these failures lay squarely with Academy members. It was these two things, the concern for the transmission of organised forms of school physical education and the education of teachers of physical education, and nothing else, that in Locke's view made physical education in higher education distinctive in terms of tasks that no other field could claim responsibility for. His warning was that to fail to commit to these tasks risked losing something precious and 'surely will end with finality the vision of the elders who built this Academy' (Locke, 1998: 248).

Rikli's (2006) Amy Morris Homans' lecture provided her with the occasion to review the highlights of this debate about the future of the field in higher education once again, but to then move on to propose a solution to the over 40 years of fragmentation and disunity. After concluding that an appropriate home organisation for the entire field of researchers and practitioners does not currently exist, her solution was the formation by 2010 of an 'American Kinesiology Association', modelled on similar home organisations such as the American Psychological Association. Whether such an association could provide a solution to the three sources of conflict identified by Lawson is, however, arguable.

Lawson (2007) himself considered that a focus on the renewal of the 'core curriculum' provides a means of renewal of the field writ large. The core curriculum, for Lawson, is 'what every undergraduate major should know and be able to do'. To identify a core curriculum, Lawson suggested that a concept of the 'field' needs to replace the dichotomy of the 'discipline' and the 'profession' as the unit of analysis, modelling other service, or 'helping' other fields such as social work, nursing, medicine and law. This more unified concept rests on a special ontology and epistemology which seeks to reconfigure social relationships, power, authority and responsibility. Discipline and profession, argued Lawson, are based on a technocratic hierarchy that moves from 'basic research' through various levels of mediation to application and practice. The field, in contrast, is characterised by a direct relationship between 'experts with knowledge' and 'persons needing knowledge', and so requires the replacement of practice with praxis and a focus on service. Teachers of workers in the field will themselves have been expert workers in the field. A core curriculum then becomes a clear possibility, since its parameters are set by praxis.

Lawson also posed the possibility that fragmentation may not necessarily be the problem that much of this higher education debate suggests, and that it creates the circumstances for the production of 'several fields out of one' (Lawson, 2007: 239). This suggestion raises the possibility of a field such as physical education, which has a clear focus on schools and related sites, coexisting with a field named kinesiology or exercise science. Interestingly, a recent edition of Academy Papers to focus on its vision for the twenty-first century posed entirely the opposite proposition of *e pluribus unum* or 'many into one', which editor Clark (2008: 1) suggested 'captures perfectly the spirit of the other papers presented, as well as the discussions that ensued throughout the meeting'. Which of these proposals for the future of the field in higher education is the most credible we will return to in subsequent chapters.

Conclusion

There is widespread concern for the future of physical education, though little systematic research or explicit writing on this topic. A considerable body of writing on physical education in higher education now exists in the USA, facilitated by the NAKPEHE, its journal *Quest* and the AAKPE, much of which has had a futures orientation. Charles' (2005) report that the NAKPEHE has created a Future Directions Committee is encouraging, though in order to provide leadership to the physical education community beyond the USA this organisation would need to overcome the USA's notorious cultural myopia. The fact that the future of the field in higher education affects the readers and writers of this literature directly and personally may help explain this 'enlightened self-interest'. This body of writing is not matched in school physical education, where teachers there are less likely than university academics to resort to the written word to express their hopes and fears for the future. It is clear, however, as predicted by curriculum historians such as Goodson, that the fate of physical education in both sites is intertwined.

The futures talk that has been recorded sketches both optimistic and pessimistic scenarios for physical education, for its rise and triumph and its decline and fall. All contributors to the debates and conversations about the future of the field in both sites recognise problems in the present and, in some cases, the residue of the past. Their analyses provide us with pointers for where to look for the id^2 of physical education: in the institutions in which it is practised, in the training and socialisation of its practitioners, in the attitudes of its students, in the expectations and needs of communities, and in the research and writing of its scholars. While these analyses are mostly insightful indeed, it is important that we do not, in Locke's (1998: 248) words, 'bungle the opportunity [for genuine reform] by not understanding the problem'. While some segments of futures talk comes close to grasping the true nature of the problem, in particular in the work of scholars such as Lawson, Locke and Siedentop among others, it seems to me that the 'the problem' is not fully or widely understood. In Chapter 4, we attempt to minimise this risk by investigating in some detail the practice of physical education in the present before seeking to understand in Chapter 5 how it came to be the way it is. Or, in other words, we will seek in the next two chapters to understand fully the problem of the currently dominant id^2 of physical education-as-sport-techniques and its past, in order to prepare us to better consider physical education futures.

4   The id² of physical education-as-sport-techniques

The institutionalization of physical education, with its ideal and material interests rooted in sports and games, was also the first historical moment in its future objectification. For institutions imply historicity and social control ... to the point where a way of doing things may well become *the* way. In other words, physical education, the institutionalized profession whose dominant programs consist of sport and games, is viewed as natural process. A way of thinking about, and doing, physical education tends to be the dominant way. This view of physical education becomes part of the common sense disseminated through societal socialization.

(Lawson, 1988: 271)

Lawson captures very nicely in this statement the level at which the id² operates. It is hegemonic in the sense intended by Gramsci (1971) in that it works at the level of assumption, of common sense. The id² of physical education-as-sport-techniques seems so natural and has been the dominant id² for so long that it is, indeed, *the* way of thinking about physical education. But as Gramsci took care to point out, the hegemony of an idea or an ideology is never uncontested, even though it operates for most of the time beneath the level of consciousness. As a 'structure-in-dominance' (Hall, 1985), the id² is a living entity since it exists primarily when it is realised in the practices of teachers and students. As such, it is constantly reasserting its dominance as conditions surrounding it change.

Lawson's statement contains a number of important points which we will come to in the course of this chapter and again later in the book, in terms of this historical process of being made and remade through institutionalisation and socialisation. His description of the dominant configuration of physical education at the time of writing his paper, probably in 1986 or thereabouts, is worthy of our immediate attention since it is of central importance to our consideration of the id² in this chapter. He wrote that the dominant programme in physical education consists of games and sport. In this, I believe, he was correct in the mid-1980s and would be correct in 2009 also. However, as I plan to show here, it is the precise approach to games and sport that is a matter of utmost importance to understanding the pervasiveness of the id², which is the pride of place given to the techniques of games and sports over the performance of the games and sports themselves.

This chapter has three purposes. First of all, I want to explain in some substantive detail what the id^2 of physical education-as-sport-techniques is and to explore the id^2 in its complexity. The language of 'physical education-as-sport-techniques' may suggest that it produces a simplistic form of the subject. I aim to disabuse readers of this notion should they be entertaining it. Teaching and learning sport-techniques forms the centrepiece of the id^2, but surrounding these techniques is a complex of other forces that give the id^2 its considerable reach and durability. Second, I want to show why the language I have used, 'physical education-as-sport-techniques' is an appropriate way to describe the id^2, since in the manner of Lawson's claim that 'the institutionalization of physical education ... was also the first historical moment in its future objectification', the notion of sport-techniques provides the historical link to the id^2 that preceded it, and also provides the clue to its characteristics which will bring about its demise or, perhaps, its transformation into something else. My third purpose in this chapter is to explain why the id^2 has been able to survive as the dominant practice of physical education even when critics can provide evidence that its fundamental articles of faith have not been realised, in the face of claims from physical education researchers from different parts of the world, working in different educational systems and out of different paradigms, that physical education is in crisis and in need of radical reform (see, e.g. Puhse and Gerber, 2005).

First, then, I need to explain that skill is typically decontextualised in the common practice of physical education and rendered 'technique', despite the centrality and fundamentality of the word 'skill' in the discourse of the id^2. Next, I seek to demonstrate through a close examination of the 'skill' lesson and unit how school physical education's subject matter is 'molecularised' (Rovegno, 1995). I then outline the challenge to the id^2 presented by Teaching Games for Understanding (TGfU) and in the process seek to expose the basic assumptions of the id^2. Finally, I explore research on student perspectives and on the institutionalisation and reproduction of the id^2 to complete this analysis.

Skill versus technique: The decontextualisation of skill

Throughout the physical education research literature and within the physical education community more broadly, the words 'skill' and 'motor skill' are used more often than technique. However, following Thorpe et al. (1986), it is important to be clear about the distinction between these terms. Sport-techniques are specific movements that are designed to be effective in achieving a clearly identified goal. The technique of the dig in volleyball, for example, requires players to make contact with the ball with their arms straight and elbows locked, their hands held together in a specific way, their backs straight, heads up and knees bent. The dig is usually the first contact a team makes with the ball on its side of the net when an attacking shot such as a spike needs to be controlled so that a counter-attack can be set up. The technique of the dig, where the ball strikes the fleshy part of the forearms, is designed specifically for this purpose. Typically, in order to be able to perform these movements in a coordinated and effective manner, and since sport-techniques are often complex and difficult to perform well, they need to be practised in isolation from the game of volleyball itself. This lifting out of the dig from volleyball, or in other words this decontextualisation of the movements, is a key feature of sport-techniques.

In contrast, according to Thorpe et al., a *skill* is an amalgam of technique and cognition in context. This is because skilful performance in sport involves not just the effective and efficient movement of the body in specific ways determined by the rules and customs of a sport, it also requires the player to choose to move in the most appropriate manner to suit the prevailing conditions of the play, particularly with so-called 'open' skills where the environmental conditions are apt to change regularly. Skilful performance in sport, this amalgam of techniques, decision making and tactical knowledge, is strongly contextualised. To speak appropriately of the dig as a 'skill', then, would require the performance of this technique in a game, at the right moment in the play, as the best, most suitable movements to perform, given the prevailing conditions confronting the player. It is entirely possible for a player to be able to perform the technique of the dig effectively but to be unable to perform the skill; in other words, to perform the movements correctly out of context, but to be unable to decide when to use this technique rather than (say) the volley, or to misread the flight path of the ball and therefore to be in the wrong position to use the technique to best effect, or to misdirect the ball once contact is made. Indeed, as we will see, the possibility of this disparity between a technique and a skill is one of the enduring problems of physical education teaching and of research on skill learning.

Thorpe et al. are correct then to insist that we make a distinction between these words 'technique' and 'skill'. This is all the more important when we examine the research literature on the practice of school physical education, since, as I aim to show, researchers and teachers alike regularly speak of skills when they are actually referring to techniques. Since the practice of teaching and learning decontextualised sport-techniques forms the basis of school programmes informed by the id², my use of the term physical education-as-sport-techniques is very carefully chosen.

The centrality and fundamentality of 'skills' in the id²

'Skills' are considered to be central and fundamental to the id² of physical education-as-sport-techniques. Lest we think this may have been true once but surely can no longer be the case, Lounsbery and Coker (2008) mount a strong argument for the development of skill-analysis competency in physical education teachers. They, in fact, use three terms interchangeably in their paper – 'skilful movement', 'motor performance' and 'motor skill' – to describe the central and fundamental phenomenon of the id². Their argument for the centrality and fundamentality of skill goes like this. 'Skill proficiency and confidence are paramount to developing a lifelong commitment to being physically active.' Consequently, one of the primary objectives of physical education is 'for students to become skilled movers who are physically fit' (Lounsbery and Coker, 2008: 255). They go on to write:

> Because there is both theoretical and empirical evidence that supports the association between skilfulness and perceived competence and a significant proportion of environmental opportunities for school-aged children to be physically active require skill (e.g. sport and intramural participation), it is our contention that an important function for physical education is the development of motor skill proficiency.
>
> (Lounsbery and Coker, 2008: 257)

They cite the National Association for Sport and Physical Education (in the USA) to support their claim that:

> A foundation for continued motor skill acquisition should be provided and conceivably, it is this foundation that ultimately facilitates successful and advanced motor performance which, in turn as we have already asserted, increases the likelihood of sustained participation in physical activity.
>
> (Lounsbery and Coker, 2008: 257)

Having made these claims about the centrality and fundamentality of skills to physical education, Lounsbery and Coker (2008: 257) confess that 'there is little evidence to suggest that physical education has made strides in developing more successful or skilled performers', a key admission that is repeated with some regularity elsewhere in the physical education research literature.

To make this point about the centrality and fundamentality of 'skill' even more explicit, O'Keeffe et al. (2007) claim that there are generic, fundamental skills that children must acquire before they can move on to learn more sport specific 'skills'. They argue that:

> If a child has not acquired particular fundamental motor skills they would not be able to participate with success in sporting activities that require these fundamental skills or variations of them. For example, one should have a basic throwing pattern before undertaking the learning of specific skills such as the badminton overhead clear and the javelin throw. Gillgren (1991) had similarly stated that young children should be first taught throwing in ways that are not sport specific.
>
> (O'Keeffe et al., 2007: 90)

Notwithstanding the veracity of this claim, which is what their study and other studies like it (e.g. Miller et al., 2007) seek to establish, O'Keefe et al. demonstrate quite clearly in this statement that what they are naming a 'fundamental skill' is more properly described as a generic throwing or striking *technique*, since the movements they study are even more decontextualised than the techniques of the badminton overhead clear and the javelin throw.

In a 1998 study, McKenzie et al. made clear what most other authors mean when they describe skill as central and fundamental to physical education. 'Historically, the development of motor skills, including manipulative, locomotor and non-locomotor capabilities, has been a primary goal of physical education. ... Skill performance is necessary for successful performance in game and sport play' (McKenzie et al., 1998: 327). Operationalised in their study, these manipulative, locomotor and non-locomotor capabilities become 'catching', 'kicking' and 'throwing' a ball.

> Children's ability to catch, kick and throw a ball was assessed in the current study. Object control is a skill requirement in game and sport forms commonly available to children both at school and in the community (e.g. baseball, basketball, soccer, softball). It has been shown that children must master object control before they can use specific manipulative skills successfully in game strategies. ... Mastery of basic manipulative skills enables children to attempt more specialised and complex movements that are part of more dynamic game and sport play, and mastery of advanced skills is typically required if adolescents are to be retained in youth sport.
>
> (McKenzie et al., 1998: 329)[1]

The id² rests then on the assumption that the teaching and learning of sport techniques (most often called 'skills') are of such central importance that these activities define the purpose of physical education. The techniques in question are typically sport specific (badminton overhead clear) or, even though more generic and fundamental, nevertheless sport related (throwing, catching and kicking a ball). Another key assumption within the id² is that physical education is a preparation for lifelong physical activity (a matter we examine in some detail in Chapter 6) and that unless school-age children master the prerequisite skills to play sports and games, mastery contributing to feelings of competence, they are unlikely to be lifelong participants. The format of lessons locates these assumptions at the heart of the teachers' and students' day-to-day practices and experiences of school physical education.

The skill lesson and unit

Writing in the early 1970s about what he called the 'traditional methodology' of teaching physical education, Hoffman offered the following description.

Traditionally, 'good teaching' has incorporated the processes of explanation, demonstration, drill and practice on basic skills, lead-up activities, and game participation as fundamental elements. The entire
sequence of phases may not be represented during every class but it is
generally reflected in a long-range plan for progression within individual
units of instruction. These specific elements may be modified, rearranged
and occasionally even omitted; nevertheless, a cluster of characteristics
always shows through even the most camouflaged forms of traditionalism.

(Hoffman, 1971: 51)

While, as Hoffman suggests, the specifics of lessons may be modified, most
of these elements of the traditional methodology feature at some point over
a unit of work. For example, in a study comparing basketball skills using
mastery and non-mastery learning methods, Blakemore et al. (1992) used the
following lesson formats.

(Mastery) Warm-ups (about 5 min), formative testing (about 10 min),
correctives and enrichments practice with feedback (about 10 min), and
competitive game play (about 10 min), ... (non-mastery) warm-ups (about
5 min), skill instruction, practice, and game play (minutes determined by
the unit plan).

(Blakemore et al., 1992: 238)

Although the mastery lesson contained elements that differed from the non-
mastery lesson, the formats are underpinned by the same logic, which is that
the lesson begins with a skill-related warm-up, the middle part and majority
of the lesson focuses on skill instruction and practice (and in the case of the
mastery treatment, assessment and feedback), and then a game in which the
skills learned are then to be applied.

Another example is supplied by Lee and Solmon (1992) in a study of students' thoughts during a unit of tennis instruction. It is worth considering
their description of the lesson format in detail.

The lesson plan the teacher followed listed the critical features of the
skill to be covered, the specific learning cues to be used, and the questions needed to check for understanding. ... The teacher followed a
model of direct instruction that included task presentation, controlled
practice, and individualised practice. During the presentation phase on
Day 1, the subgoals of the task were defined (e.g. make a V with the
thumb and forefinger, grasp the racket as though you are shaking hands,
swing level) and their relationships to the primary task (i.e. hit the ball
forward toward a floor target) were discussed. Along with the explanation of technique, demonstrations for the grip, footwork, swing, and
follow-through were provided. During controlled practice the students
were led through a step-by-step progression of the technique. Following

the teacher's cues, the students as a group performed each component of the skill (grip, backswing, forward swing, follow-through) along with the teacher. After several trials, the teacher asked the students to demonstrate the forehand grip, and individualised feedback was provided for each student. The teacher then asked the students to demonstrate the technique for the forehand drive. Using the predetermined list of observation cues, the teacher again provided individualised feedback. During guided practice for the forehand drive, the teacher checked to see if the student's side was toward the net and if the foot opposite the swinging arm was forward. Next, the teacher looked for a level swing. If both of these elements were present, the focus of the observation was to determine if the follow-through was up and over the target. ... The last 15 min of the lesson consisted of individualised practice.

(Lee and Solmon, 1992: 258–59)

In this example, Lee and Solmon show clearly the central role of the teacher and the use of 'direct instruction' as the teaching method. In this case, the movements that make up the technique of the forehand drive are demonstrated by the teacher and copied, step by step, by the students. The teacher determines precisely what information is to be communicated, in what order, and whether students have performed appropriately. Note too, in this example, that there is group instruction, where the entire class follows the teacher's lead, feedback from teacher to student as the class perform aspects of the technique, and then a period of individual practice which the teacher monitors. A final point to note from this example is that it is not just the whole technique of the forehand drive that is isolated from the game of tennis. The technique itself is disassembled and the various parts – the grip, footwork, swing and follow-through – are isolated and practised in turn, before being reassembled as one action.

Lee and Solmon are describing an introductory lesson for beginners who had no prior experience of tennis. The case for this lesson format would appear to be compelling. If tennis is a game played with a racquet and a ball, clearly students need to begin by learning how to hold and swing the racquet before they can make contact with the ball. Then once this has been mastered to a satisfactory level through supervised practice, other more complex skills may be taught and learned, such as the backhand drive, the lob, the serve and the smash. The logic of this approach is captured by Blakemore et al. (1992: 35), who argue that 'skills should be taught in a hierarchical order from simple to more complex, and students should clearly demonstrate the ability to master the easier skills before attempting more advanced skills'.

At the beginner stage of learning described by Lee and Solmon, the concern is not for the *skill* of the forehand drive, since, by Thorpe et al.'s definition, the term 'skill' would imply use of the forehand in a game, which requires a player to select the forehand as the most appropriate shot to play in the prevailing conditions, to position herself to meet the ball, to play the shot with a purpose in mind relating to the rules and tactics of the games, and to execute the movements efficiently and effectively. Building on the same logic as the beginner's lesson in tennis, Boyce et al. (2006) provide the example of practice variability as a key principle informing how, over a series of lessons within a unit of work, a student would progress from learning the techniques of sports skills to performing the skills.

> The curriculum in the secondary setting is predominantly activity based ... and consists primarily of units in sports (e.g. volleyball, soccer, softball, archery) or fitness activities (weight training, aerobics, Pilates) lending itself more easily to the implementation of repeated-blocked or random scheduling. The activity-based units typically span 2–5 weeks depending on the unit and grade level. Middle school students tend to experience shorter units (2–3 weeks in duration) while high school students would experience longer units (3–5 weeks in duration). These units are covered in consecutive days or days that follow a block time class schedule and focus on a variety of skills that make up the sport activity. For example, a softball unit could cover many motor skills (batting, base running, catching, throwing, fielding, etc.).
>
> (Boyce et al., 2006: 338–39)

In the context of this 'multi-activity curriculum', Boyce et al. continue:

> practice variability is used primarily as it relates to how the skill will ultimately be used in a game situation and is applied in combination with other skills. For example, in the game of softball the teacher may have students practise different defensive scenarios to help students use a variety of skills (fielding and throwing to the correct base, catching and tagging an offensive player and possibly throwing to another base). In addition, the use of stations as an organising element for the class would allow students to practise a set of skills related to softball and are an excellent way to incorporate repeated-blocked or random practice. ... The practice of multiple skills helps students develop motor patterns for use in improving their game or lead-up game play. Lastly, there are many situations where practice is both variable and random in nature. For example, in modified game play (lead-up or culminating activity), the defensive person must react to the offence by using a series of skills that are dependent on the offensive tactics. Also, in tennis, the forehand and backhand (multiple skills) could be practised in the same practice session in addition to varying the type of ball feed, target location, and/or area on the court from which the learner hits.
>
> (Boyce et al., 2006: 338–39)

We can see in this example that the focus of Boyce et al.'s study, variability of practice, depends on control over the sequencing of lessons and requires that the teacher has the time to consolidate the techniques of games such as softball and tennis before varying the conditions of practice of those techniques so that they become skills that can be used in the whole game. This style of programming is characterised by Ennis (1999) and others in the USA as the 'multi-activity' programme and is practised widely elsewhere. It might also be described as foundationalist and hierarchical, where the structure of units of work within the physical education programme is a macrocosm of the lesson structure in Lee and Solmon's example.

Boyce et al. suggest that the progression of technique to skill depends on the inclusion of lead-up activities such as modified game play incorporating variability of practice, a principle that is taken up elsewhere in the literature on skill learning in physical education. For example, Rink et al. (1991) investigated the use of a four-stage model for students learning the volleyball set and serve which included introduction, extension, refinement and application. The study supported the notion of a carefully planned and monitored progression of learning from elementary to more complex tasks. However, a major difficulty, as Rink noted in relation to her four-stage model, is that 'the most neglected stages of development of games skills in physical education programmes have been stages two and three. ... It is not uncommon to see units of instruction established that move directly from stage one to stage four' (Rink, 1993: 253). In other words, as Bunker and Thorpe (1982) argued in introducing their TGfU approach, the techniques introduced and practised in physical education lessons never become skills that can be used effectively to play games. Rovegno (1995) has very appropriately described this commonplace practice within school programmes informed by the id² of physical education-as-sport-techniques as a 'molecular' approach to physical education.

The molecularisation of physical education

Rovegno (1995) argued that a molecular approach to teaching and learning dominates the practice of school physical education. By molecular she means a foundationalist, linear and hierarchical approach in which advanced skills are added on to basic skills and tactics are learned after skills have been mastered at a level that enables a game to be played. Rovegno explains what she means by this notion of a molecular approach through a case study of a student teacher's dividing and sequencing of subject matter.

> Ted divided volleyball and badminton content into skills and games. He divided skill content into components of the biomechanically efficient body positions of mature performers. He focused solely on telling about and reinforcing these body positions. Teaching meant telling the children about a molecular component of the mature body position. In the bump [dig], for example, he demonstrated and explained about keeping the elbows straight, knees bent, feet in a stride, and thumbs together. He

had the children stand in this mature position and he tossed the ball onto their forearms. Ted discussed the mature pattern of skills as the 'correct way' of performing; developmental patterns were 'problems', 'incorrect', or 'infractions'. Learning meant hearing about and then making 'specific changes' in body components to the biomechanically efficient, mature positions.

(Rovegno, 1995: 292)

Rovegno comments that Ted went directly from Rink's first to fourth stage, from the introduction and practice of this biomechanically informed technique learning to playing modified games. Not only did he fail to recontextualise these techniques, but he also treated what were components of an open skill requiring adaptations to the variable environmental conditions of game play as a closed skill. This meant Ted neglected to teach the students about the perceptual aspects of the skill, including anticipation, and the effort aspects in terms of timing and quality of movement such as the application of force.

Rovegno concluded that Ted's division and sequencing of subject matter was informed by a 'hegemony of biomechanics' that included an unquestioned assumption that there is one correct mature movement pattern that constitutes each of the skills of volleyball and badminton.

I am using the term *hegemony* not only to emphasise Ted's taken-for-granted privileging of the biomechanically efficient position over other knowledge but also because such privileging is pervasive and colors much thinking about motor skill teaching. For example, notions that pupils must be taught the correct technique or they will develop bad habits and that pupils should develop the mature pattern of fundamental skills before developing those skills as game skills or using those skills in game situations are common conceptions about teaching and sequencing content. In addition, the convictions that any movement pattern that is not the mature, efficient pattern is an 'error' and that allowing children to explore when learning a skill will lead to errors and is therefore not effective for skill development are widespread and reflect the privileging of the biomechanically efficient body position. ... The phrase *hegemony of biomechanics* is also meant to call attention to the hidden curriculum. ... The hidden curriculum of the privileging of molecular components of the mature body position makes primary that motor knowledge which is efficient, objective, and decontextualized.

(Rovegno, 1995: 299)

Rovegno's conceptualisation of the molecular approach lies at the heart of the id² of physical education-as-sport-techniques. Her use of the term hegemony confirms Lawson's point that this is a highly institutionalised and deeply sedimented practice that, for many teachers of physical education, is rarely open to question let alone critical scrutiny. Rovegno thinks Rink's four-stage approach is less linear than the molecular approach, possibly better described as 'spiral', though I suggest we can still see in it and in the version of the unitised programme outlined by Boyce et al. the foundationalist and hierarchical characteristics of the molecular approach. She means Ted's case study to represent not an extreme version of this approach applied by one individual, a novice teacher, but to stand instead for an institutionalised molecularisation of school physical education. Nowhere can we see the assumptions of the molecularised nature of the id^2 of physical education-as-sport-techniques more clearly expressed and exposed than in the research literature on TGfU.

Challenging the molecularisation of physical education: The case of TGfU

The TGfU approach developed from the work of Rod Thorpe and David Bunker at Loughborough University during the 1970s and 1980s (Thorpe et al., 1986; Bunker and Thorpe, 1982). It generated enormous interest from pedagogy researchers in physical education from the mid- to late 1980s and later from sports organisations such as the Australian Sports Commission (1997), the Canadian Soccer Association (Holt et al., 2002) and the Rugby Football Union in England (2000). Effectively, Bunker and Thorpe challenged the centrality and fundamentality of the teaching of sports-techniques in games, and proposed that games teaching should begin not with practice of the prerequisite skills but with participation in a game modified to suit the level of experience and ability of the players.[2] So, for example, rather than play tennis with a standard racquet, ball and court, beginners could play with short plastic racquets, sponge balls, lower nets and smaller courts. A modified game of volleyball might include lowering the net and permitting players to catch the ball then throw it rather than begin with dig, volley and spike. Their priority was for players to understand the game and develop tactical awareness that could aid decision making.

The modifications made to the game were of the utmost importance and, as Bunker and Thorpe recognised, required considerable depth of knowledge on the part of the teacher, both of the game and of children's development and learning. Not only did the modified game need to match the current experiences and abilities of the players. It also had to conform to two principles, representation and exaggeration. The modified game had to represent all of the main features of the full game, so that even in a 3v2 rugby game, for example, the game-like qualities of rugby such as attacking to score a try and defending to prevent a score are retained. The modifications to the game also had to exaggerate particular tactics, such as in a 3v2 modified rugby game the ways in which an attacking team might use its extra player to disorganise the defence and score a try, for example, on the overlap, or by splitting the defence.

Bunker and Thorpe maintained that techniques should be practised and skills developed in the usual fashion – that is, through demonstration, feedback and variable practice – but only as the need for the skills became apparent in the course of the players' growing understanding of the game concept and developing tactical awareness. For example, learning the technical aspects of making a lateral pass in rugby – such as how to hold the ball, swinging the arms across the body, aiming in front of the receiver and using the hips to add force – is only relevant when the ball needs to be passed over some distance. In modified small-sided rugby games played on areas of say 10 metres by 5 metres, learning the technique of the lateral pass is not needed in order for this modified game to be played, so long as players can execute a throw of some kind. Bunker and Thorpe's view was that the technique of the lateral pass (for example) could wait until players moved on to a bigger playing area where the possibility of gaining some advantage by being able to pass accurately over a relatively long distance becomes apparent.

Given the central and fundamental role of technique within the id² of physical education-as-sport-techniques, the first studies of TGfU unsurprisingly sought to compare TGfU with the so-called 'traditional' (skill-based) approach (for example Lawton, 1989; Turner and Martinek, 1992; Griffin et al., 1995; Turner, 1996). This rush of studies may have been a sign of enthusiasm for the idea of TGfU or a symptom of researchers' dissatisfaction with the dominance of the technique-led molecular approach. Whatever these researchers' motivation, these comparative studies proved to be disappointingly inconclusive.

In an important and influential contribution to this research, Rink et al. (1996) concluded that comparison between the various studies of TGfU was difficult and results were ambiguous due to researchers' use of different games, lengths of unit, ages of students, and so on. In a very thorough fashion, Rink and her colleagues discussed some of the challenges presented by TGfU for research, adding to the issues already mentioned the matter of the valid measurement of learning outcomes. I have already noted Rink's own line of research within the skill-based programme, her four-stage approach and her concerns that teachers too often moved directly from stage one to stage four. In this context, she and her colleagues gave TGfU very serious consideration, theoretically, methodologically and practically.

Their conclusions are revealing, not just for highlighting key aspects of learning and teaching games that the id² of physical education-as-sport-techniques in its most sophisticated forms has championed. On these matters, Rink et al. (1996: 490–94) concluded that a minimal level of 'object control' was an essential prerequisite to learning to play games such as basketball, volleyball and baseball. Even though these games could be modified, they argued that players still needed to be able to catch, throw, kick and strike in some fashion, and so 'skill' remained fundamental to learning to play games. This is a point that Bunker and Thorpe always readily accepted and indeed endorsed, their response being that the adult form of a game could often be retained through application of the principle of representation using elementary forms of throwing, catching, kicking and striking. They understood that within the so-called 'traditional' approach to games teaching, the skills define the game. 'Tennis' is defined by the use of a racquet and a ball; without the racquet and ball and the various skills that make use of them, according to the traditionalists, it is not possible to play tennis. In contrast, in TGfU, Bunker and Thorpe believed that rules defined the game and that something like the game of tennis could be played without a racquet. The point at dispute here for them was, in other words, a matter of degree rather than an absolute barrier. They accepted the fact that some level of 'enabling skill' was required to play games; they did not accept the interpretation of this fact that game play was impossible without conventional equipment and the relatively mature, sports-specific skills required to use it, or that the skills defined the game, rather than the rules and the tactical possibilities they allowed.

More telling was Rink et al.'s point (1996: 491) that the development of skill and strategy are interdependent, and that the 'ability to execute skills constrains decision making'. This is an argument one imagines Bunker and Thorpe would be ready to concede. Indeed, their point had always been that skill development and tactical understanding needed to advance together, simultaneously, rather than either tactical knowledge or skill taking absolute precedence over the other. Rink et al. (1996: 492) reinforced their argument with the claim that there was an important relationship between cognition and language development. In other words, the students in their studies who had learned to name specific skills had a more sophisticated vocabulary for communicating about game play.

In addition to these important and helpful points of clarification, Rink et al. also reached some more controversial conclusions. On the basis of their studies, they claimed that in skill-based approaches it was possible for students to pick up tactics without explicit teaching. This may be true for some players, but does not mean that this is a good practice to adopt for all. Similarly, contradicting the conventional wisdom that a skill-based approach required direct teaching methods, they claimed that some skills are acquired through indirect teaching (Rink et al., 1996: 492). Again, this could also be true on some occasions but does not make this observation a recommendation for good practice either. Rather more controversially, they stated (p. 493) that there was no advantage for either approach when effective teachers were used, a point McMorris (1998) among others (e.g. Holt et al., 2006) have restated since, claiming that the alleged failure of a traditional approach to games teaching is simply the problem of poor teaching. They did not, however, address the more significant issue of pedagogical content knowledge and the need for teachers to have a high level of understanding of a game rather than merely the techniques of the game in order to use the TGfU approach effectively.

Rink et al.'s conclusions are also revealing because they show clearly the error of assuming that the so-called skill-based approach and TGfU are equivalent 'models' of or for games teaching. The 'skill-based' or 'traditional' approach is much more than this. It is a manifestation of the id² of physical education-as-sport-techniques. TGfU is not part of this configuration since it challenges some of the most cherished assumptions of this id² concerning the centrality and fundamentality of 'skill' and the molecular approach. But TGfU offers no wide-ranging perspective on physical education beyond games, whereas the id² of physical education-as-sport-techniques pervades all aspects of the practice of conventional physical education. To be sure, we might argue that TGfU belongs to a different id² of physical education, one that is yet to be identified. Despite its popularity with researchers (Griffin et al., 2005; Oslin and Mitchell, 2006) the fact that TGfU has continued to be hailed as an innovation in physical education almost 30 years after its introduction to the physical education community provides support for my point that the 'skill-based' approach and TGfU are not equivalent levels of practice and conceptualisation. To compare them as equivalent models of games teaching and learning makes little sense.

For our purposes in this chapter, the value of TGfU is the challenge it presents to the id² of physical education-as-sport-techniques, exposing the strength of the assumptions concerning the centrality and fundamentality of skill and the molecularisation of physical education. One other matter researchers' interest in TGfU underscores is the search for ways of improving the effectiveness of physical education, underpinned by a growing acknowledgement that the dominant form of practice does not only fail to produce skilful participants in lifelong physical activities, as noted earlier in this chapter by Lounsbery and Coker (2008) among others (e.g. Rink, 1993). Much worse, this approach may very well be responsible for widespread and increasingly evident disaffection with physical education among students. Indeed, according to Locke (1998: 247), physical education based on the traditional approach is not just an impediment to learning: 'too often adults have to recover from experiences as adolescents in physical education'.

Student perspectives and the id² of physical education-as-sport-techniques

Even where studies have sought to capture student thinking (Lee and Solmon, 1992; Langley, 1995), likes and dislikes (McKenzie et al., 1994), and learning-method choices in problem-solving (Vincent-Moran and Lafont, 2005), in other words, aspects of cognition, this programme of research has worked within the id² of physical education-as-sport-techniques, accepting that 'skill' learning is central and fundamental in physical education. However, some studies have suggested that the assumption of the centrality and fundamentality of sport-techniques may be a source of student disaffection. Researching the perceptions of high-school students involved in a badminton unit, Tjeerdsma et al. (1996) found that students preferred game play and competition to skill practices. Rikard's and Banville's (2006) investigation of high-school student attitudes to physical education echoed this finding. In their study, they reported the following.

> If the activity was new, their skill levels did improve, but if the activities were those repeated year after year like soccer or basketball, the challenge was insufficient and skill levels were not advanced, especially when skill grouping were heterogeneous.
>
> (Rikard and Banville, 2006: 396)

If units of work within the multi-activity curriculum model typically consist of ten lessons or less on one topic, the possibilities for advancing skill levels may be seriously limited.

Some studies of student attitudes to physical education have addressed sources of disaffection more directly. While the focus on techniques is not always mentioned explicitly, we might reasonably suppose it to be implied, given the strength of connection we have seen evidenced so far in this chapter. Flintoff and Scraton (2001) among other researchers have noted a connection between physical education and gender, usually to the disadvantage of girls. They found that some of the young women they interviewed in their study who were physically active outside school, participated in sport despite their unhappy experiences of physical education and 'were, at best, indifferent to PE; at worse, hostile'. They concluded that 'it is unlikely ... that a traditional games-based curriculum will attract many young women into an active lifestyle' (Flintoff and Scraton, 2001: 18).

Penney and Evans (1999) argued that the 'traditional' approach to physical education, dominated by masculinised forms of games and sports, had managed to survive the invention of the national curriculum in England and Wales, and in the process perpetuate gender and other inequalities in and through physical education. Williams and Bedward (2001) added:

> As far as the 1992 and 1995 Physical Education National Curriculum Orders are concerned, the centrality of 'traditional' team games reflecting a dominant central government view of physical education as synonymous with particular forms of sport, has, in the judgement of some (Penney and Evans, 1999; Williams and Woodhouse, 1996), privileged a curriculum which has much greater relevance to boys than to girls and which reflects a particular and Eurocentric view of physical activity.
>
> (Williams and Bedward, 2001: 53–54)

Smith et al.'s survey of 15 and 16 year olds in the north of England reiterated these points in the context of the National Curriculum Physical Education (NCPE).

> Although the introduction of NCPE was intended to bring about more equitable PE and sporting opportunities among young people, it has, in

fact, kept in place some of the preconditions for persistent inequalities in participation between young males and females within and between individual schools. The continued emphasis on invasion games and the sex differences in participation therein serves to illustrate this.

(Smith et al., 2007: 186–87)

Smith et al. offer two important qualifications about the continuing dominance of the id² of physical education-as-sport-techniques that are worthy of note here. The first is that the actual games and sports available to students in this age group depended very much on the schools they attend, with considerable variation between the seven schools in their study. Moreover, the percentages of girls and boys participating in particular games also varied according to school. Their second qualification is that there is a difference in emphasis on skills between Key Stage 3 (KS3) (ages 12–14) and Key Stage 4 (KS4) (ages 15–16), a feature Underwood (1983: 70) also noted some 25 years earlier.

When reflecting upon their past experiences of PE, pupils suggested that lessons at KS3 were more often than not characterised by a greater degree of skill learning. ... Moreover ... it is clear that young people consider PE, for the most part, to be about learning in the physical. ... [Some] pupils were critical of the almost exclusive use of KS3 PE for the development and learning of skills and, correspondingly, were more likely to suggest that they enjoyed PE less as a result. (Rosie, a GCSE pupil: 'It's boring until Year 10, you have to learn all the skills and do the same stuff over and over again.')

(Smith et al., 2007: 47)

With few specialist teachers in primary schools in the Britain, physical education teachers have often regarded the first two years of secondary school as an occasion for 'remedial' work, in which 'basic' skills have to be taught in the wide range of activities that constitute most secondary school programmes. This emphasis on skills in KS3 identified by Smith et al. may be a manifestation of this attitude among specialist teachers that many students come to secondary school lacking 'the basics', the prerequisite skills they require to play games and sports. According to Smith et al., KS4, in contrast, was less skills focused and considered by these students to be more enjoyable as a result. Most schools offered some choice of activity, something that was strongly endorsed by the students, though Smith et al. (2007) note along with Flintoff and Scraton (2001) that often choice was limited by facilities, the timetable and teacher interest.

The id² of physical education-as-sport-techniques seems to be strongly implicated in these reports of student disaffection. The extent to which disaffection is widespread may be arguable; Tinning (1987) wrote that physical education makes both enemies and friends of young people. Some individuals would no doubt argue that where the molecular approach is taught well, students enjoy physical education and benefit from it. The evidence presented so far in this chapter not only suggests that the teaching of sport-techniques is pervasive in physical education, but also that it does not seem to result in the development of sports skills to any sophisticated level that could be used to play games. Moreover, though many students may be well disposed towards physical education, the studies just cited suggest there is, to say the least, considerable room for improvement. While the evidence is not conclusive, it could be that, no matter how well teachers teach, the molecular approach may be a chief source of student disaffection, exacerbating gender inequity and failing to connect with the forms of physical culture to which young people relate most closely, matters we will turn to in Chapter 6. As decontextualised techniques, it may be that young people don't see the connection, so obvious to their teachers – many of whom are sportspeople – that techniques must be practised over and over in order for them to be used, eventually, to play games; in other words, it may be that young people 'don't get it' (Kirk et al., 2000).

In the next section, I want to explain why the id² of physical education-as-sport-techniques remains dominant contemporaneously. It does so even in the face of its apparent widespread failure to produce young people who are skilful, enthusiastic and knowledgeable players of games and sports. This apparent failure renders problematic core aspirations of the id² of physical education-as-sport-techniques, that prerequisite skills of games and sports equip young people to go on to lead physically active lifestyles as adults, a matter we investigate in more detail in Chapters 5 and 6.

The institutionalisation and reproduction of the id² of physical education-as-sport-techniques

Having sought to demonstrate in this chapter that the dominant id² of physical education contemporaneously involves, in Rovegno's words, a molecularised approach, informed by the hegemony of biomechanics and concerned primarily with teaching decontextualised sport-techniques, I want in the final part of the chapter to highlight some of the factors that seem to me to be most influential in its continuing institutionalisation and reproduction. Lawson's statement quoted at the beginning of this chapter suggests that the reasons for the durability, resistance to change, and pervasiveness of the id² of physical education-as-sport-techniques are complex, and have deep roots in history. An investigation of the emergence of this id² from a different id² of physical education-as-gymnastics is the topic of Chapter 5. This section seeks to form a bridge from the present to the past.

First, at the level of curriculum, physical education must fit the school timetable. In secondary schools, where the majority of physical education programmes with specialist teachers are to be found, length of lessons varies. In some places, blocks of an hour or more may be available. In others, lessons can be as short as 40 minutes. In these latter circumstances, the actual time available for engagement in the subject matter of physical education may be very much less than 40 minutes, after students have made their way to the outlying part of the school in which physical education departments often tend to be found, changed clothing, completed the other aspects of the changing-room ritual (O'Sullivan and Dyson, 1994; O'Donovan and Kirk, 2008), and brought out and distributed equipment or set up a playing area. Within this context, the multi-activity programme seems to present itself as a viable option for curriculum organisation. As Cothran notes:

> From a curricular perspective, what physical education has been is the multi-activity model. This framework of numerous sport or movement activities offered in relatively short and frequently changing units holds a near monopoly on secondary programs. ... The multi-activity model's purpose is to provide students with an exposure to a wide variety of sport and movement while maintaining student interest with its fast changing focus.
>
> (Cothran, 2001: 67–68)

We noted earlier that within the multi-activity programme units of work can be short, according to Ennis (1999) as short as 4 or 6 lessons, though, of course, in some places enlightened head teachers will permit some units that will be longer. We also noted that this kind of structure works against the development of a level of learning beyond the elementary because, as French et al. (1991: 273) pointed out, 'motor skill acquisition takes time'. The exposure of students in secondary-school programmes to a wide variety of sports is often justified by physical educators in the claim that by this method each student has the chance to find a game or sport they may be good at or could develop an interest in that could sustain lifelong participation, an argument we will scrutinise in Chapter 6. On the other hand, as Cothran remarks, these short units of activity may be driven by the more pragmatic concern to prevent student boredom by providing variety.

The practice of the multi-activity curriculum appears to be widespread in the USA, Britain and beyond (Puhse and Gerber, 2005). In Britain, as we learned earlier in this chapter, a number of studies report that the NCPE has had little impact on altering its main features of sport-techniques, direct teaching styles, gender inequity and short units of work (Smith et al., 2007; Green, 2000; Curtner-Smith, 1999; Penney and Evans, 1999; Williams and Bedward, 1999). The ubiquity of programmes informed by the id² of physical education-as-sport-techniques can be accounted for to a considerable extent by the similarity of schools as subject-centred institutions in which the timetable is a fundamental organisational tool. Although writing in the early 1970s, Chanan and Gilchrist's characterisation of the secondary-school timetable and its effects remain salient and informative.

The conventional musical-chairs timetable is based on an assumption of a norm of pupil passivity and recalcitrance. Pupils have to be told what to do; they cannot be trusted; they do not want to learn; they have to be made to learn; this involves imposed discipline; they don't like discipline and are liable to rebel; they therefore need constant supervision. Professing to cope with this situation, the timetable exacerbates it. Sustained concentration, rhythmic development of learning to a natural climax, is impossible. At the sound of the bell, everything must change – the room, the subject, the teacher, sometimes the group. Half the energy of every lesson is taken up by the attempt to establish borders, procedures, norms for an arbitrary unit which will be abandoned again in a few moments. The overriding criterion of timetable planning is to make sure that all classes are occupied in all contact hours. The effect of adjacent lessons on each other, the effect of the cumulative sequence of lessons, is not considered. ... The overall effect is an imposed superficiality, a self-fulfilling prophecy of pupil passivity, uninvolvement, restlessness and all that follows.

(Chanan and Gilchrist, 1974: 16)

In physical education's quest to move from the margins of school life and to be taken seriously as a school subject, it has been forced to accept that it should then be treated just like any other subject (Kirk, 1988). This structure may be able to produce genuine learning experiences in other subjects such as mathematics and geography, though on Chanan and Gilchrist's account, this would seem unlikely. What is clear from the physical education literature is that this commonplace timetabling arrangement creates a constraint on what might be possible in terms of learning. It is little wonder that when the overall effect of such timetabling is 'imposed superficiality', decontextualised, molecularised sport-techniques present themselves as appropriate subject matter for physical education. Moreover, it is understandable that teachers may wish to focus on something tangible, discrete and capable of disassembly and reassembly in a short time, such as sport-techniques.

If the structure of the multi-activity programme and the hegemony of the school timetable delimit what it might be possible to do and to achieve in physical education, research at the level of the lesson provides some insight into other forces at work which support some aspects of the id^2 of physical education-as-sport-techniques, such as the ubiquity of direct instruction as the main mode of interaction between teachers and students. In one of the earliest studies of the ecology of secondary-school physical education lessons, Tousignant and Siedentop (1983) noted that, implicit in the command-style teaching method, teachers and students 'got the work done' through subtle processes of negotiation. They noted that teachers were prepared to compromise the integrity of the instructional task system – the system most concerned with learning the subject matter of physical education – for the sake of maintaining the managerial task system.

This important insight has been noted and developed by others. Schempp's (1985: 165) study of student teaching reached the conclusion that 'student teachers defined progress and no progress in becoming a better teacher as the ability to develop and implement tactics and techniques in order to dominate and control the collective social behavior of their students'. Tinning (1988), also studying student teachers, found that the process of learning to become a physical education teacher was largely shaped by the contingencies in operation in the here and now of the school setting. He argued that 'the pedagogy developed by student teachers is a pedagogy of necessity. There is little sense of a pedagogy of the possible' (Tinning, 1988: 82–83).

Further developing the notion of tacit negotiation between teachers and students in this context of necessity and the pressures of the here and now, O'Sullivan et al. (1994) discovered, like Tousignant and Siedentop, that teachers did not permit students to sidetrack or modify the managerial system in the manner allowed by the instructional task system, and that 'teachers spent inordinate amounts of time establishing, monitoring, and maintaining the managerial task systems of their programs' (O'Sullivan et al., 1994: 422). In these cases, O'Sullivan et al. suggested that the teachers believed their work was not taken seriously in their schools and that little of what they did really mattered. Consequently:

> The curricula offered by these teachers were remarkably similar and traditional. The programs of study were sport oriented with a multi-activity format. While district syllabi highlighted increased capacity for skill and strategic play in sport activities such as fencing, badminton, volleyball, and basketball, the nature of the instructional ecologies of these programs could only allow for modest gains at best. While none of these teachers could be said to have thrown out the ball, we observed instructional ecologies that might best be described as casual rather than learning environments in which students engaged seriously with learning activities. While teachers achieved for the most part classrooms in which students respected each other and the teacher, these classes were less enjoyable and rewarding experiences for students who were less skillful in general and were least enjoyable for less skilled girls in particular. The competitive nature of some learning activities within this casual non-goal-oriented environment allowed more assertive students, who were predominantly male in most (though not all) cases, to act as the steering group and control the tempo or pace of the class.
>
> (O'Sullivan et al., 1994: 425)

As we learned in Chapter 3, O'Sullivan et al. concluded that there is a 'co-dependency' of physical education and the school as an institution. In circumstances where physical education lacks the educational status of other fields of study, they suggested that teachers are more likely to see the management of students' behaviour as of greater priority than their learning of the subject matter.

This point, that teachers have different goals for their work from those stated in official curriculum documents or assumed by researchers or, at least, some goals have a higher status for them than others, is supported by Parker's (1995) study of secondary-school teachers' views of effective teaching.

> Findings drawn from these investigations [teachers' views on effective teaching] seem to indicate that from the teachers' point of view, student learning may not be the most important criterion of effective teaching. Much of the previous research on teacher effectiveness has been process-product in which the behavior of the teacher constitutes the process, and student learning is regarded as the product. ... Although this research has value, the use of student learning as the major dependent variable limits its applicability when, as the literature reviewed here suggests, teachers may have other objectives and measures by which they judge their effectiveness.
>
> (Parker, 1995: 128)

Just as the teachers in O'Sullivan et al.'s study felt that their work was not valued as equivalent to other subjects, so the research on students' attitudes reveals a similar marginalisation among students. Smith et al. (2007: 54) noted that 'there was a near-universal acceptance among pupils that physical education served as a break from other "academic" aspects of school life and was a context in which they can have fun and enjoy themselves by participating and interacting with friends'. Similarly, Flintoff and Scraton found this in contrast to physical activities undertaken outside the school, which offered opportunities for socialising and keeping fit

> The purpose of school PE was less clear. At best it was seen as a break from academic work; at worse, an unnecessary imposition impacting negatively on their academic studies, and one in which they rarely learned new skills useful for their out of school lives.
>
> (Flintoff and Scraton, 2001: 11)

In these circumstances, it may hardly be surprising that teachers and student teachers measure their competence according to the criteria of their students being 'busy, happy and good' ahead of learning skills. However, as the passage quoted earlier from Channan and Gilchrist showed, the timetable and the institutional assumptions underpinning its arrangements present a powerful force delimiting what teachers can do. Thus, as Brown (1999) noted, the prioritisation of control over learning is not simply a matter of choice for teachers. Their concern for management and control of student behaviour ahead of learning of subject matter has a gendered dimension and, indeed, there is an expectation that 'good' physical education teachers will display particular kinds of behaviour consistent with dominant forms of, in the case of his study, masculinity. Brown reflected:

> There is a very real concern for controlling classes and trying to fit into such a strongly regulated institution such as a school. Children, teachers and parents often demand strongly gendered displays from male PE teachers if they are to be considered legitimate and worthy. Given this combination of factors, even well meaning male PE teachers such as Joe and Derek, are likely to be drawn towards demonstrating complicit masculine teaching identities, and so remain active intermediaries in the reproduction of the gender order.
>
> (Brown, 1999: 156)

Brown and Evans (2004) developed this argument, suggesting that particular dispositions in new teachers can be traced to relationships with other physical education teachers, especially those experienced in a pupil–teacher and athlete–coach relationships. They suggested that these relationships may be viewed as inter-generational links which form key moments in the process of cultural production, in particular the production of gendered forms of physical education. This argument finds support in the work of Green (2002) on teachers' everyday philosophies and their figurations of values. Green claimed that these values are grounded in personally successful sporting experiences, complicit teacher education programmes, and a workplace culture that reproduces a particular physical education teaching *habitus*.

Lawson (1983; 1988) has drawn on research into occupational socialisation to argue that this inter-generational reproduction is how institutionalised forms of professional practice sustain themselves.

> Assuming that all social institutions aim to reproduce themselves, the joint effects of education and sport on the aspiring teacher-coach should be very powerful, indeed. Most such persons should be oriented toward acts of curriculum maintenance, resulting in the continuing dominance of the sport education model. Very recent work on the occupational socialisation of physical educators appears to confirm this suspicion. … The subjective warrants of recruits into physical education teaching are resistant to their teacher education programs, the programs themselves are not designed to have a high impact on these subjective warrants, and teacher educators can't agree in any case what the main focus of their subject is or should be.
>
> (Lawson, 1988: 274)

The very nature of the field, grounded as it is in competitive success in organised physical activities such as games and sports, tends to attract individuals with similar physical attributes and dispositions. At least, this was the case until the academicisation of the field of physical education teacher education was fully under way by the 1980s (Whitehead and Hendry, 1976: 52). Even though physical competence perhaps has counted for less than it did up to the mid- to late 1970s, as we will see in Chapter 5, recruits to physical education continue to express the same or similar subjective warrant as earlier generations. The sheer visibility of physical competence or lack of it, on display daily to the hypercritical community of young people in schools, continues to demand a particular kind of physicality from physical education teachers. Macdonald's and Kirk's (1996) discovery of the pressures felt by young teachers of constant surveillance suggests that the *habitus* of the physical education teacher remains even today relatively narrowly defined.

Producing a different kind of teacher may offer the possibility of change. But as the research on socialisation into teaching shows, the pedagogy of necessity and the peer pressures of workplace culture soon wash out any radical ambitions that may reside in neonate teachers (e.g. Stroot et al., 1993). Those who discover that teaching physical education offers a different kind of challenge from the one they expected may move on to other occupations, as the work of Macdonald (1995) suggests. But this attrition is in itself a further mechanism of selection, ensuring that only those teachers who are committed to 'acts of curriculum maintenance' persevere with the hardships and pleasures of teaching physical education.

As I argued in Chapter 1, the need to have some acquaintance with most of the very wide range of subject matter that many physical education programmes now contain adds a further powerful force to the perpetuation of the id² of physical-education-as-sport-techniques. If it is only possible to have expertise that is 'a mile wide and an inch deep', if the academicisation of physical education has squeezed the space available for the development of expertise in practical physical activities so that teachers 'are so unprepared in the content area that they would be described as "ignorant" if the content area were a purely cognitive knowledge field' (Siedentop, 2002a: 369), then the impetus towards molecularisation is accelerated. In place of the deep knowledge required of teachers to teach games for understanding, for instance, there is an irresistible draw to apply the biophysical knowledge that now occupies pride of place in the preparation of most physical education teachers and to treat learning as a technical biomechanical process of acquiring mature, discrete and decontextualised techniques.

There may be a parallel here with Harold Benjamin's 'Saber-Tooth Curriculum' (Peddiwell, 1937). In his satire, Benjamin's Palaeolithic teachers persisted with a curriculum that included saber-tooth tiger-scaring-with-fire, woolly-footed horse-clubbing, and capture of fish-with-the-bare-hands even when the environmental conditions for using these skills had changed. The tigers were replaced by bears who were not easily scared by fire, the woolly footed horses became extinct and the rivers became too muddy to see the fish. The curriculum was culturally and economically obsolete. Even when this was pointed out to the traditionalists among the Palaeolithic teachers, they argued that the educational value of these activities lay precisely in their lack of direct relevance to the real world (see Lave, 1997). While the environment has changed in terms of the physical culture of society, as I will argue in Chapter 6, physical educators have continued to teach decontextualised techniques of an ever-widening programme of games and sports with an ever-decreasing expertise to do so, particularly in terms of understanding how techniques become skills and how the use of skills is determined by an understanding of games and sports. Despite clear calls on physical education to make a contribution to ameliorate the alleged obesity crisis, it is not scepticism about the reality of this crisis that has prevented teachers from subscribing wholeheartedly and implementing faithfully forms of health-related exercise (Harris, 2005). It is as if physical education gains greater educational status as its subject matter becomes, like the saber-tooth curriculum, more decontextualised, more technical, but ultimately superficial and less meaningful.

Conclusion

My purpose in this chapter has been to offer an account of the currently dominant id^2 of physical education. I have sought to show that 'skill' learning has been viewed, unproblematically for the most part, as central and fundamental to physical education, and that this molecular approach (Rovegno, 1995) is ubiquitous, long living and resistant to change. In fact, and more accurately, I have argued that physical educators are concerned less with skills and more with the techniques of a wide range of games and sports. There is a hegemony of biomechanics that physical educators sustain on a daily basis as they teach the same short units of elementary sport-techniques 'again and again and again' to increasingly disaffected students. Moreover, this hegemony is perpetuated as *the* way (Lawson, 1988), through an intergenerational process of cultural reproduction, whereby like-minded and socialised individuals are recruited and socialised into 'acts of curriculum maintenance'. To change the dominant practice of physical education would appear to require a wholesale change in the perspective of physical education teachers and teacher education. If there is to be a shift in the id^2 of physical education, it may seem to require, as I will argue in Chapter 7 along with Locke (1998), radical reform.

But are there signs of an impending crisis? Alternative forms of physical education have emerged such as TGfU and health-related exercise that have challenged the id^2 of physical education-as-sport-techniques. Physical education fails, by its own admission, to develop skills and thereby to facilitate lifelong physical activity, a claim we will interrogate in some detail in Chapter 6. Young people appear to be showing dissent. Physical culture is, most certainly, in constant process. And governments have expectations that appear to far surpass the modest offerings of current practice. It seems to me that change is something that can happen to physical educators or, alternatively, they can take an active part in bringing about change, even if this action works against the current self-interest of traditionalists.

I have suggested that the currently dominant id^2 of physical education-as-sport-techniques emerged around the 1950s from a formerly dominant id^2 of physical education-as-gymnastics. How did this shift occur? Was it through revolution, or evolution? By studying the conditions of the emergence of the id^2 of physical education-as-sport-technique we may be in a better position to understand the circumstances in which this change happened, and to identify any lessons in these events for what the future may hold for physical education. At the very least, by studying the emergence of the current id^2 and its early days, we may be better able to understand the hopes and aspirations of those early pioneers of the 'new' physical education (as it must surely have been), and to see which of these if any have been realised, changed or forgotten over time. We need to search, in other words, for the 'first historical moment of its future objectification'.

5 Continuity and discontinuity
The residue of the past in the present

The term 'physical education' has been in general use for a few years; before that the term was 'physical training', which in turn was preceded by an activity known as 'drill'. A further, and very descriptive term – 'physical jerks' – is familiar to many, and recalls the quality of movement that used to be regarded as an effective means of setting up physique and ensuring discipline. ... The use of these different phrases is interesting because they reflect the gradual development of certain ideas. The 'physical education' of the present day not only embraces a much wider scope of activities than the 'drill' lesson of the beginning of the century; it also reflects a different relationship between the teacher and the class, and a different conception of discipline. Drill was inherited from military manoeuvres; physical education has emerged from the observation and study of the needs of growing children.

(Ministry of Education 1952: 83–84)

In Chapter 4, I argued that contemporary practice of physical education can best and most appropriately be conceptualised as the id^2 of physical education-as-sport-techniques. The question this chapter seeks to address is how was this id^2 of physical education socially constructed? What was this id^2 of physical education's 'first historical moment of its future objectification'? How has physical education come to be practised in the way it has and how might we explain its resistance to change? In this chapter, I suggest that answers to these questions might be found in a study of the historical roots of contemporary practice. What we are seeking to do in studying the past is not, as the authors of *Moving and Growing* appeared to believe, to map the gradual 'progress' of ideas and practices. It is instead to understand both the continuities and discontinuities between past and present. Which past practices have disappeared, and which have continued in a residual form to impress themselves on the present? In other words, how much of drill and physical training has remained within physical education?

The chapter draws together original historical research I have conducted in Britain and Australia since the late 1980s, and published in two books, *Defining Physical Education* (Kirk, 1992a) and *Schooling Bodies* (Kirk, 1998a), and also in numerous papers in journals and in book chapters. The majority of this work has focused on school physical education, though some has also

taken the form of theoretical and empirical investigations of physical education in higher education, with a particular concern for physical education
teacher education (Kirk, 2000a; Kirk and Macdonald, 2001). I base the
chapter heavily on Australia and Britain as countries, but, as I have done
elsewhere in this book, seek to point out major differences in the patterns of
events in other countries where I am aware these exist. For the purposes of
this book, which seeks to use a study of the past to understand better both
present and possible futures, there is much nuanced and important detail
that is omitted. The curious or sceptical will need to refer to the books and
papers referenced here and to other histories of physical education.[1]

We begin with an account of the id[2] of physical education-as-gymnastics,
it origins in the work of German and Swedish gymnasts, and its institutionalisation in schools in a 'drilling and exercising' form of physical education.
Next, we consider physical educators' criticisms of the past and hopes for
the future during the transition period between the two id[2]s of physical
education, mainly from the 1930s on, which contain insights into the demise
of the id[2] of physical education-as-gymnastics. We then seek to understand
change and continuity between the two id[2]s of physical education and the
residual influence of the 'old' physical education on the 'new', particularly
the concept of skill learning as linear progression and the effects on physical
education of the school as an institution. Finally, this study of the continuities
and discontinuities of the past and present considers how the academicisation of the physical activity field in higher education, discussed in detail in
Chapter 4, impacted on physical education teacher education and on its part
in the social construction of the id[2] of physical education-as-sport-techniques.

The id[2] of physical education-as-gymnastics

The historical roots of physical education lie in gymnastics, which formed
the basis of a curriculum activity in schools from the middle to late nineteenth century until around the early to middle twentieth century, variously
named 'drill', 'gym' or 'physical training'.[2] There were two main forms of
gymnastics which influenced the substance of the school subject, one origi-
nating in the nineteenth century work of Friedrich Ludwig Jahn in Germany
and the other in Per Henrick Ling's work at the Central Gymnastic Institute
in Stockholm, Sweden. Many other gymnasts built on Jahn's *Turnen* and
Ling's Swedish gymnastics, and throughout the nineteenth and early twentieth centuries there was much adaptation and development. In Britain, the
Swedish version of gymnastics was adopted for all government schools as
the basis for physical training and was enshrined in several official syllabuses
between 1909 and 1933. Swedish gymnastics was most radically challenged
by the women gymnasts who based their work on Rudolf Laban's modern
educational dance, and, for a period beginning from around 1940 on into
the 1950s in Britain, educational gymnastics vied with Swedish gymnastics
and later with the emerging sport of Olympic (now Artistic) gymnastics (a

version of *Turnen*) as the defining form of physical education. As I recounted this history in *Defining Physical Education* (Kirk, 1992a), by the 1960s Swedish gymnastics had all but disappeared from the curriculum and by the 1980s the mainly female educational gymnasts lost out on two counts, trumped by a fast-growing number of men in their field and by a male-driven sport-related form of the subject, the id^2 of physical education-as-sport-techniques.

The detail of the emergence of these forms of gymnastics and their various fates in different countries is important and can be found in a number of excellent histories cited earlier. For our purpose here, more important still is for us to understand some of the key features of gymnastics, and some of the values that underpinned these embodied practices so that we can better appreciate the issues and problems physical educators were addressing when they sought to replace the id^2 of physical education-as-gymnastics with a new id^2 of physical education.

A.D. Munrow (1963) argued that the Greek concept of 'gymnastics' during the classical period, as it appeared for example in Plato's *The Republic*, was concerned with education through the medium of the body. He noted that in the intervening 2000 years the concept had undergone some considerable changes in emphasis, but that this notion of 'education through the physical', as we will see, remained important in twentieth-century thinking about physical education. Munrow (1963: 11–14) also pointed out that these two forms of gymnastics derived from the work of Jahn and of Ling had mistakenly been included under the same umbrella term of gymnastics, despite the considerable differences between them.[3] For instance, Jahn's gymnastics used apparatus such as rings, pommel horse and bars to execute movements that became increasingly formalised over time. Munrow pointed out that this form of gymnastics had from its beginning a competitive element. Swedish gymnastics, on the other hand, was created with mainly therapeutic purposes in mind, and was closely linked to medicine. While Jahn's gymnastics developed strength and muscularity, particularly of the upper body, Ling's system of free-standing exercises was aimed at the development of supple, flexible joints, some cardiovascular and local muscular endurance, and good posture. Both forms required high levels of manual dexterity and coordination, but only *Turnen* could be considered a sport. Both also included, more through accident than design according to Munrow, vaulting and agility, which in some British physical education circles by the 1950s had come to be regarded as the pinnacle of gymnastic work (mistakenly, in Munrow's opinion, pp. 16–17). Moreover, both *Turnen* and Swedish gymnastics, either from their origins or through appropriation, were connected to military practices.

Munrow's purpose in *Pure and Applied Gymnastics* (1963) was to produce a precise and, in his view, accurate definition of gymnastics which eventually and controversially in his day excluded most of Olympic gymnastics and vaulting and agility but included all free-standing Swedish exercises and some technique practices for educational gymnastics. For our purposes, it is more appropriate to consider all this activity as part of the dominant id[2] of physical education of the time, of a configuration of the field best named physical education-as-gymnastics. While one version used apparatus and the other did not, and one could be practised as a competitive sport (though in schools it more often was not), both, along with their many adaptations, were more similar than different, particularly in their detailed and precise attention to the effects of particular exercises on the body, but also in their explicit moral expectations of gymnasts. By attending to these similarities, we can learn something of the values that underpinned and informed these highly specialised 'techniques of the body' (Mauss, 1973).

Absolute precision of movement lay at the heart of the id[2] of physical education-as-gymnastics. In Swedish gymnastics, 'correctness of performance' (Kirk, 1998a) was manifest in the precise movements of large groups of gymnasts in unison, as can be seen in surviving film footage of the annual Lingiads, freely available on the internet. Not only had movements to be performed correctly, literally 'by the book', but the timing of up to tens and even hundreds of people had to be exact. In *Turnen*, work on apparatus meant that individual activities were of greater importance than mass, synchronised movement but, nevertheless, imprecise movement not only failed aesthetically but it could also be dangerous to personal safety. Significantly for our study here, gymnastic movements consisted almost entirely of what in more modern parlance came to be known as 'closed skills', skills that are performed in circumstances in which there is relatively little variability in the environment, such as moving objects, opponents, or changing conditions such as wind (in sailing) or snow (in skiing). In other words, variability of the environment is relatively low and *technique*, including the coordination and timing of the actual physical movements of limbs, trunk, head, hands and feet, is a matter of prime importance during learning and performance. This factor is highly significant for our understanding of the id[2] of physical education-as-sport-techniques, as we will come to see in the course of this chapter.

Swedish gymnastics allied the concern for correctness of performance with a systematic mapping of the entire range of gross muscular movement of the body, a concern that is not apparent to the same extent in Jahn's approach, where there was no concern to be systematic. According to Munrow (1963: 10), while Jahn developed the earlier work of the German Guts Muths in relation to his apparatus, Ling developed Muths' work in relation to the classification of exercises along anatomical lines. This classification formed the basis for Munrow's judgement that Ling's was a *system* of gymnastics, whereas Jahn's was not. Ling based his entire pedagogy on his classification of exercises, and each lesson of each level of Swedish gymnastics sought to train the body's capacities in detail, both developmentally and systematically.

Significant also is the fact that from their beginnings, both *Turnen* and Swedish gymnastics in their pure forms, outside the school context, were strongly gendered. Indeed, the various adaptations made to both versions over time often sought to make them *more* feminised or masculinised by, for example, introducing more rhythmic movements to music in the case of the former and more powerful movements in the case of the latter. Daring, spectacular athletic feats of vaulting and agility, for example, became a very masculine province until at least the 1960s. Munrow noted that Jahn's over-riding interest in developing *Turnen* was to foster patriotism, and male gym-nasts would often march to and from gymnastics sessions singing patriotic songs. In Australia, even though, like Britain, Swedish gymnastics was selected as the official system for government schools, concerns about cadet training for boys prior to the First World War resulted in hybrid forms of practice that included Swedish exercises coupled with squad drill and rifle practice (Kirk, 1998a). Not only were the gymnastic movements adapted to make them more suitable for women and men, but classes were also usually strictly single sex. This aspect of the id^2 of physical education-as-gymnastics was to have a long and powerful residual affect on the contemporary id^2 of physical education-as-sport-techniques, particularly as it found its place in the curriculum of compulsory mass secondary schooling from the mid-twentieth century in Britain.

The id^2 of physical education-as-gymnastics also made various claims about the relationship of specific versions of gymnastics and health or, more precisely, specific effects on the body. Our current understanding of the exercise–health relationship only took shape from the 1930s as scientists began to understand how the application of the principle of progressive overload could impact on strength and endurance (Kirk, 1992a: 137–47). In the nineteenth and early twentieth centuries, the effects of gymnastics on health in Britain was most often conceptualised as balanced or harmonious physical development, by the 1930s enshrined in the notion of 'posture' (McIntosh, 1968: 212). The British 1909 *Syllabus of Physical Exercises for Schools* stated that the physical effect of physical training had three health-related benefits: to general health through efficient functioning of the body; remedial benefits in terms of correcting poor posture; and developmental benefits in terms of assisting the natural pattern of growth of the child (Board of Education, 1909). Munrow (1963: 13) argued that one of the rea-sons why *Turnen* was unpopular in educational circles in the first half of the twentieth century was that it produced 'ill-balanced physical development', particularly enlarged muscles of the upper body.

Each aspect of the id^2 of physical education-as-gymnastics provides some insight into the values of its creators and practitioners of these specialised techniques of the body, and perhaps of the wider societies in which they lived and worked. Use of the term 'gymnastics' made a connection to clas-sical Greek culture with its educational connotations, suggesting a need to provide these practices with a respectable heritage that raised them above mere animalistic movements. In the Swedish system and its derivatives, gymnastics could also be valued as a form of physical therapy, and thus was closely aligned with medicine. The fact that gymnastics was adapted to express contemporary notions of femininity and masculinity should not surprise us, either. At the same time, we might note both the social class and the emancipatory dimensions to this idea that women could have the freedom, the capacity and the time to exercise, and the reality of the struggles women faced that prevented the majority, particularly working-class women, from doing so (McCrone, 1988; Vertinsky, 1992). The link between gymnastics and militarism is also notable, particularly explicit in the activities of vaulting and agility shared by both versions of gymnastics, since vaulting had antecedents in horsemanship and the training of cavalry (Munrow, 1963: 14–17).

There is, however, a more subtle link between gymnastics and militarism that also recommended gymnastics to educationalists charged with the task of establishing the first systems of compulsory mass schooling in the mid- to late 1800s. The id[2] of physical education-as-gymnastics was characterised, especially as we have noted in its Swedish form, by precision of performance of large groups of people en masse. Such precision required a high degree of conformity and a willingness to submerge individual behaviour to the needs of the collective. As I argued in *Schooling Bodies* (1998a), this version of gymnastics was a creation of a period of history Michel Foucault (1977) characterised as 'disciplinary society', in which power was shifting from the central authority of the sovereign to be distributed or capillarised throughout society, and from an external to an internal locus of control. This capillarisation took place, according to Foucault, through a proliferation of what he called 'little practices' centred on the regulation of the body in space and in time within the new institutions of industrial society, including factories, barracks, prisons, asylums, hospitals and schools. The trajectory of disciplinary society was self-regulation or the policing of the self in harmony with the imperatives of industrialised, capitalist nation-states.

Transposed into the emerging industrial-age school (Lawson, 2009) as an institution of mass, compulsory education, gymnastics took on a particular form with a particular purpose. While the physical effects or benefits were no doubt genuine aspirations, it was the so-called educational benefits of moral rectitude, self-discipline and obedience that attracted the interest of the creators of the first state schools for the masses. Swedish gymnastics was viewed as one means of instilling order and discipline among cohorts of children as the school began to establish itself as an institution. In order for the school to function, the compliance of the children was of paramount importance. All unruly aspects of human behaviour, from control of bodily functions to peaceful interactions between pupils to cooperative relationships between pupils and teacher had to be regulated before the school could function as a school. Compulsory mass schooling as it took shape in the final decades of the nineteenth century required children to sit still for lengthy periods of time, a highly unnatural act in itself. They were required to concentrate for prolonged periods, and to undertake difficult tasks, such as learning to read, write and count. Movement about the school also had to be orderly, and there were rules even for this, such as walking only on one side of corridors or stairs when moving in a particular direction. Transgression meant certain and often brutal punishment.[4]

Children's bodies were of central importance to this task of creating and maintaining order. The timetable, as we learned in Chapter 4, and the classroom were two devices essential to this task. The timetable designated what activities were legitimate at any given point in the school day, when they would take place and for how long; the timetable mandated where children should be and where they should not at any given moment. The classroom was in Foucault's terms a 'differentiating space', in which the worth of each child was constantly displayed by their positioning in the classroom, and by the freedoms of movement and special status (such as 'monitors') they enjoyed. This is the context into which gymnastics was transposed. From its very beginning in schools for the masses, and notwithstanding whatever other rhetoric was used to justify its inclusion in the school curriculum, gymnastics was a form of physical training that was seen to literally embody the school's institutional imperatives for order by regulating children's bodies through meticulous attention to the detail of movement. It provided a microcosm of the regulation of children's bodies in time and in space.

We need to look inside physical training lessons themselves to fully appreciate how Swedish gymnastics was so well suited to this task of corporeal regulation in compulsory mass schooling. As we have already noted, lessons were conducted en masse, with the expectation that all children would perform the exercises in the same way at the same time. I recount in *Schooling Bodies* (1998a) that each exercise is described in close detail, and each child was expected to perform exercises precisely as they were set out. There was no room, in other words, for individual interpretations or variation. As it appeared in the 1909 and subsequent British syllabuses, and also in the Australian adaptations of these, Swedish gymnastics was structured by many tables of exercises that were carefully graded by their level of difficulty. Here we find, at the centre of the id^2 of physical education-as-gymnastics, a linear notion of *progression* which, as we saw in Chapter 4, also lies at the heart of the id^2 of physical education-as-sport-techniques in relation to skill learning. Teachers were required to follow the progressions to the letter, to work through each table of exercises in precise sequence.

More than this, in the syllabuses up to and including the Board of Education's 1933 *Syllabus of Physical Training for Schools*, each lesson was scripted, detailing the various parts of the lesson, what would take place in each, and what 'words of command' would be used to initiate particular responses from pupils (such as 'head backwards – bend!', 'left foot sideways – place!', 'trunk forward and downward – stretch!' and 'knees – bend!'). The lessons, tables of exercises, and entire *Syllabus* covered systematically all the major muscle groups and joints of the body. This was, indeed, a *system* of physical training; in the words of Lingian disciple Gustav Techow (1866: xii), gymnastics sought to cultivate a 'systematic culture of the muscles'.

We should recall that most of the teachers in the early elementary schools who were expected to teach physical training lessons had no specialist training. Since the system required precision of movement and, notwithstanding the tightly scripted lessons, many would have experienced considerable challenges to achieving the desired effects, as indeed observers of the time reported (see Kirk, 1998a). For instance, writing in the mid-1950s, Bert Willee of the University of Melbourne wrote:

> Though it has been said that a good teacher can make of 'heel raising and knee bending', a wild adventure, and though one may agree with the sentiments, many have found the doing beyond their powers. It is generally agreed that ... many teachers have found that they cannot make Part 1 of a 1933 Syllabus Lesson either interesting or meaningful to the primary school child.
>
> (Willee, 1955: 1–2)

Nor in elementary schools could teachers afford to observe the nuances of gender that were so crucially important among the trained specialist gymnasts. In Britain, women gymnasts were far in the majority of trained specialists from the 1890s to the 1950s, and they worked mainly in private schools for girls. In the state elementary system, prepubescent boys and girls were effectively treated, for the purposes of physical training, as androgynous (Kirk, 2000b), the needs of social regulation outweighing the social construction of femininities and masculinities. With the addition of quasi-military practices such as marching, physical training in these schools was a hybrid, shaped by and for the institution's needs, and might most accurately be described, as I have done elsewhere (e.g. Kirk, 1998a), as 'drilling and exercising'.

Before we move on from this brief account of the values underpinning gymnastics and its use in compulsory mass elementary schooling, it is worth recalling also that sport had little or no place in physical training in these schools at this stage, though particular games and sports were by the end of the nineteenth century already firmly entrenched in the private, mainly secondary schools, serving the social elite classes of Australia and Britain. Games also featured as minor activities in the early gymnastics training programmes for women and in some high schools for girls (McIntosh, 1968: 13). My argument in *Defining Physical Education* (Kirk, 1992a) was that sport, or more accurately sport-related practices, only became part of the curriculum of physical education in Britain in the 1940s and 1950s with the beginning of compulsory mass secondary education. This is not to say, though, that no sport was played in elementary schools prior to the mid-twentieth century in Australia and Britain. In both countries, highly organised inter-school competition in particular sports, mainly for older boys, appeared in the early 1900s (Kirk, 1998a). But sport in this context was an extra-curricular activity and was not considered to form part of the core curriculum of physical training.

Hopes and visions for the future, criticisms of the past: The demise of the id^2 of physical education-as-gymnastics

Dating precisely how long the id^2 of physical education-as-gymnastics remained dominant is not without difficulties. Local events played an important part in shaping practices between and also within countries and regions, all the way down to the individual school level, as we saw in Chapter 4 with Smith et al.'s (2007) survey of schools in England. Advocacy for change regularly appeared before changes actually manifested themselves in noticeable ways.[5] We can do little more, perhaps, than suggest that in Britain, for example, the id^2 of physical education-as-gymnastics was dominant from the mid-1800s to the mid-1900s, but that during this 100-year period its dominance waxed and waned. As a means of conceptualising the practice of physical education, gymnastics was in the ascendancy until the early 1920s or thereabouts in Australia, Britain and the USA, though it persisted longer in Britain because of the rich history of specialist training first of women then of men that preceded Australian specialist institutions by up to 50 years. We might also suggest that its practice persisted in schools beyond the certainty among some thinkers and writers that its days were numbered. At the same time, as I have recounted elsewhere (Kirk, 2006a), as late as 1954 Scottish male and female physical education associations were predicting that the future of physical education for boys in their secondary schools would be centred on Swedish gymnastics rather than educational or Olympic versions.

We might argue as I have done in *Schooling Bodies* (1998a) that the form of society that gave birth to the id^2 of physical education-as-gymnastics, that is, Foucault's disciplinary society, was changing as the Industrial Revolution was consolidated. In the nineteenth century the practices of capillarising corporeal power were, in Foucault's words, 'heavy, ponderous, meticulous' whereas, by the middle of the 1900s, specialised techniques of the body such as physical education required a 'looser form of power over the body', one that was moreover increasingly diffused, individualised and internalised. The need for the heavy, ponderous and meticulous practices of drilling and exercising may, by the decades after the First World War, have diminished. Dating the decline and fall of the id^2 of physical education-as-gymnastics is not, then, straightforward. What we can do, though, in order to trace and better understand the process of its decline and replacement by the new id^2 of physical education is to note the criticisms of the past contained in expressions of hopes and visions for the future.

Ennis (2006) has suggested that the decline of the id^2 of physical education-as-gymnastics began in the USA following the end of the First World War. In its place, a new id^2 was articulated under the heading of the 'New Physical Education'. Critics of gymnastics claimed that these physical training programmes were 'education *of* the physical'. Strongly influenced by the work of John Dewey among other progressive educational and social thinkers,

American physical educators argued that physical education was 'education *through* the physical' which, we might recall, was, according to Munrow, the classical Greek conception of gymnastics. Consistent with child-centred principles of the day, physical education was to focus on the 'whole child' and to engage the mind as well as train the body. Ennis argued that by the 1930s, the New Physical Education was inspiring school programmes that focused on games and sports for boys, and dance and other less competitive physical activities for girls. She noted, also, that the New Physical Education was at one and the same time a rejection of 'foreign' systems of physical education and an affirmation of the place of physical education in supporting American democracy.

Similar currents were flowing in Australia and Britain at this time where it was popular, and widespread, belief that the shift from physical *training* to more frequent use of physical *education* as the name for the field was based on the influence of child-centred ideas. Writing in retrospect in the Carnegie research papers series in 1966, the first warden of Carnegie Physical Training College, Ernest Major, observed that:

> During the period 1919–39 the scope and conception of Physical Education in the schools were considerably broadened to include not only Physical Training in the narrow sense, but also games, swimming, dancing and athletics, and in many areas camping was also introduced.
>
> (Major, 1966: 5)

Carnegie was one of the first specialist training colleges for men in Britain, established in 1934 with the aid of a grant from the Carnegie Foundation. A close examination of the teacher training course offered by Carnegie in the late 1930s registers some broadening of the curriculum, though the College's 1937–38 *Syllabus* (Carnegie College of Physical Education, 1937) showed that Swedish gymnastics ('modified to suit British conditions') continued to dominate the timetable.

The 1955 Carnegie *Syllabus* tells a different story. This *Syllabus* is presented in considerable detail, but we need to search the document to find gymnastics. In an entry under the heading 'Theory of Physical Education and Teaching Technique', gymnastics is discussed in terms of its suitability for primary and secondary schools, involving for the former 'a wide variety of small apparatus and large climbing apparatus' and for the latter 'the use of portable and fixed apparatus'. Nowhere is there mention of Swedish gymnastics, which we can only assume (with some support from Peter McIntosh, 1968: 262–63, himself a Carnegie student of the 1930s) was in the process of being squeezed out of a rapidly expanding curriculum. At the same time, gymnastics did not quite disappear overnight. 'School gymnastics' retained 112 hours in the 1955 Carnegie timetable in contrast to 84 hours of training in major and minor games, 56 hours each of athletics, swimming and camp craft, and 42 hours of national dancing, supplemented by a substantial portion of time devoted to teaching practice and a growing list of theoretical subjects (Carnegie College of Physical Education, 1955: 19–20).

There can be no question then that, consistent with the New Physical Education in the USA, the curriculum of physical education in Britain was expanding first in the specialist colleges but very soon after in the schools. Developments in physical education for primary school children in Australia also echoed the New Physical Education's concern for child centredness, the education of the whole child, and education through the physical. In the Australian monograph *Physical Education for Victorian Schools* which replaced the 1933 Board of Education's *Syllabus*, the Medical Inspector of Schools wrote:

> Formal exercises are artificial, unrelated to life situations, and generally lacking in interest; they also completely ignore the very important influence that the emotions exert on the physical well-being of the individual. Enjoyment and enthusiasm are necessary if the exercise is to have a stimulating and beneficial effect. We therefore insist that every child has the right to play, and that this right must be restored to all children who have lost it.
>
> (Education Department of Victoria, 1946: vi)

The notion that 'formal exercises' were in some sense 'unnatural' was a criticism of Swedish gymnastics repeated more and more frequently from the 1930s. Increasingly too there was expressed a concern that physical activities should be *meaningful* for children if they were to engage with physical education fully. Both sentiments form themes running through Willee's (1955) book *Small Apparatus for Primary School Physical Education*. He commented that:

> In the past it has been customary to regard gymnastics of the 'artificial', 'constructed', 'manufactured', type as the only way in which systematic, preparatory, body training may be given. To young children, therefore, Part 1 [of the 1933 Syllabus Lesson] has been unreal, lacking in meaning.
>
> (Willee, 1955: 37–38)

For Willee, the challenge for teachers was to use 'small apparatus' – bean bags, lengths of rope, hoops, bands and so on – to make exercises more meaningful for children. He stated that physical education was based on two fundamental characteristics of children, 'the urge to move and the urge to play'. It followed then that:

> Since physical education is education through movement and through experiences which arise from and are inherent in moving, the physical education teacher needs to learn as much as possible about the way in which children do move in a given situation.
>
> (Willee, 1955: 17)

This concern for the meaningfulness of movement for the individual child represents a major break with Swedish gymnastics in which, as I noted earlier in this chapter, allowed no room for individual interpretation. Even so, while the rhetoric of child centredness, individual freedom and expression inspired some physical educators such as Willee, it was nevertheless a source of considerable disagreement and conflict within the physical education community. In *Defining Physical Education* (Kirk, 1992a) I showed that criticism of 'traditional' gymnastics and a vision of the future that was child centred had also come from within the ranks of the specialist-trained gymnasts in Britain. Building on work carried out by Swedish and Danish women gymnasts in the 1920s and 1930s, the women gymnasts in Britain led the construction of a new version of gymnastics that sought to counter the 'manufactured' and 'unnatural' exercises of Swedish gymnastics with a form of movement based on the radical approach of Rudolf Laban to modern educational dance. By the mid-1940s, this critique had completely riven the female gymnasts' tight-knit community in Britain into the camps of the 'old' Swedish gymnastics and the 'new' educational gymnastics. Pleas for moderation fell mostly on deaf ears, with the 'new' gymnasts accused by a visiting Australian, Marjorie Swain, of acting like 'a mystic cult of initiates' and described by historian Sheila Fletcher as a 'mystic cult of female groupies' (Kirk, 1992a: 62).

Some writers of the time, such as Willee and Randall, attempted to steer a middle course. Willee advised, for example, in a chapter on 'suggestions for students and reminders for teachers' and under the heading 'freedom' for children:

> With command-response methods there was little opportunity for self-expression and little actual freedom; in the modern lesson the pendulum must not be allowed to swing to the other extreme. It is undesirable that our children should be trained either in docility or to be without respect for authority.
>
> (Willee, 1955: 46)

Martin Randall (1967: 97), writing originally in 1952 in *Modern Ideas on Physical Education*, noted the growing feeling that the 'traditional type of physical education lesson is inclined to be too rigid'. The difficulty this created was that, using traditional methods, teachers could not hope to cater for the 'vast variety of children with their differing backgrounds, taught under varying conditions' (p. 98). He proposed that the problem of 'teacher domination' of lessons might be avoided by allowing children scope to practise, to experiment and invent, and some choice of activities. He echoed Willee's view that maintaining a balance between teacher domination and children's freedom was a matter for 'common sense' (Randall, 1967: 101)

In expressing their hopes and visions for the future of physical education, even 'moderate' reformers were highly critical of the form of physical training that established the subject in schools in Europe, the USA, the Antipodes and many other places from the mid- to late 1800s up to the early to mid-1900s. Little wonder, perhaps, that those who remained loyal to Swedish gymnastics were, by the 1940s, bewildered and defensive. The passionate embrace by some physical educators of child-centred principles and notions of self-expression, meaningfulness and individuality by the mid-century is somewhat startling given the highly structured, teacher-dominated physical training programmes of the preceding 70 years or more.

If, in at least its less satisfactory manifestations, a drilling and exercising version of Swedish gymnastics had been repressive, with an explicit agenda of corporeal regulation, then an extreme reaction in the opposite direction, to advocacy for 'absolute' freedom and liberation of movement, is perhaps not so surprising. At the same time, we can understand why there was as much concern expressed over the implications of these progressive principles for the practice of physical education as there was joy over their liberating possibilities. The mix of child centredness and Laban's 'mystic' influence was, as Fletcher (1984: 132) observed, heady indeed for the women gymnastics who embraced the 'new'.[6] But, notwithstanding the apparent radicalism of the times, the institutional context in which physical education had developed meant that there was to be a high level of continuity between the 'old' and the 'new', with residual effects that persisted in highly subtle ways. And in British physical education from the 1950s on, men for the first time became the majority of specialist teachers. It is to these changes and continuities we turn in the next section.

Change and continuity: The residue of the 'old' physical education

Just as physical educators began to take seriously and incorporate child-centred principles into their writing and practices during the 1940s and 1950s, several events created significant change. In Britain, the first of these was the commencement of compulsory mass secondary education and the raising of the school leaving age to 15, in England and Wales from 1946 and in Scotland from 1948. Mainly as a result of this event, more specialist teachers of physical education were required for the new secondary schools, both men and women. The existing colleges did not have the capacity to meet the demand for teachers and a long-running expansion of physical education teacher education was set in process during the post-war years.[7]

In this context, the long-established private colleges for women that had supplied the vast majority of specialist gymnastics teachers for over 70 years and which were the main site initially for the struggle over the 'old' and the 'new' physical educations were suddenly in the minority. While the community of physical education was expanding all around them, and as the politics of the post-world war settlement were being worked out between the left and right wings of British politics, the main proponents of progressive educational ideals in physical education were locked in a fierce and bitter civil war with their backward-looking colleagues. Notwithstanding the insularity, elitism and Victorian 'familism' of their colleges noted by Sheila Fletcher (1984), it would in any case have been difficult for the women gymnasts to take forward the radical impetus of the child-centred, Laban-inspired moment. The concentration of teachers in the new secondary schools did not augur well for child-centred ideals that supporters such as Willee admitted, and others such as Munrow (1963: 280–81) argued more forcefully, had a more natural home in the primary school where physical education was in the hands of generalist, mainly female, teachers.

We noted earlier that while the specialist gymnasts were highly sensitive to the gender-appropriateness of Swedish and other versions of gymnastics, elementary schools had more urgent priorities for social control and tended both in policy and practice to treat prepubescent children as androgynous. When they began to populate the new secondary schools, however, the physical education specialists discovered children already in adolescence. Androgyny in these circumstances was out of the question, and the sex-differentiated curriculum student teachers experienced in their single-sex colleges found a comfortable home in the secondary school. What this meant was that the men, unencumbered by civil war and tradition, and not required to consult with their female counterparts, could take forward their own curriculum.

While the language of child centredness peppered their discourse through the 1950s and beyond, the men took forward progressive ideals selectively. For example, the technology of fitness development was greatly advanced during the war as armed forces sought to turn conscripts into soldiers. Out of this work emerged schemes such as circuit training, pioneered by Morgan and Adamson (1961) at the University of Leeds. For many male physical educators, circuit training not only had a basis in the emerging science of exercise physiology, but it also satisfied the progressive principle of catering for individual needs and was, additionally, more likely, they argued, to appeal to adolescent boys than educational gymnastics.

It was, in fact, the areas of continuity rather than change that became sources of conflict between female and male physical educators as the gymnastics wars of 'old' versus 'new' finally began to fritter out by the mid-1950s. One of the areas of continuity from Swedish gymnastics to educational gymnastics was the foundational concept of 'generalisation before specialisation', that physical education provided first and foremost a general and systematic training of the body. Willee, as we have noted, was a strong critic of the old style of gymnastics and an equally forceful advocate of child-centred methods. He continued to argue, however, that a *system* of physical training remained an essential feature of new approaches to physical education.

> If one is convinced that systematic body-training is essential, that generalization must come before specialization, that all-round development

must be a fundamental aim of any programme of physical education, then Part 1 of a physical education lesson may well be transformed from a set of small, subjective, invented, meaningless, manufactured exercises, into objective,[8] natural, meaningful activities, achieving nevertheless the same avowed purposes as the original.

(Willee, 1955: 2)

Here, Willee is describing a crucially important continuity between Swedish gymnastics and educational gymnastics, a residual influence that the emerging male physical educators were to use against the female educational gymnasts. Paradoxically, this notion of generalisation before specialisation also lies behind the arguments of contemporary proponents of fundamental motor skills, as we saw in Chapter 4, a matter we return to later in this chapter.

M.E. Squire, in the mid-1940s principal of Anstey Physical Training College for women, captures the notion of a generalised physical training that lay at the centre of Swedish gymnastics. She claimed that Swedish gymnastics:

Is the only form of physical education which systematically attempts to affect bodily structure and to remedy possible defects of posture; therefore it should be the basis of all physical education in that it prepares a sound moveable instrument upon which all other forms of physical education should play harmoniously.

(Squire, 1945: 101–4)

The educational gymnasts rejected all the alleged formalism and artificiality of Swedish gymnastics, but remained faithful to this idea that the purpose of gymnastics was to develop this general physical educated-ness, which they named 'body awareness' or 'body concept', a general kinaesthetic capability, that underpinned all other physical activity.[9] This notion was, however, criticised by various male and female physical educators. Martin Randall, for example, argued that:

The use of gymnastics as a means of acquiring a general faculty of skill has been discussed and, excepting so far as it contributes along with all movement experience to a general fairly low level of bodily coordination, this claim must be rejected. Above this level ... , which is attainable through a varied physical education rather than gymnastics alone, skill tends to be highly specific.

(Randall, 1967: 65)

Barbara Knapp, a colleague of both Munrow and McIntosh at the University of Birmingham, in her widely read book *Skill in Sport* (1963), went further.

It cannot be claimed that educational gymnastics develops a central factor of physical activity for many attempts have been made to isolate a general motor factor but without success. Suggestions that it develops 'body awareness' or 'kinaesthetic sensitivity' should also be accepted with caution. ... Research indicates that skills are highly specific ... and similar skills which are not identical can interfere with one another.

(Knapp, 1963: 112–13)

R.E. Morgan (1973), Director of Physical Education at the University of Leeds between 1945 and 1973,[10] took a much more sympathetic line, discussing skill in the context of 'quality of movement', a clear attempt to connect the men's interests in skill with those of the women educational gymnasts. He argued that physical educators had made the common error of believing that skill is an act when in fact it is, following Oxford philosopher Gilbert Ryle (1990), a disposition. As such, the disposition to act in a particular manner will always be shaped by the conditions in which a movement has previously been practised, with each new performance being shaped by previous performances and in turn shaping those to come. Morgan suggested that skill is much more fluid than many physical educators had argued in the 1950s and 1960s, and adaptability rather than replication is of central importance; skill is, in other words, a productive rather than a reproductive process. Moreover, he wrote, skill is 'specific' only insofar as it relates to facility of performance in a particular field of behaviour, but at the same time is neither a general capability nor a mere stimulus–response reaction.

Morgan also had something to say on this topic directly to educational gymnasts. He argued that mimicking a cricket stroke using Laban's effort actions, which, for all intents and purposes, requires the body to move in an almost identical way to a cricket stroke played in a match, is not adequate preparation for learning to play a cricket stroke and far less for learning to play cricket. He wrote:

> The ability to reproduce movement forms is of great value in many situations, particularly those associated with expression or communication or with purely locomotor actions. ... But it is not the heart of the skill. The ability to make a flowing cricket shot (as many a dancer could make after a short period of initiation) would be of no value without the quite different ability to connect with a bouncing ball.
>
> (Morgan, 1973: 30)

Although he does not use the terms, I suggest Morgan here is effectively distinguishing between a skill and a technique consistent with the manner I outlined, with the help of Thorpe and Bunker, in Chapter 4. Skill is specific in the sense that it involves a disposition to act in a manner appropriate to the circumstances in a given field. The rehearsal of the movements that make up a cricket stroke may resemble a skill, but no matter how closely they do so does not make the movements the skill. This, as I will argue towards the end of this chapter, is a key insight of Morgan's, assisting us to understand the social construction of the id[2] of physical education-as-sport-techniques.

A further continuity between both Swedish gymnastics and *Turnen* and the sport-based form of physical education that was championed by male physical educators in Britain after the Second World War was a preoccupation with skill as a concept and its location at the heart of physical education. Ennis (2006) notes that in the USA leading physical educator Delbert Oberteuffer (1951) was instrumental in returning the focus of physical education to a notion of education *of* the physical by stressing the importance of motor-skill learning and of the scientific principles that informed skill acquisition. We have noted the key difference in understanding of skill between Swedish gymnastics (in particular) and the post-Second World War concept that skill is not a generalised physical capability but is instead specific to particular fields of action. While this distinction was argued consistently by British male physical educators in their post-war debates with the female educational gymnasts, I suggest it was not necessarily adhered to in the sense described by Morgan and, indeed, for both conceptual and institutional reasons, was not well understood in practice.

In the orthodoxy of the time, it was believed that 'motor skills' (sometimes also referred to as 'perceptual motor skills') existed on a continuum of closed to open skills. The location of a skill on this continuum was determined by the degree of variability in the environment in which the skill was regularly performed. Making a pass in soccer is a relatively open skill because the passer has to take into account the positions of her teammates relative to her own position, the positions of opponents, her own passing ability and the ability of the target player to receive and control the pass, matters which will, in turn, determine the force of the pass and its precise direction, and to consider the state of the game and other options of shooting or dribbling. Playing a shot in golf is relatively less open than a soccer pass since the ball is stationary and there are no opponents to contest possession of the ball. Nevertheless, the golfer has to account for the lie of the ball, its position in relation to and distance from the hole, club selection and weather conditions, each of which varies from one shot to the next. The performance of a shot put is, again, relatively less open than a golf shot, since the throwing surface and other conditions seldom vary except, perhaps, in extreme weather.

Morgan (1973: 27), arguing against this conventional wisdom, suggested that the notion of a closed skill is a misnomer, since a characteristic of skilful performance is adaptability to changing conditions. No two shot puts will ever be exactly alike since one precedes, and therefore inevitably influences, the next. Less esoterically put, in a sport, various competitive effects such as anxiety, motivation, concentration, audience and so on will have some influence on performance and so will have to be taken into account by a performer. But what Morgan fails to account for explicitly, as we noted earlier, is the difference between a skill and a technique, even though he demonstrates the difference in his example of the dancer and the cricket shot.

Munrow captures this contrast between a skill and a technique more explicitly by focusing on the crucial issue of how much variability in the environment can be tolerated when a skill is being learned.

> At an early stage in skill acquisition, it is necessary to eliminate all the environmental factors which are not essential to performance and to standardise others. Thus, for example, kicking, trapping and heading a ball do not require at this stage any opponents in the field of vision, certainly not the challenge of opponents, nor even necessarily a goal or other relevant target. Practices, however, do need enough of the environment to give the task meaning. We move immediately into an area of controversy. How much environment is needed to give meaning? Can one usefully practise cricket strokes with a bat but without a ball? Is there a useful stage in tennis serving practice with no throw up but with the hitting of a suspended ball?
>
> (Munrow, 1963: 248)

The issue Munrow is raising here is how decontextualised a task or activity can be before it is rendered either meaningless or of little value in learning a skill because the part that is 'learned' (that is, capable of reproduction) cannot be transferred to the whole skill and its performance in context. Munrow's response to these questions is that however far decontextualisation is taken, this must only ever be a transitory phase, and that 'the sooner it is over the better'. He goes on:

> One needs to be outward looking and to relate the movements to the environment to which they are essentially a response. The standardised environment needs randomising so that the performer can deal with the varieties of speed, direction and angle of the oncoming ball. The other factors of the environment – which may quite fundamentally affect the nature of the response – need reintroduction so that ultimately one is reacting to the full array of environmental information.
>
> (Munrow, 1963: 248)

Rink (1993) would certainly recognise the challenge to practise Munrow has identified here. Her four-stage model of skill acquisition, which we noted in Chapter 4, was concerned specifically with this process of reducing the environmental complexity of skill learning while keeping in view the circumstances under which skills will be employed. Introduction, extension, refinement and application, the key teaching strategies within this process, including the need to build in variability, are the substance of the simultaneous outward- and inward-looking activities of the teacher in designing learning experiences for pupils.

Munrow certainly appreciated the controversial nature of this issue, of how decontextualised a skill could become and still remain a useful aspect of learning to play games and sports. He also noted the relatively wide range of views on the issue or, perhaps, the different levels of comprehension among his peers. Following the passages quoted above, he goes on to cite Walter Winterbottom, first coach to the England men's football team, who, according to Munrow, insisted on forms of practice that were strongly contextualised, requiring skills to be learned as close to the game situation as possible (Munrow, 1963: 248–50). To design learning experiences of this kind is demanding of the teacher's and coach's knowledge of the activity in terms of knowing just how much complexity to allow. It is demanding too of the players, who must learn to cope with the inflow of a range of information in a short period of time. It is significant that Munrow (1963: 249) wrote: 'such principles of skill training have application over a wider range of sports than at present employ them'.

While there was then, from the 1940s on, an emerging base of knowledge about skill learning, particularly sports skills, much of it deriving from experimental studies, and while some writers of the time clearly understood the challenges skill learning presented, there would in all likelihood, as Munrow seems to suggest, have been a wide range of comprehension among teachers of the implications of this knowledge for practice in schools. As we have seen, the historical roots of school physical education were in gymnastics, in particular in a form of drilling and exercising. The primary focus of drilling and exercising was on education *of* the physical, despite the aspirations of the New Physical Education in the USA and educational gymnastics elsewhere to the contrary. Consequently, it is entirely to be expected that (male) physical educators (in particular) in the 1950s and beyond would accept unquestioningly 'motor skill' as *the* most significant dimension of their subject matter.

I have suggested that the notion of generalisation before specialisation, so central to Swedish gymnastics, continued to thrive within educational gymnastics, while elsewhere in physical education the received wisdom of the day was that 'skill is specific', and so it was not possible to achieve a generalised physical education that could be transferred to more specific activities. Morgan's (1973) writing reveals some of this thinking to have been muddled both in terms of how a (specific) skill related to the more general concept of skill, and in what sense a skill might be said to be specific. I suggested that beneath his example of the dancer mimicking a cricket stroke there was the issue of technique, a highly decontextualised form of the actual skill of playing a cricket stroke. Given a lack of shared understanding among physical educators of the era on these issues surrounding skill, it seems to me that there may be more continuity than we might formerly have suspected between Swedish gymnastics and the sports-based form of physical education, between the id^2 of physical education-as-gymnastics and the id^2 of physical education-as-sport-techniques. There are at least three reasons to suspect that despite the rhetoric of child centredness and in particular the emphasis on the meaningfulness of physical education, the form of physical education that came to replace drilling and exercising in schools failed to resolve the challenge of making physical education individualised and meaningful.

The notion of progression and institutionalised physical education

Swedish gymnastics was structured around the notion of linear, step-by-step progression. Its tables of exercises were carefully graded according to the ages and experience of pupils, ranging from elementary to advanced. I suggested earlier in the chapter that the concept of generalisation before specialisation seemed at odds with the post-war idea that skills are specific but that, paradoxically, the advocates for fundamental motor skills we met briefly in Chapter 4 have continued to advance this concept. Researchers such as O'Keefe et al. (2007) argue that there are generic throwing patterns, for example, that must be learned in advance of specific sports skills such as the overhead clear in badminton and the javelin throw. Others, such as McKenzie et al. (1998), discuss experience of generalised abilities to catch, kick and throw as prerequisite to their use in games and sports. While it might be argued the contemporary advocates for fundamental motor skills are somewhat more specific and precise about which fundamental skills relate to sports-specific skills this, it seems to me, is only a matter of degree. The notion of linear progression, from the more general to the more specific is, I would argue, identical.

Even among those physical educators who argue that 'skill is specific', a notion of linear progression in learning is of central importance, as we saw in Chapter 4 in the examples provided by Lee and Solmon (1992) and Boyce et al. (2006), among others. Within this notion of progression, learning is considered to be additive, in the sense that skills can be disassembled and reassembled, and that the molecular parts are building blocks for larger blocks which can be built, eventually, into the whole skill and applied to the whole game. Note that this concept of skill runs counter to the notion advanced by Morgan (1973) earlier in this chapter, in which performance is not additive, but is instead transformative,[11] where adaptation to accommodate new information is a key characteristic. In Chapter 4, we learned how the Teaching Games for Understanding (TGfU) approach to games challenged this notion of progression as an additive process by proposing that children could learn to play modified versions of games ahead of mastering the mature skills. TGfU has frequently been mired in debates about cognition versus skill and whether one should be given priority in the learning process over the other. This debate, I suggest, has been deeply misleading from the outset. The real reason that TGfU has provoked resistance from some researchers and teachers is, in my view, the challenge to the profound belief that mature skills are prerequisite to game play. TGfU challenged the order of the skill-learning universe; it showed that linear progression from the molecular level of technique to the mature skill is not fundamental to playing games and sports after all.

Even in the face of these continuities with the past, with the unquestioned positioning of skill at the centre of post-Second World War physical education practice, built on a linear notion of progression and, notwithstanding the apparent confusion over this central concept of skill itself, even in the face of all this, the id[2] of physical education-as-sport-techniques may never have become a reality but for two further decisive factors relating to the school as an institution.

The first of these was the structure of the timetable in secondary schools and physical education's place within it. The institutional imperative of the school for order continued in the 1950s, as it had in the 1880s, to use the timetable and the classroom (and by extension the laboratory, workshop, gymnasium and corridors) as the means of manipulating the two principal coordinates of time and space to control children's behaviour by regulating their bodies; in other words, it retained its 'industrial-age logic' (Lawson, 2009). As physical education laid claims to the status of a subject, it was obliged to fit into the timetable as did other subjects. Typically, in junior secondary grades for children aged 11–14 in England and Wales, physical education might have been timetabled for up to two 40-minute periods with one additional double period of 80 minutes per week (Munrow, 1963: 273; Whitehead and Hendry, 1976: 23). For this age group, activities tended to be compulsory. Older pupils might have expected to receive less time than this, though typically through the 1960s to the 1980s, they would have been granted some forced choice of activity (Whitehead and Hendry, 1976; Underwood, 1983). Munrow (1963) recognised the potential problem the curriculum of physical education, with its ever-increasing number of activities, posed for schools.

> Any headmaster must feel somewhat bewildered at the prospect of timetabling a 'subject' the requirement for which may vary between twenty minutes on a squash court, an hour on the track, an hour and a half on the pitch and two days in the local hills or estuary. ... The headmaster who is sympathetic to a catholic concept of physical education is still confronted by a total timetable in which every other subject is accustomed to fitting tidily into the units of single or double periods: and these are the subjects on which his school is primarily judged.
>
> (Munrow, 1963: 273)

The problem of fitting into the regular timetable for the physical education teacher was: What could conceivably be achieved in 40 minutes with a class of up to 30 children of mixed ability and diverse experience of games and sports, and variable motivation and interest? Once time is taken for a class to find its way to the physical education department, often, as I wrote in the previous chapter, on the outer edges of the school, changed and undergone the other rituals of the changing room such as giving up valuables to the safe keeping of the teacher and getting out equipment, and then doing all these in reverse including (in some schools) the requirement for a shower, where is the time for meaningful teaching and learning? If a unit of work is as short as even six or eight lessons, this could amount to a total instructional time of two to three hours at 20 minutes per lesson. Two to three hours of teaching and learning in one block might provide an opportunity for learning. Spread over six to eight weeks, with regular interruptions due to inclement weather, withdrawal of key facilities such as games halls for examinations, assemblies, school musicals and 'harvest fayres', it is little wonder the same introductory content is taught, as Siedentop (2002a) reports, again and again and again.

Here, then, is one of the obdurate realities faced by physical education teachers during this transition from an id^2 of physical education-as-gymnastics to an id^2 of physical education-as-sport-techniques. The subject matter of physical education had widened, which was for many male physical educators a cause for rejoicing.[12] The subject by the end of the 1950s included a wide range of games and sports in addition to gymnastics, which was, over time, to decrease in importance (Underwood, 1983). The development of skilful performers who would become lifelong participants in games and sports were the worthy goals of this 'modernised' subject. But where was the time to realise these goals? What else could teachers do, given their mission to develop the prerequisite skills for games and sports, but concentrate the precious little time that was available on the development of the basic, introductory skills, which were at least discrete and self-contained? And how easy was it, when faced with large groups of children characterised by mixed interest and ability, to slip from the development of skills to the development of techniques? It is possible too to see why the command style of teaching could retain its appeal, despite the rhetoric of child centredness.

The second institutional factor was a situation that was possibly peculiar to England, but it was decisive in this context and compounded the issue of the timetable. The problem was put by Munrow (1963) like this:

> There is ... the concept of physical education as a 'subject' and therefore taught by one or two members of staff. It follows that the 'subject' takes place in a classroom (a special one called a gym ...) between certain times on certain days. This is supplemented by a double period called 'games' at which *any master* may assist when academic periods do not add up to a full working week.
>
> (Munrow, 1963: 273, my emphasis)

This unusual arrangement was widespread during the 1950s and on into the 1970s and beyond in England. Whitehead and Hendry explain why.

> Normally, there are too few physical education 'specialists' on many school staffs in England to ensure that all the physical education work is

taught exclusively by 'specialists'. Therefore it is necessary for 'academic' subject teachers to be involved in some physical education teaching. But these 'academic' subject teachers are not usually able to assist in indoor physical education lessons because local authority inspectors refuse to permit teachers without physical education training to use gymnasium equipment.

(Whitehead and Hendry, 1976: 30)

As strange as this situation may appear today, in the formative period of the consolidation of the id² of physical education-as-sport-techniques this arrangement had the effect of ensuring the gymnasium and indoor work was the sole province of the specialist. Games and sports were now on the curriculum, but the timetable had already circumscribed what might be taught in the 40-minute lessons that were afforded the specialist. Many, no doubt, saw these lessons as an opportunity to teach skills that could be applied in the longer outdoor lessons, even if these had to be led by teachers of other subjects. But what kind of facility was the 'gymnasium' at this time, and what kind of skill learning did it afford? Munrow, again, offers a view.

Throughout the early years of the century we sowed the seeds for a gymnastic approach to physical education and we have reaped the harvest of 60 ft × 30 ft gymnasia 'fully equipped'. … It is not the local authority's fault that we now find we need weights instead of wall bars [and] canoes instead of window-ladders.

(Munrow, 1963: 273)

The consequences of this indoor facility for teaching an entirely different curriculum is highlighted, in their turn, by Whitehead and Hendry in a brief account of the very popular sport of basketball in physical education for boys in secondary schools.

In the traditional type of gymnasium in England there is a 60 ft × 30 ft floor space, and normally only one basketball court is marked. This would account for only ten boys being active if a basketball game were being played. Frequently, this is the picture that is seen in schools, the remainder of the boys being spectators awaiting their turn to be called to participate. One is reminded, therefore, that though an activity is named as being a feature of a school's programme, its value as an educative medium depends upon how it is organised, what the teacher plans to be the effect of the activity, and what the pupils attempt to get from it.

(Whitehead and Hendry, 1976: 28)

The situation Whitehead and Hendry describe is one I experienced regularly as a secondary school pupil of this era. Only one court was marked because it took up the entire gym. Players throwing in from the side of the court would typically be required to put a foot up on a wall bar to show they were indeed at the side of the court. Spectating pupils awaiting their turn on court usually climbed the wall bars and either sat on top or hung off as the mood took them, or else they sat in the store room off the gym. For pupils whose attention wandered easily, spectating was an opportunity for mischief, and so games of basketball were less frequent than 'skill' sessions, where the teacher could occupy the whole class, in whole-class instruction, within the limited floor space of the gym.

Whitehead and Hendry's final comment is worth reflecting on. Because a 'game' or 'sport' is listed as an activity on the school programme, it does not mean that it is experienced as a game or a sport by pupils. As I commented in Chapter 1, the dominant id^2 of physical education is not physical education-as-sport, which would imply a whole different set of arrangements for timetable and facilities. Even though the subject matter of a lesson is basketball, introducing and practising various types of passes, shot, and ways of controlling the ball in a dribble, with little or no time for extension, refinement and application, does not add up to playing basketball.

I am arguing then that these factors were decisive in the formative years of the id^2 of physical education-as-sport-techniques in consolidating an approach to physical education that had far more continuity with the old regime of gymnastics than is at first glance apparent. This is because of the centrality of 'skill' and the linear notion of progression and its corruption to sport-techniques, particular institutionalised features of the schools such as the timetable, the responsibilities of specialist teachers and design of facilities, allied to a hostility from the men towards the excesses (as they saw them) of child-centred ideals. In Chapter 4, I sought to show that beyond these formative years and up to the present and beyond in England, this id^2 of physical education has become even more entrenched in government systems of schooling. One further matter has helped to hold this id^2 of physical education in its currently dominant position, which is the fate of physical education teacher education in higher education since the 1970s.

Teacher education: More academic content, less time for practical physical activity

I have already, in Chapter 4, outlined in some detail the processes of academicisation, scientisation, specialisation and fragmentation that have been active in the physical activity field in higher education since the 1960s to the present, and various reactions to the fate of physical education teacher education within this context. Suffice it to conclude this chapter, then, with some comments on how these processes described in Chapter 4 have impacted on the consolidation and institutionalisation of the id^2 of physical education-as-sport-techniques.

In Australia and Britain, the 1970s was the decade in which degree-level qualifications became widely available in physical education teaching, a situation that in some places preceded and in some occurred simultaneously with the emergence of non-teacher education undergraduate degrees, variously named and including kinesiology, human-movement studies, leisure studies and sports science. The availability of degrees in physical education teacher education was not by any means a foregone or inevitable conclusion of these processes of academicisation, scientisation, specialisation and fragmentation. Physical educators had to fight hard to convince university curriculum committees and bodies such as the Council for National Academic Awards in Britain that there was sufficient academic content in the field to make degree-level study possible. At the same time, during the 1960s and early 1970s, degree-qualified teachers were becoming the norm in other school subjects, and so, in part, the momentum to produce physical education teachers with degrees came from at least two sources: broader teacher education policy making and from within the field itself (Connell, 1983).

So in one respect the 'degree decades' (as I have named them elsewhere, Kirk, 2000a) of the 1970s and 1980s helped to retain physical education teacher education within the college and university alongside other emerging 'sub-disciplines' of the field.[13] At the same time, degree status came at a cost. In some institutions, physical education pedagogy (as it began to be known) was regarded as of less academic worth than some other sub-disciplines. Much worse, however, was that in order to meet the requirements of degree status, many institutions reduced the number of credit-bearing courses in practical physical activity – the substance of what student teachers would teach in schools. Anecdotes from my own professional experience provide an illustration of this process. When I studied for the first ever four-year Bachelor of Education degree in Physical Education and Human Movement at the Glasgow-based Scottish School of Physical Education (SSPE), Jordanhill (1975–79), the students in the year group ahead of me were completing the College's three-year diploma in physical education. These students participated in gymnastics every day for the three years of their course. My year group participated in gymnastics once per week for the first two of four years, with an option to specialise in gymnastics in years three or four. Unsurprisingly, the diploma-qualified teachers had highly superior gymnastics skills compared with the majority of my year group. When I took up my first academic post at the University of Queensland in 1984, physical education teacher education students studying for a four-year Bachelor of Human Movement Studies (Education) degree undertook what were called at the time 'movement laboratories', which were practical sessions in physical activity, but they could not gain credit from these courses towards their degree. Part of the selection process for entry into the course at the SSPE in 1975 was a practical test of 'basic skills', which was a common practice in British courses at this time (Whitehead and Hendry, 1976: 52). These tests are no longer conducted, even in courses such as the BA Physical Education at Leeds Metropolitan University, a three-year non-teaching course, containing a relatively and uncommonly high level of practical physical activity.

The physical educators of the 1960s and 1970s who fought hard for degrees in physical education teacher education could not have known that the academicisation of the field would lead to the drastic reduction of practical physical activity content. But there is no question they set in motion a process that has had disastrous consequences, unintended though they undoubtedly were. The push towards the inclusion of more academic content in courses was borne out of a number of perceived needs and desires. There was clearly the need to survive in the face of policy reform in teacher education and rapidly changing circumstances in higher education. There was also a desire, if not for academic status as such, at least to confound the stereotypes of the 'dominant competitive, aggressive, not-too-bright individual ... [the] companionable "man of action", but not someone with whom to engage in professional dialogue' (Whitehead and Hendry, 1976: 75). While all stereotypes contain grains of truth, and physical educators often self-consciously chose to act in ways that confirmed these stereotypes, physical education teacher educators were just as keen to deny the possibility that physical education teachers 'wore their IQs on their backs'.

The push for more academic content also came from a deep ambivalence about the role of physical performance in physical education teacher education. At the inauguration of the Leeds Physical Training College in 1934, there was much official talk that the course was intended to produce teachers, not 'acrobats' (Connell, 1983). In 1958, Hugh Brown (1958: 93), Director of the SSPE, stated emphatically that 'the emphasis ... is first, last and all the time on *teaching*. ... However desirable it may be, personal ability in the gymnasium, swimming pond or playing field ... is no substitute for teaching ability'. Whitehead and Hendry (1976: 52) noted that the purpose of practical physical activity work in teacher education was not always clear within the specialist training institutions. They concluded, on the basis of a short study of marks for teaching practice and markers of sporting prowess, that no relationship could be shown between student teachers' ability levels in sports and games, and their teaching. At best, practical sessions were intended to develop what we would now call pedagogical content knowledge, knowledge of how to teach or coach a particular game or sport, rather than depth of understanding of the activity itself.

As I will argue in some further detail in Chapter 6, this ambivalence about the purpose of practical physical activity in teacher education courses is related to an apparent inability to identify standards of excellence and to state clearly what it means to have 'ability' in school physical education. Assessment of student learning in practical physical activity units exposed physical educators' lack of confidence in this area, or else their muddled thinking. The problem was exacerbated when physical education achieved examination status in high schools in England and Wales, Australia and New Zealand. How, for example, should a junior international volleyball player be assessed alongside his peers who had never played the sport before? Since, by the 1970s, students inevitably came to physical education teacher education courses with different experiences of this broad-ranging subject, some would be beginners and some advanced-level performers in specific games and sports. And as the curriculum expanded through the 1960s and 1970s to include more and more games and sports, how could a teacher develop a level of practical competence in all of them? The retreat to the notion that practical work was an opportunity for students to learn how to teach physical activity content merely begged the question, as Siedentop (2002a) had posed it: How without some practical experience of physical activities could student teachers acquire the content knowledge needed for them to develop pedagogical content knowledge?

At the same time, while there was considerable variability of practice in assessing practical performance in teacher education, from recruitment through to graduation, in Britain, perhaps more than other countries such as the USA and Australia, some level of practical competence was required up until the early to mid-1980s. Not all students could expect to be all-rounders, but most would be expected to excel in at least one physical activity. One of the lasting memories of my experience of being a young teacher was spending many free periods and lunch times in the gym or on the playing field practising the techniques of various sports and games I was required to teach in order to perfect them to a level that would pass the scrutiny of my pupils when it came to the time for me to demonstrate. In those areas where there was no possibility that I could achieve even a basic performance, for example in gymnastics, the last resort was to hope there would be at least one pupil in the lesson who could demonstrate on my behalf.

I suggest there is a relationship between the academicisation of physical education teacher education and the survival of the id^2 of physical education-as-sport-techniques. From the 1950s to the 1970s, as Swedish gymnastics disappeared from the curriculum and physical education expanded to include a wide range of sports, games and outdoor pursuits, and for a time, educational gymnastics and dance, teacher education courses retained their essentially practical focus, even in the face of policy directives to mainstream courses and to increase their length. The average teacher produced by these courses arguably understood the subject matter they would teach in schools much more thoroughly than their contemporary counterparts. Nevertheless, the residual influence of gymnastics and the institutionalisation of physical education in compulsory mass secondary education set very real limits on what teachers might achieve in physical education. The focus on sport-techniques was tangible and demanded a reasonable level of detailed technical knowledge of physical activities. As I have already noted, however, the invention of degree-level study for teachers immediately reduced the amount of practical physical activity in teacher education courses in Britain from the middle to the end of the 1970s. From this time forward, student teachers received less and less formal practical instruction as the timetable was required to included more and more academic content. Some individual student teachers bring to their courses particular expertise in one or more games and sports. Others spend time coaching in community clubs and other contexts in order to supplement their university experiences. Arguably, none today could possibly match their predecessors of the 1970s and earlier for depth of experience and knowledge of physical activity.

One possible conclusion we might reach then is that the id[2] of physical education-as-sport-techniques has endured for so long in schools in part because teachers, through no fault of their own, lack the content knowledge to take students beyond elementary sport-techniques. Indeed, most teachers educated between 1980 and the present, with only a few exceptions, are far better suited to teach the sport and exercise science content of the senior high school examinable forms of physical education than they are the practical physical activities of the middle and lower secondary grades. Moreover, as Fletcher (1984) argued, the pursuit of academic status in physical education from the 1960s was driven primarily by men, and the women's tradition suffered a further setback that led to eventual amalgamations with larger colleges or to closure. In the courses for women that remained single sex beyond the 1960s, their content increasingly came to resemble that of the men's courses as they too established degree programmes (Whitehead and Hendry, 1976: 65–66). By the 1980s, as single-sex institutions also began to disappear and women experienced the same courses as men, the women's tradition in England was greatly diminished.

Conclusion

Whitehead and Hendry (1976) come to two important conclusions following their study of physical education in England up to the early 1970s. The first is that while there was a widespread impression that physical education had undergone radical change, they found that school programmes for both boys and girls were much as they had been as they took shape during the 1950s, the main categories of activity being gymnastics (including vaulting and agility), athletics, major and minor games, swimming, outdoor activities and dance. This curriculum formed the core and compulsory experience for most secondary school pupils, with some limited choices, though less curriculum time, for older boys and girls. The second is that while physical education teachers enjoyed tremendous freedom in secondary schools to develop their own programmes, a situation that was to last until the introduction of the National Curriculum Physical Education in the early 1990s, there was remarkable convergence of practice across schools, despite considerable diversity between teacher education institutions (Whitehead and Hendry, 1976: 73). Almost a decade later, Underwood (1983) noted a common pattern in the secondary school curriculum.

> Most schools nowadays operate a system in physical education which insists that all children follow a basic course for two, three or four years. This is followed by some limited choices before there is finally a free

choice from a large range of options. Without exception, every school in this sample believed that children should be exposed to a common core of activities which generally comprised athletics, major games, gymnastics, swimming and dance (for girls). The emphasis and range varied slightly according to the staffing, facilities and philosophy of the school.

(Underwood, 1983: 70)

As we saw in Chapter 4, Smith et al. (2007) argued that the National Curriculum Physical Education in England and Wales had done little to disturb this pattern of curriculum organisation and, indeed, was responsible for perpetuating it. Notwithstanding the variability of 'emphasis and range' of actual games, athletics events, gymnastics exercises and so on offered by individual schools, we can only conclude that the id^2 of physical education that emerged in the middle of the twentieth century in Britain and around this time elsewhere remains intact in all its essential features. In the first four years of secondary school, where most state school pupils first encounter specialist teachers, physical education is activity based. The activities consist in the main of the techniques of a wide range of games and sports, activities are usually compulsory for all pupils, and teachers mainly use command-style methods supplemented with some reciprocal peer teaching. This is the practice of physical education that can be conceptualised as the id^2 of physical education-as-sport-techniques.

This chapter has sought to trace continuities and discontinuities with the past in order to understand better how this particular version of physical education came to take the form it has. I showed that from the middle of the 1800s, physical education was constructed and constituted by gymnastics. In its manifestation in compulsory mass elementary schools, gymnastics took the form of drilling and exercising in order to meet the institutional imperatives of the industrial age school for social order within what Foucault described as 'disciplinary society'. As the perceived need for 'heavy, ponderous and meticulous' corporeal practices receded, the id^2 of physical education-as-gymnastics met with widespread criticism, particularly for its alleged 'artificiality'. Child-centred philosophies, in particular the work of John Dewey, made a considerable impression on physical educators, leading to advocacies for a more humane and 'natural' approach to physical education. Just as child centredness was taking root in physical education thinking and practice, the women gymnasts of 1940s Britain encountered the work of Rudolf Laban and so began a civil war, first among the women, and then between the surviving women and the men.

The discontinuity in this process was the removal of gymnastics from the centre of physical education and its replacement with games and sport. We noted that physical educators of the time, between 1930 and the 1950s, saw this process as a welcome broadening of their curriculum, not as a removal of gymnastics but as the addition of many other activities, some of which, games and some sports such as athletics and rowing in particular, had been grown and developed in the private schools of the minority social elite. Contrary to McIntosh's (1968) notion that the 'two traditions' of physical education 'fused' during the 1940s and 1950s, instead there was a struggle to accommodate and legitimate games and sports as activities for the masses. Some perceptive physical educators, some of the so-called 'old-guard' Swedish gymnasts, could see that what was afoot was not a benign broadening of the curriculum towards a catholic concept of physical education but, far more malignant, the extinction of the id^2 of physical education-as-gymnastics.

They may have lost the battles both with the 'new' educational gymnasts and with the sportsmen and scientists, but we might conclude that they won the war. The continuities from the id^2 of physical education-as-gymnastics to the id^2 of physical education-as-sports-techniques are plain to see. The id^2 of physical education-as-gymnastics was rooted in an authoritarian pedagogy of command–response. While contemporary physical educators may not now bark words of command such as 'trunk forward and downward – stretch!', they nevertheless continue to use a close cousin of this style for much of their teaching. As I sought to show in this chapter, they are left with little alternative, given the institutionalisation of the subject to meet the imperatives of the school and its timetable. Moreover, contemporary physical education has retained the gymnasts' concern for skill. Some would argue that it is a different concept of skill, since 'skill is specific', but even there we hear contemporary advocacy for the existence of fundamental motor skills. In any case, the continuities with gymnastics run deep at this level. Physical education has retained a focus not on skill as Morgan described it but with the decontextualised, prerequisite techniques that it is assumed pupils require in order to play games and sport.

This historical investigation has sought to help us understand why it is technique and not skill that forms the bulk of the practice of physical education. It has also sought to show how, in discontinuity with the past, the academicisation of physical education teacher education has supported rather than challenged this process, since in their education, teachers do not receive the content knowledge required to teach beyond the introductory unit underpinned by a molecularisation of skill and a concept of linear progression in learning.

While contemporary physical education practice, with games and sport rather than Swedish gymnastics at its core, may constitute a 'looser form of power over the body', it nevertheless remains enmeshed in a process of schooling bodies. Armed with our understanding of continuities and discontinuities from the past, it is to issues of the wider social purpose and relevance of the id^2 of physical education-as-sport-techniques that we turn next. This is crucial, since the id^2 of physical education-as-sport-techniques rests on at least two aspirations that imply a reach beyond the school. The first is that pupils will become skilful performers of games and sports, or at least of one game or sport they have come to enjoy, chosen from the wide range they experience in school. The second is that, as skilful performers, they will be equipped to become lifelong participants in physical activity, thereby contributing one component to a healthy lifestyle. In light of these two aspirations that lie at the heart of the currently dominant id^2 of physical education, and before we can finally come to address the question of 'physical education futures?', we must understand how the id^2 of physical education-as-sport-techniques is informed and legitimated by the wider physical culture of society, how it serves young people in their lives now and in their futures beyond the school, how standards of excellence are constructed and thus ability is conceptualised to define the practice of physical education, and how it contributes, if at all, to cultural transmission and renewal.

6 Four relational issues and the bigger picture

After all, what would be the point of work or of political brinkmanship or, for that matter, of life, if there were no pursuits we humans find intrinsically satisfying that make life worth living in the first place, that is, worth all the struggle and hardship that are an inescapable part of life? And since play, games, and sports are best conceived, as the philosophical literature suggests, as just such intrinsically good things, they are among the most important and serious of human activities, and they are the very activities which things like work derive whatever seriousness they possess.

(Morgan, 2006: 102)

I argued in Chapter 2 in discussing the possibility of 'the idea of the idea' of physical education that too often physical educators have spent energy struggling over *ideas* of physical education and in the process much of the time have failed to see the bigger picture: the id^2 of physical education and how it is constructed and constituted through its relationships to wider issues in society. A good example of this which I mentioned briefly in Chapter 5 is the debate in Scotland, in November 1954, over which version of gymnastics should form the future of physical education for boys in Scottish secondary schools. Representatives from the Scottish Physical Education Association (the men's association) and the Scottish League of Physical Education (representing the women) met in Edinburgh to discuss the topic of 'Physical Education Today and in the Future', later reported in *The Leaflet*, 56 (1), 1955. After prolonged and at times heated debate, the delegates could not reach an agreed position and a further four one-day meetings were organised. Finally, an outcome was reached. The status quo prevailed. It was agreed that boys' physical education would continue to be based on Swedish gymnastics. We know from Chapter 5 that they made the wrong choice. Swedish gymnastics was barely to survive the decade, while educational gymnastics thrived into the 1970s, though mainly in girls' physical education and in primary schools, while the least considered contender, Olympic gymnastics as it was then known, became the main version of gymnastics in schools from the 1980s, though no longer the centrepiece of the id^2 of physical education.

The point of this example is not that these physical educators made what turned out in hindsight to be the wrong decision. It is to point out that they seemed to possess little awareness, collectively, that a shift was under way from the bigger id^2 of physical education-as-gymnastics to the id^2 of physical education-as-sport-techniques. The future, in other words, was not a gymnastics-based form of physical education, but another form grounded in games and sports in which gymnastics would play only a minor role. It seems to me these kinds of debate feature large within the physical education community, creating the impression that we are fractious and disputatious. For instance, another, more contemporary, example of debates over *ideas* of physical education would be Teaching Games for Understanding (TGfU) versus 'the traditional approach' to games. Arguably, TGfU belongs to a different, perhaps yet to be defined, id^2 of physical education from the currently dominant sport-techniques form, but this point is missed by many debaters. A further example is the (again interminable) 'discipline versus profession' debate that has consumed academics, particularly in the USA, since the 1960s.

How might we recognise an *idea* of physical education for what it is, merely one version of a bigger configuration of knowledge, the id^2 of physical education? Or, to put this question differently, how might we see the bigger picture in which *ideas* of physical education such as TGfU or various versions of gymnastics might be located? My response to these questions, suggested in Chapter 2, is that we might locate school physical education in relation to four issues that I suggest all institutionalised forms of knowledge must consider. These relational issues are culture, transfer, excellence and renewal. In this chapter, we will consider each of these issues in turn, and their part in constructing and constituting the id^2 of physical education-as-sport-techniques. The purpose of this exercise is not just to see the bigger picture, though this is important. It is to understand better whether and to what extent the id^2 of physical education-as-sport-techniques is legitimated by contemporary physical culture, whether it meets its aspirations for transfer of learning beyond the school, how it defines standards of excellence and associated notions such as ability, and the role it plays in social and cultural transmission, reproduction and renewal. Understanding the relationship of forms of school physical education to these issues allows us to consider, as we will in Chapter 7, physical education futures.

Physical culture

Physical culture, as I have developed this concept elsewhere, is one form of a broader corporeal discourse that is concerned with all aspects of meaning making centred on the body (Kirk, 1993; 1999).[1] I have suggested that physical culture is a specialised form of corporeal discourse concerned with at least three highly institutionalised and codified forms of human movement that relate most closely to school physical education, sport, exercise and active leisure. To this earlier analysis I would add here two other physical cultural forms which may have some influence on school physical education, including dance (Gard, 2001) and perhaps, as appropriate, to particular societies, meditative and martial arts such as yoga and karate, respectively (Brown and Johnson, 2000). Sport as a category of physical culture includes activities in which the competitive contest is a central, defining feature. Exercise includes activities specifically designed and intended to produce a benefit to health. Active leisure may include some activities such as walking, and others that also appear in the sport category, such as skiing and swimming, but as active leisure do not involve the competitive contest. Dance includes the wide range of activities specifically concerned with aesthetics, expression and communication, such as ballet, and modern, folk, ballroom and street dance. The meditative and martial arts also include a wide range of possible activities, which in the latter category, when the competitive contest is of central concern, may also be sport.

An important feature of the concept of physical culture is that it counteracts the tendency in physical education to consider only or mainly the body in nature (the biological and mechanical body) and to ignore or dismiss as irrelevant the body in culture (the signifying and symbolising body). The notion of physical culture proposes that the human body is in nature and culture simultaneously, and that neither can be reduced to the other.

Marcel Mauss's (1973) account of the 'techniques of the body' provides an illustration of this point, and of the concept of physical culture more broadly. Writing originally in 1934, he argued that a wide range of activities, including the examples he provides of swimming, digging, marching, walking and running, can be described as techniques of the body. He makes two points about this notion. The first is that these are not merely biological and biomechanical phenomena. They have a clear psychosocial dimension that he captures in the concept of the *habitus* (popularised much later by Pierre Bourdieu). He explains:

> I have had this notion of the social nature of the '*habitus*' for many years. Please note that I use the Latin word – it should be understood in France – *habitus*. The word translates infinitely better than '*habitude*' (habit or custom), the '*exis*', the 'acquired ability' and 'faculty' of Aristotle. ... These 'habits' do not just vary with individuals and their imitations, they vary especially between societies, educations, proprieties and fashions, prestiges.
>
> (Mauss, 1973: 73)

While the habitual[2] character of many of the techniques Mauss mentions such as walking, running, sleeping and so on are performed adroitly and routinely and so may appear to require no conscious effort, he makes an important second point that all these techniques are an outcome of education.

> In all of these elements of the art of using the human body, the facts of *education* were dominant. The notion of education could be superimposed

on that of imitation. For there are children with very strong imitative faculties, others with weak ones, but all of them go through the same education. ... What takes place is a prestigious imitation. The child, the adult, imitates actions which have succeeded and which he has seen successfully performed by people in whom he has confidence or who have authority over him.

(Mauss, 1973: 73)

Some of the techniques of the body Mauss discusses, like walking, appear to be acquired informally in the course of everyday life, while others, like marching and swimming, typically require formal instruction. But Mauss cites an example of Maori mothers in New Zealand who drill their daughters to walk in a particular way, with a 'loose-jointed swinging of the hips' termed *onioni*, which is much admired, to make the point that all techniques of the body are learned. Closer to home, he points out that wearing shoes transforms the position of the feet when walking, something we notice immediately we attempt to walk without them.

Mauss argues that in order to qualify as a technique of the body, an action must be both effective, that is, it must accomplish some purpose with facility, and it must be 'traditional'. On this latter point, he writes, 'there is no technique and no transmission in the absence of tradition. This is above all what distinguishes man from the animals: the transmission of his techniques and very probably their oral transmission' (Mauss, 1973: 75). Mauss's point is that techniques of the body are meaningful actions that have a purpose and are part of a shared culture, even though there is some differentiation among social groups, nations and so on. His account of techniques of the body allows us to appreciate the extent to which they are transmitted and learned, not only those which require explicit instruction. This in turn allows us to see that techniques of the body are socially constructed and reconstructed over time, that they are meaningful and value laden, and that they are purposeful. The creation, selection, development and maintenance of particular techniques of the body are underpinned by and reflect deeply held values and beliefs about embodiment in any given society.

Physical culture consists, then, of many highly specialised techniques of the body that find expression in sport, exercise, active leisure, dance and meditative and martial arts. Note that Mauss's use of the word 'technique' emphasises both the physical and the cultural. His addition of the notion of the *habitus* captures the sense that these are techniques embedded in and indeed constituting *la vie quotidienne*, the course of everyday life, that they are routine and purposeful but at the same time meaningful. Techniques of the body signify. They signify since they have specific purposes achieved with facility and they are part of the collective resources of human society generated over time, forming 'tradition'. They are typically transmitted through educative processes, either formally or informally. His use of the word technique sits closer to our discussion of *skill* in Chapters 4 and 5 than the notion of sport-techniques as a decontextualised form of skill. Nevertheless, even here, although sport-techniques may be decontextualised from their proper context in a game or sport, they nevertheless signify, except that in school physical education lessons they express a different meaning in the context of the institutionalised practices of the school. This point is of crucial importance, as we will see, for transfer of learning, not merely in the sense usually intended in the skill-acquisition literature of the transfer between skills or from skill practice to a performance, but also transfer from school to other aspects of life.

As I have argued elsewhere (Kirk, 1998b), physical culture provides the raw, non-pedagogical materials out of which school physical education is constructed. Put differently by Anne Williams (1985), the producers of physical culture outside the school in the communities of, in her examples, 'sport' and 'health', act as 'legitimating publics' for innovation within the school curriculum. They make judgements about the worth and coherence of forms of school knowledge. In this sense, physical culture can be regarded as equivalent to Basil Bernstein's (2000) notion of regulative discourse within his theory of pedagogic discourse. Regulative discourse is produced in Bernstein's primary field of knowledge production. He claims that distributive rules operate in this primary field to regulate power relations between social groups by distributing different forms of knowledge and consciousness. Distributive rules regulate the relationship between what is thinkable and unthinkable by creating a space where the 'yet to be thought' can be conceived (Bernstein, 2000: 30). The primary field is therefore a differentiated field, one in which different social groups have different and inequitable access to the processes of knowledge production. This means that knowledge at its point of generation has already embedded in it the values of particular social groups and their sectional interests.

In the physical cultural sphere, these distributive rules permit social groups to bring pieces of knowledge into relationship with each other, in other words, to construct 'truth'. So, for example, our understanding of exercise, its effects on our bodies and its relationship to health is shaped in particular ways by the distribution of this knowledge by social groups such as scientists, doctors and other agents, including sections of government. One popular and dominant configuration of this particular 'chain of signification' (Hall, 1985) is that exercise acts on the body to reduce weight and that an exercised, slender body is evidence of good health ('exercise = slenderness = health', Kirk and Colquhoun, 1989; Kirk, 1992b). While individuals with some knowledge of the relationships between exercise, body shape and health would understand these connections to be merely *contingent*, that is to say, there is no guarantee that exercise will produce a slender body nor that a slender body is evidence of good health, some knowledge producers operating in the primary field can and indeed often do present these connections in such a way as to suggest they exist in a *necessary* relationship, thereby doing 'ideological work' (Eagleton, 1991; Kirk, 1992b).[3]

The construction of this 'truth' about exercise, body shape and health is not pedagogical at this stage. According to Bernstein, it must be 'de-located' from the primary field (of physical culture), 'recontextualised' by specialised agents such as educational policy makers, curriculum developers and other 'experts', and 'relocated' in the secondary field (of education) in the form of instructional discourse, as, for example, a health-related exercise programme or a weight-loss camp, where it may continue to do ideological work if programmes are not sufficiently socially critical, a point to which we return in considering the fourth relational issue of social and cultural transmission, reproduction and renewal. Bernstein argues, then, that the instructional forms of school subjects, such as physical education, are embedded in nonpedagogical practices that have been de-located from their original, primary field of production and relocated to the secondary field of education through a recontextualising process.[4] This embedding of the instructional discourse of school physical education within the regulative discourse of physical culture thus creates the pedagogic discourse of physical education or what we are calling in this study the id^2 of physical education.

Given this mediated relationship between school physical education and physical culture, it is of some importance that we consider what changes, if any, may have taken place in the physical culture of economically advanced societies. Indeed, a major force to consider is the ongoing globalisation of particular aspects of physical culture, emanating primarily though not exclusively from countries such as the USA, converging on a high degree of uniformity of practices there and elsewhere. The commodification of sport is an example of this process of globalisation as individual sports are reshaped to increase their capacity to generate profit, not only through the sale of sports to spectators as a form of entertainment, but also through the generation of merchandise such as branded sportswear and equipment. For example, established sports such as basketball and rugby have changed their rules to become more entertaining for spectators. New forms of sport such as one-day cricket have emerged to suit the medium of television. We can see similar processes impacting on and reconstructing exercise and active leisure. An entire 'fitness industry' has emerged to cater for our collective obsession with exercise, body shape and health. New activities such as bungee jumping and white-water rafting and forms of sport tourism extend the range of active leisure possibilities. Both the media and technology have been central to the globalisation of commodified sport, exercise and active leisure, particularly in combination, increasing the reach of these physical cultural forms further and further into people's everyday lives. Allied to these processes, sport at elite levels has been professionalised, not just for performers but also increasingly for coaches and administrators.[5]

As the id^2 of physical education-as-sport-techniques was being consolidated in the 1950s, countries such as Britain had little television and few televised sport contests. A scientific understanding of the relationship between exercise and health had only just emerged around training principles such as progressive overload and was still in the process of being applied, as we noted in Chapter 5, in practices such as circuit training. While the notion of 'recreation' was being promoted as a means of broadening physical training from the mid-1930s, there were few municipal facilities available to ordinary people who, in any case, had yet to achieve the reduction in hours of work that would provide the free time and wages that would fund organised active leisure. Sport was, moreover, staunchly amateur with only a few notable exceptions including, in Britain, men's football, rugby league and boxing. With mass media in an early form of digitisation, physical culture was shaped more by local than global forces and traditions, which is why Marcel Mauss, writing in 1934, could claim on the basis of evidence from anthropologies of primitive societies that there was great variation in techniques of the body between social groups, a claim that is rather more difficult to make in the age of the World Wide Web.

There are at least two observations we might make about the relationship between the practices of school physical education and physical culture then and now. First, it could be argued that the shift of subject matter from gymnastics to sport was forward looking. In *Defining Physical Education* (Kirk, 1992a) I proposed that a sport-based form of physical education was perfectly aligned to a number of broader trends in British society and beyond, including the movement towards increasing government intervention in sport policy and the provision of municipal facilities, a popular egalitarian movement towards 'sport for all',[6] the idea that success in international sport could compensate for declining performance as an industrial and colonial power, and the widespread view, nationally and internationally, that sport was a common denominator that could overcome divisive relations of social class, religion and nationhood. A form of physical education based in sport was in tune with the times of the mid-twentieth century, and the addition of new sports over time captured the increasing availability of some, though not all, sports that had in the previous half-century been accessible only to a privileged minority of British society.

It was, at the same time, a concept of sport that remained rooted in the late 1800s and early 1900s, and so was archaic in many respects. There was the strong amateur ideal, which carried with it the social-class interests in which it originated within the primary field of knowledge production, and amateurism's disdain for professionalism (Hargreaves, 1986). Coaching was tainted as a result, and was not widely encouraged. While some sports were distinctly working class, the majority of participants in the 1950s remained middle- and upper-middle-class men. Women's sport was still in its infancy, while working-class women's participation was more or less non-existent. Spectatorship at live events massively outbalanced participation. Commissioned by the Central Committee for Physical Recreation (CCPR), the writers of the Wolfenden Report (1960) *Sport and the Community*, expressed their puzzlement that few working-class youth chose to play sport after leaving school, a concern confirmed by a CCPR (1961) survey of secondary-modern school leavers in 1960. As Ken Roberts (1996: 52) was moved to observe in the face of pronouncements by government, the BBC and other experts that sport participation among young people was falling in the 1980s: 'the past Golden Age when the mass of young people were heavily involved in physically active recreation is pure myth'.

Second, the institutionalisation of physical education in schools and the need to accommodate the school's imperatives for social control centred on children's bodies, manifest, as I showed in Chapter 5, in the organisational arrangements of the timetable, the division of teaching duties and the spaces available for teaching and learning, augmented by the central place awarded to sport-techniques and their linear progression towards the development of skills, meant that physical education was backward looking in its pedagogy, despite advocacy for child-centred philosophies. The old regime of corporeal regulation expressed in the drilling and exercising form of gymnastics took a less ponderous and meticulous form in sport-techniques, but nevertheless this focus of physical education remained as a strong residue from the past, informed by what Lawson (2009) has called 'industrial-age logic'.

We can see in these two dimensions of school physical education, the forward looking and the backward looking, the seeds of a misaligned relationship with physical culture. On the one hand, sport and allied activities of exercise and active leisure are even more culturally salient for the mass of the population now than they were in the mid-twentieth century, suggesting that physical education is a highly culturally relevant school subject of interest to a number of important communities occupying Bernstein's primary and recontextualising fields. I suggest that this apparently obvious relationship to contemporary physical culture has been behind the widespread endorsement of physical education by government in Britain since the introduction of the Physical Education, School Sport and Club Links (PESSCL) initiative and its successors. On the other hand, if the institutionalised forms of physical education both in schools and in higher education are constructed and constituted in the ways I have described in detail in Chapter 4, rooted in and continuing to be informed by the historical events and circumstances described in Chapter 5, then the possibility for school physical education to realise the high expectations being set for the subject must be limited. Despite its close alignment to contemporary physical culture in terms of its field of knowledge of sport, exercise and active leisure, the institutional manifestation of the id^2 of physical education-as-sport-techniques can be described as culturally obsolete, archaic and largely irrelevant to current societal needs and interests.

Transfer of learning

We saw in Chapter 5 that the notion of transfer of learning emerged as a matter of central concern and debate in the 1940s and 1950s as the Swedish gymnasts' principle of generalisation before specialisation was challenged by new research on skill acquisition. For both the 'old-guard' gymnasts and their successors, the educational gymnasts, mastery of general forms of movement was a basis on which more specific movements, such as the skills of games and sports, could be built. The new researchers of skill acquisition argued that this transfer of generalised to specialised movement forms was not possible because 'skill is specific'. If a player wished to learn to perform an overhead smash in badminton, they must practise the overhead smash. As the body of knowledge began to accumulate, researchers occupied themselves with different questions about transfer of learning, such as the possibilities of transfer (both positive and negative) between similar skills (such as the overhead smash in badminton, the similar skill in tennis and the volleyball spike), and between skill practices and their performance in a game or sport. In Chapter 4 we learned that a particular strand of pedagogy research has been much concerned with this latter form of transfer, and the intricacies of developing extension, refinement and application tasks and building game-like variability into skills practices in order to ensure that skills are used appropriately in game play.

There is, however, a further sense of transfer of learning that has occupied educational researchers in fields such as science and mathematics, which is the extent to which school knowledge transfers beyond the school gates, both to young people's lives outside the school and to their future lives in adulthood. Taking a situated learning perspective, Jean Lave (1997) ques-tioned traditional mathematics teaching that rests on the view that appro-priate mathematical learning is abstracted from specific contexts. She referred to this view of learning as the 'culture of acquisition', in which it is assumed that it is the task of the school to transmit to children the valued accumulated factual knowledge of a society, and it is children's task to acquire and reproduce this knowledge. She claimed it is further assumed that:

> Cognitive benefits follow only when the process of learning is removed from the fields in which what is learned is to be applied. This belief underlies standard distinctions between formal and informal learning, so-called context-free and context-embedded learning, or logical and intuitive understanding. Schooling is viewed as the institutional site for decontextualizing knowledge so that, abstracted, it may become general and hence generalizable, and therefore transferable to situations of use in the 'real' world.
>
> (Lave, 1997: 18)

We noted in Chapter 4 that the traditionalists among the Palaeolithic tea-chers in Benjamin's satire of the saber-tooth curriculum argued in a similar fashion that the educational value of activities such as saber-tooth-tiger-scaring-with-fire lay precisely in their lack of direct relevance to the real world. Developing a critique of the 'culture of acquisition', Lave drew on ethnographic studies of shoppers and dieters to suggest that their practices for solving problems of calculation bore little resemblance to the ways in which children are taught mathematics in school. Moreover, citing research in a school mathematics class, she showed that children could produce correct solutions to problems without using the strategies taught by their teachers. She proposed that the process of doing mathematics in school is in itself a *situated practice*, and argued that this in turn makes the possibility of transfer of school knowledge to other situations in the 'real world' highly problematic. Building on Lave's work, Walkerdine (1997) added that the culture of acquisition remains valued and dominant in schools because it forms part of a larger set of discourses concerned with civilised rationality and governmentality.

I suggest, on the basis of the evidenced marshalled in Chapters 4 and 5, that the id² of physical education-as-sport-techniques produces similar forms of abstracted, decontextualised knowledge consisting in the main of sport-techniques. This molecular approach (Rovegno, 1995) to physical education is shaped to fit the institutional context of the school. The logic Lave exposed that underpins traditional mathematics teaching is, I suggest, the same logic that informs the id² of physical education-as-sport-techniques. It conforms to the belief that abstract knowledge is more general and therefore more generalisable and suitable to application in specific instances in the 'real world' of games and sports. Despite the insistence of motor-learning researchers that skill is specific, the residual gymnastic principle of generalisation before specialisation may be continuing to work within the id² of physical education-as-sport-techniques since the institutional structures of the school, its timetable, classrooms and methods of assessment support it.

Furthermore, Lave makes the insightful point that the abstracted and decontextualised form of mathematics is in itself situation specific and contextualised or, in her words, it is a *situated practice*. Abstracted and decontextualised maths, like abstracted and decontextualised sport-techniques, only makes sense as practices of the school. Mauss's use of the word 'technique' to describe the signifying and symbolic properties of the body in movement and repose confirms that all techniques of the body mean something, even when they take place out of their usual context, such as calculating portions and amounts as a dieter and shopper, or playing a game of soccer.⁷ Here, then, is an additional institutional imperative for the id² of physical education-as-sport-techniques. In abstracting the rich and complex configurations of knowledge that are games and sport and rendering them as sport-techniques, physical educators have not merely been pragmatic in terms of what is possible in relation to timetable arrangements, class sizes and constitution, facilities and their own expertise. They have practised a form of physical education rooted in sport-techniques because, as Walkerdine (1997) argues, the discourses of civilised rationality and governmentality rooted in industrial-age logic require school knowledge to be configured in this way. To act against these powerful forces would be to undermine physical education's credibility as a school subject just like any other.

There is, however, a further difficulty for physical education that may or may not be faced by mathematics and other academic subjects. This is the ubiquitous aspiration of the id^2 of physical education-as-sport-techniques, its raison d'etre. This aspiration is to equip young people with the prerequisite skills of games and sport and provide them with some experience of a wide range of games and sports so that they will find at least one activity to be enjoyable and interesting and will, consequently, gain pleasurable experiences of sport, exercise and active leisure both in their lives outside the school and as lifelong participants throughout adulthood. If skills form the basis of participation in games and sports, then transfer of learning will be from the skills learned in school to participation in sport, exercise and active leisure in community contexts.

It is worth, first of all, acknowledging the ubiquity of this concept of transfer of learning at the heart of the aspiration for lifelong participation. In the late 1990s in England and Wales, for example, an earlier version of the National Curriculum Physical Education (NCPE) claimed 'learning ... leads to increasing competence and, thereby, personal confidence and self-esteem. This provides the basis for lifelong learning in and enjoyment of physical activity and the ability to continue learning independently' (Qualifications Curriculum Authority, 1999: 1). Sport England argued in similar fashion in 2002 that the Active Schools programme demonstrated 'Sport England's commitment to encouraging every child to stay physically active for life. It highlights the importance of physical activity as an essential part of a healthy, active lifestyle' (Sport England, 2002). This aim for lifelong participation was not, however, new in the late 1990s. Foreshadowing the emergence of the id^2 of physical education-as-sport-techniques, Sir George Newman wrote in the prefatory memorandum to the Board of Education's 1933 *Syllabus of Physical Exercises for Schools* 'physical training at school should form the ground work of healthy exercise and recreation in after life [life after school]' (Board of Education, 1933: 8).

Nor was this concept of transfer of learning confined to England. In Australia, the indigenous 1946 *Physical Education for Victorian Schools* in Victoria that replaced the 1933 British *Syllabus of Physical Exercises for Schools* was underpinned by the view that:

> Each individual shall be enabled to develop to his maximum potential and ... each one shall acquire a sufficient degree of proficiency in at least one form of physical activity to enable him to maintain an interest in healthy activities throughout his adult life.
> (Education Department of Victoria, 1946: vii)

Meanwhile, in the 1972 Scottish *Curriculum Paper 12*, it was claimed that 'through satisfying participation pupils develop positive attitudes towards physical activity and are therefore favourably disposed towards continuing to participate in appropriate activities in later school years and in adult life' (Scottish Education Department, 1972: 9).

This notion of transfer of learning to life beyond the school and, in particular, the aspiration for lifelong participation among a majority of the adult population, is integral to the id[2] of physical education-as-sport-techniques and has been since its emergence in mid-twentieth century to the present day. Significant then that, in a much cited paper on the contribution of secondary school physical education to lifelong participation, Fairclough et al. (2002: 69) note evidence that some physical activities are likely to have greater transfer value to life beyond the school than others.[8] They explored the likelihood that the aspiration for lifelong participation in physical activity might be achieved through a survey of secondary schools in which they asked teachers to report on the ratio of 'lifetime' activities (such as aerobics, jogging, circuit training, dance, tennis and swimming) to team games within their Key Stages 3 and 4 curricular and extra-curricular programmes. They discovered that significantly more lifetime activities were available as extra-curricular options than as part of the core curriculum, which was dominated by team games, and that female teachers offered more lifetime activities during curriculum time than their male counterparts. They concluded that:

> The restrictive nature of the NCPE, traditional biases as to what activities boys and girls should follow, teacher expertise and influence of the media may conspire to affect the content and future relevance of curricular and extra-curricular programmes. As a result many schools place a significant emphasis on team games, as opposed to lifetime activities. In order to promote the PE goal of preparing students for lifetime participation in physical activity, physical educators must recognise which activities have the greatest carry-over value into adult life. HoPE[9] should aim to provide more opportunities for all students to experience these lifetime activities, both within and outside curriculum time.
> (Fairclough et al., 2002: 81)

These authors seem convinced that if there is to be effective transfer of learning from school physical education to adulthood, the team games and sports which currently dominate curriculum time are the least effective means of realising the aspiration of lifelong participation. In this, they would appear to be well supported by research evidence of adult physical activities and participation rates. Surveys of adult physical activity in Australia and Britain dating from the mid-1940s to the mid-1990s tell more or less the same story. The majority of adults do not participate regularly in the team games and sports that dominated their physical education programmes and only a minority are active in some, though not all, of the lifetime activities Fairclough et al. list. On the basis of this evidence, I concluded (Kirk, 2002a) that in the 50 or so years since the emergence of a multi-activity, sport-based form of the subject, physical education had failed to achieve the goal of lifelong participation for a majority of adults.

Green et al. (2005) have recently disputed my claim, arguing on the basis of surveys by Sport England and the Sports Council of Wales, mostly published on or after the date of my 2002 presentation, that:

> Overall, the trends in PE and leisure-time sport and physical activity among youth reflect a broadening and diversification of participation rather than a wholesale rejection of sport and physical activity *per se*. In this regard, it is simply not the case that sport – and especially competitive games – are notable by their absence from young people's activity portfolios the moment that school ends and leisure begins. There is a body of evidence in England and Wales (Sports Council of Wales, 2003; Sport England, 2003a, b) to suggest that not only are overall levels of participation among young people in sport and physical activity higher than is commonly assumed, but also that participation patterns are somewhat more complex than claims regarding the supposed neglect of, or undue emphasis upon, games and sport might suggest.
>
> (Green et al., 2005: 31)

I believe that Green and his colleagues are correct to claim that the number of physically active young people has been increasing since at least the mid-1980s, and that more young people are active now than at any point in the past century. I also believe Ken Roberts, one of Green's co-authors on this 2005 paper, has been for the most part a lone and courageous voice in saying so in the face of widespread official and 'expert' pronouncements to the contrary (Roberts, 1996). Nevertheless, their attempts to argue that the multi-activity, sport-based form of physical education and physical education teachers' collective determination to promote a sport for all ethos since the 1970s have played an important part in this increase does not fit what we know about the id^2 of physical education-as-sport-techniques nor with the evidence on adult participation in physical activity.

Green et al. (2005) argue that since the 1970s physical education has responded to the 'new conditions of youth', akin to the 'new times' of Tinning and Fitzclarence (1992) and the third wave of post-industrial, digital society of Fernandez-Balboa (2003). They claim that secondary school physical educators have broadened their curriculum and included new activities in order that young people might individualise and customise their own leisure 'portfolios', creating what Lawson (2009) has described somewhat derisively as the 'cafeteria curriculum'.[10] This multi-activity curriculum, they claim, has been decisive in increasing participation among youth and young adults.

Notwithstanding their qualifications that they are not suggesting there is a causal relationship for physical education's influence on lifelong participation, we must view these claims with some scepticism. To begin with, the latest survey data for adult participation in physical activity in England available at the time of writing, from the *Taking Part* study (Department of

Culture, Media and Sport, 2009), states that 22% of adults in the sample participated in physical activity for 30 minutes on at least three separate days in the week prior to the survey. The survey period was 2006–7. This study reports that swimming, fitness activities in a gym and recreational cycling were the most popular 'active sports', with participation rates between 10% and 15% of active adults. Meanwhile, the latest data from the Sport England (2009) *Active People* survey states that 21% of the adult population met the criterion for participation of at least three 30 minute episodes of activity in the previous week, with the most popular recreational activity overall being walking. They claim that over eight million adults aged 16 and over or 20% of the adult population walked at least once for at least 30 minutes in the previous four weeks. These figures are entirely consistent with the survey results from Australia and Britain that I cited in 2002. They may very well show an increase in participation as Green et al. claim the 2003 surveys reveal, but they could hardly be cited as evidence that school physical education has since the 1970s made an impressive impact on lifelong participation of adults.

The latest data from the *Taking Part* (Department of Culture, Media and Sport, 2009) study of young people aged 11–15 shows that 95% had participated in an 'active sport' during the previous four weeks. The more detailed analysis reveals that football, swimming and cycling were the most common activities outside school, and that 75% of young people had participated in an 'active sport' outside school in the previous week. While this data does not support claims for the transfer of learning of the specific activities of the school physical education programme, what we might call 'strong transfer', it does at least support Green et al.'s claim that 'sport' occupies a significant place in the leisure culture of many young people in this age group. Nevertheless, there is no evidence from these surveys of participation to claim that school physical education in its current form makes a particular and positive contribution to this leisure culture.

Green et al. (2005) note that the increased availability of municipal sport and leisure centres in Britain from the 1970s accounts in part for the increasing prominence of participation in physical activity beyond the school gates. What they neglect to mention is the enormous increase from the 1980s in the availability of club-based sport in local communities for children as young as 5 or 6 years of age, which has resulted in some children arriving at secondary school physical education already having 'sampled' (Côté and Hay, 2002) a range of sports, while their 'non-sporty' peers have had a limited experience of sport, thereby increasing even further the range of pupil ability and interest with which teachers must deal in physical education lessons (Kirk, 2005). And even though class and gender divisions may be 'blurring', as Green et al. claim, it is nevertheless the case that club-based sport participation is by and large the province of the wealthier sections of communities in Britain (Kay, 2000) and Australia (Kirk et al., 1997).

If Green et al. are to make a decisive argument for transfer of learning between physical education and life beyond the school, it cannot be couched in the terms that physical educators themselves have used. Integral to the id^2 of physical education-as-sport-techniques, as we have seen in Chapters 4 and 5, is the claim that physical education provides young people with the opportunity to learn the prerequisite skills of particular physical activities. The studies of skill learning cited in Chapter 4 show that there is little evidence to suggest physical education generally is successful in realising this goal. Moreover, even if there has been an increase in participation among young people, it has not for the most part been in the specific activities that form the substance of physical education programmes; there is, in short, little evidence of strong transfer. For older adults, walking remains the most popular leisure-time physical activity, as it has since adult participation trends have been recorded.

The only basis on which Green et al. might make a convincing argument that some kind of transfer of learning occurs is on the basis of fostering positive dispositions among young people to be active for life. It is not at all clear that the id^2 of physical education-as-sport-techniques does this or is the best means of doing this. It is also a somewhat weaker case than needs to be made in order to retain a place in the crowded school curriculum. In the culture of acquisition, while knowledge might be abstract and decontextualised, other subjects claim that students learn something worthwhile. In so doing, other subjects also claim to be able to identify the outcomes of learning in terms of the developing competence and expertise of pupils to complete algebraic equations, play a musical instrument, provide an account of the confluence of factors that brought about World War 1, to explain a chemical reaction, and to speak a foreign language. While these different forms of expertise may or may not find a ready transfer value outside the school, they nevertheless represent tangible efforts to engage with and achieve some mastery of bodies of knowledge. Providing experiences of games and sports in the somewhat vague hope that young people may enjoy them and in so doing develop a disposition to be physically active beyond the school does not suggest an equivalent engagement with a body of knowledge nor a convincing argument for physical education's presence in schools. These considerations raise a third challenging issue for the id^2 of physical education-as-sport-techniques, which is how excellence is defined and how such a definition is manifest in the notion of 'ability'. These notions, of excellence and ability, more than any others focus our attention on the coherence of a field, the status of the knowledge that constructs and constitutes it and, ultimately, whether it can achieve the aspirations it claims for itself.

Excellence and ability in physical education

John Evans (Evans, 2004; Evans and Penney, 2008) has for some time been a lone voice in insisting physical educators must pay attention to how ability is conceptualised in physical education.[11] He noted that physical education

Increasingly centred attention on and justified its existence discursively and pedagogically in terms of just about everything other than that which is distinctive and special about itself and its subject matter. ... This ought to strike us as very odd indeed. We would be hard pressed to find, for example, maths or English teachers justifying their existence principally in terms of what they can do, not for a child's literacy or numeracy, but their mental health, self-esteem or social welfare in and out of school.

(Evans, 2004: 96)[12]

Evans's concern is that narrowly defined and implicit notions of ability have come to dominate physical education, influenced primarily by the sectional interests of sport and health communities, while the issue of what it means to be physically educated is no longer debated either by physical educators or the wider policy community. He employs the notion of the *habitus* to argue that any definition of ability in physical education must take account of the different physical capital young people bring to school physical education from their differentiated social class, ethnic, religious and family backgrounds. He claims that without such a perspective, children from some backgrounds will be considered to be 'in deficit' of, for example, the ability to achieve a particular body shape or perform range of physical skills.

For Evans, the need to discuss ability is prompted, properly, by concerns for social justice and for forms of state-funded education that will benefit all young people. In this, he is drawing on Bernstein's (2000) theory of the social production of pedagogic discourse which maintains that 'evaluative rules' operate in the secondary field of the reproduction of knowledge. Evaluative rules are concerned with what counts as valid acquisition and realisation of the subject, both in terms of its curricular content and its social conduct, character and manner, and reflect the social interests of the agents who have produced and recontextualised knowledge to construct a school subject, thereby creating the possibilities for inequalities, a matter we will return to in the final section of this chapter.

There is another compelling reason why conceptualisations of ability are important for school and university subjects hinted at in Evans' statement quoted earlier. This is that definitions of ability in a particular social practice, whether it is a discrete activity such as football or a school subject such as physical education, contain within them standards of excellence. These standards are not necessarily fixed for all time, but neither are they arbitrary. According to Alasdair MacIntyre (1985), they are inherent in practices in the form of 'goods' and so are partly definitive of the practice. Striving to achieve these goods internal to a practice systematically extend what MacIntyre (1985: 187) calls 'human powers'. When an individual engages seriously and wholeheartedly in a practice, they are bound

To accept the authority of those standards and the inadequacy of my own performance as judged by them. It is to subject my own attitudes, choices, preferences and tastes to the standards which currently and partially define the practice. Practices ... have a history: games, sciences and arts all have histories. Thus the standards themselves are not immune from criticism, but nonetheless we cannot be initiated into a practice without accepting the authority of the best standards realised so far. ... If, on starting to play baseball, I do not accept that others know better than I when to throw a fast ball and when not, I will never learn to appreciate good pitching let alone to pitch. In the realm of practices the authority of both goods and standards operates in such a way as to rule out all subjectivist and emotivist analyses of judgement.

(MacIntyre, 1985: 190)

Mauss's point, noted earlier in this chapter, that techniques of the body are 'traditional', is similar to MacIntyre's comment that practices have a history. In both cases, some standard of quality defines specific techniques and practices, and these standards are social in origin. They are constructed collectively though not necessarily democratically. Standards are not above criticism but they can only be legitimately criticised by someone on the inside of a practice. In other words, as MacIntyre argues, a beginner must accept the authority of the definition of ability that is integral to a practice. It is of some importance then that any highly codified, institutionalised form of social practice such as a school subject in which learning is of central concern is able to identify standards of excellence and in the process say what would count as 'ability'. The process of striving to meet the standards of excellence in a practice provides access to the goods internal to the practice, indeed, provides a novitiate with the ability to recognise goods *as* goods in the first place, and then the extent to which these standards are met provides a measure of ability.

Since physical education is a social construct, it is constituted by knowledge that is not only valued by a society but that in itself conveys particular values. For example, a game such as rugby union conveys the values of its creators, the male pupils and teachers of Britain's socially elite schools of the nineteenth century. As a number of feminist scholars have noted, sports such as rugby constitute a 'male preserve' (Theberge, 1985). Rugby union was created *by* boys and men *for* boys and men of a particular social class, and so the game's rules, the skills and the strategies as well as its etiquette tell us much about the values of these boys and men and about the goods they believed to be intrinsic to playing rugby (see Mangan, 1981). To protest that rugby is 'too rough' or that it unreasonably favours players who are strong and fast and requires players to play with controlled aggression makes no sense. The goods to be gained from playing rugby derive from its requirement for physical contact, strength, speed and controlled aggression. Standards of excellence related to these goods define what it is to possess and display ability in rugby.

Within the id[2] of physical education-as-sport-techniques, it may be that it is the commitment of teachers to the aspirations of sport for all and universal lifelong participation reported by Green et al. (2005) and Green (2000) that lies behind physical education teachers' reluctance to discuss or to make explicit the matter of ability. This may be because these egalitarian principles appear to be at odds with the fact that practices such as games and sports, as MacIntyre (1985) shows, contain standards of excellence and goods intrinsic to these practices. The issue of ability can only be avoided at a cost, however, which is to the coherence of the school subject. If the id^2 of physical education is to have, as a central aspect of its subject matter, games and sports, then these activities bring with them standards of excellence, goods and ability defined in specific ways. It is not surprising that Bailey and colleagues (2004) have had considerable difficulty in identifying a multifaceted notion of ability in physical education *beyond* the activities of the school programmes that are the manifestations of the id^2 of physical education-as-sport-techniques. Nor is it surprising that physical educators in similar fashion struggled to construct practical means of assessing pupil learning when this became a requirement for programmes in England and Wales at the end of Key Stage 3.

Physical education is a social construct like all other school subjects. It is constructed and constituted by configurations of knowledge that carry forward the sectional interests of the producers of knowledge influenced by Bernstein's distributive rules, mediated by agents in a recontextualising field, and realised in terms of what children actually learn through the activities of teachers according to evaluative rules operating in the secondary field of schools. It is this reality of social constructed-ness that explains why some young people experience physical education differentially, according to the intersections of their social class, gender, religion, ethnicity and ability from where they acquire their physical capital and construct a particular *habitus*. The fact of this social constructed-ness does not contradict Macintyre's point that all social practices require standards of excellence that define the goods inherent in the activity. Nor does this fact deny that these practices, again in MacIntyre's terms, systematically extend human powers. Some of the physical cultural practices that construct and constitute forms of school physical education, such as sport, do indeed extend human powers, notwithstanding the ever-present danger of their corruption by the pursuit of goods external to sport (Kirk, 2002b). But in so doing they inevitably relay in a highly powerful form the sectional interests of their creators and contemporary practitioners. These realities need to be confronted and understood, as do their implications for the practicalities of defining excellence and ability in physical education. If they are not, we unwittingly support instead a situation described by Evans where physical education defines ability in terms other than its subject matter but then allows the most inequitable aspects of the sectional interests of its creators to construct implicit notions of ability. In order to confront these issues, we must consider then the part played by school physical education in social and cultural transmission, reproduction and renewal.

Social and cultural transmission, reproduction and renewal

The idea that education and schooling more specifically play an important part in the transmission of the knowledge and values of given societies has a long history, particularly in terms of the transmission and preservation of the cultural heritage, the 'stock of knowledge', of society (Chanan and Gilchrist, 1974). In the years between the first and second world wars in Britain, advocates for a broader concept of physical training in government schools drew heavily on the games ethic of the private schools to suggest that the values inherent in games playing were worth preserving and transmitting to new generations of children. I argued in *Defining Physical Education* that a sanitised version of this games ethic was active by the 1950s, reworking the original function of games to *emphasise* social divisions to one of *overcoming* them. Many child-centred advocates for games in school physical education, such as members of the Wolfenden Committee, sincerely believed that all young people from all positions in the social hierarchy could become better people through playing games. They saw games and sports as universal goods, and while they were critical of the excesses of some sections of the private school and sport communities, they nevertheless believed sincerely in the educational value of games and sport.

In the 1970s and 1980s, educational researchers became interested in how schools reproduced social inequalities, despite the existence in Britain from the 1950s of comprehensive schools which were explicitly intended to create equal opportunities for all (Rubenstein and Simon, 1966). It was noted that 'achievement' in schools seemed to be distributed unevenly, along the lines of social class particularly, with young people from wealthier and 'mainstream' social groups outperforming their poorer and minority group peers (Floud, Halsey and Martin, 1956). More detailed analyses followed at the level of specific practices of the school, including analyses of particular school subjects, where it was confirmed that in some subjects achievement was also distributed along class and gender lines, so that in mathematics and sciences the wealthier achieved more than the less wealthy and boys outperformed girls (Apple, 1979; Giroux, 1981; Whitty, 1985).

In physical education, Hargreaves (1986) and Evans (1986) among others noted how a multi-activity, sport-based form of the physical education in schools reproduced hegemonic masculinity, 'the irresistible occupation of space (and) the ability to operate on space or the objects in it' (Connell, 1983: 18), and a cluster of associated values including controlled aggression and assumptions of white, male superiority. The dominant form of physical education was thus recognised as a means of advantaging a privileged few able-bodied young people, mostly boys, and disadvantaging many other girls and boys. Rather than acting as a common denominator as its advocates had intended, the studies of sociologists of physical education suggested that instead sport-based physical education reproduced social inequalities. What began as a trickle of research in the early 1980s had by the late 1990s become a flood. On the back of sociological studies of sport more generally (Maguire, 2004; Coakley and Dunning, 2000; McKay, 1991), researchers in physical education told much the same story in increasing detail, concluding that school physical education was a site of the reproduction of social inequalities and injustices (Evans and Davies, 2008; Flintoff and Scraton, 2001; Green, 2008; Wright, 1997).

In the face of these discoveries, the faith of the creators of the id^2 of physical education-as-sport-techniques in the educational value of games and sports, drawing on a sanitised version of the games ethic, is difficult to credit or to sustain. Indeed, notwithstanding (or perhaps because of) the enthusiasm of government in the benign influence of games and sport, it has become in some academic circles unfashionable, certainly suspect, even naively dangerous, to argue for the educational value of games and sport. And yet, if we follow through the logic of the id^2 of physical education-as-sport-techniques, we find that some researchers have been too ready, as Lois Bryson (1990) notes, to 'read-off' from some elite performance sports the characteristics of all forms of sport (see also Kirk, 2003).

To do so would be a mistake. This is because the logic of the id^2 of physical education-as-sport-techniques considers excellence to be found in the mastery of sport skills, and thus views 'ability' to be the successful acquisition of a wide range of sports skills. The acquisition of these skills is not difficult to assess, in principle at least. In any case, the acid-test is that these skills can be put to effective use in playing games and sport, while again not unproblematic practically, is not beyond the wit of physical educators to measure (Grehaigne et al., 2005). The purpose of becoming skilful as a player of games and sports is, as we saw earlier in this chapter, to be enabled to lead a physically active life. Far from being sculpted as a plan to oppress the working classes, women, disabled people and minority groups, the ideals behind the id^2 of physical education-as-sport-techniques were, as I recounted in Chapter 5, child-centred and egalitarian. They were based on the profoundly-held belief that if playing games was part of what it meant to be socially 'privileged', then all young people should be so privileged by having access to the 'goods' of games and sport. In principle at least, the id^2 of physical education-as-sport-techniques provided young people with opportunities to learn and practise not just the prerequisite skills of games and sport, but the social goods of cooperation and teamwork, deferred gratification, respect for rules, the umpire, opponents and fair play, and the unselfish prioritisation of group over individual needs. These goods, which in Macintyre's terms reflect the virtues of honesty, courage and justice, are internal to games and sport.

With these historical roots, it is easier to understand 'a clear tendency among PE teachers to view their broadened PE curricula as the best way of encouraging maximum participation in the spirit of "sport for all" and in a manner that might extend young people's participation into their out-of-school and post-school lives' (Green et al., 2005: 39). When confronted with the bad news that school physical education reproduces social inequalities, in my experience many students of physical education and many practising teachers are affronted. Beyond their sincere intentions, there may have been an even better reason for their commitment to the realisation of egalitarian principles through an id^2 of physical education based in games and sports if these social practices existed in another institutional setting. But as we saw in Chapter 5, transposed to the school as an institution, the worthy ideals of the advocates for multi-activity, sport-based physical education set challenges that physical educators have found difficult, if not impossible, to overcome.

If, in other words, the logic of the id^2 of physical education-as-sport-techniques could be worked through to its inexorable and ideal conclusion, teachers would move pupils from the introductory molecular level of sport-techniques by tasks that apply, extend, refine and vary these techniques through to the development of effective skills in a range of games and sports which they would play with more or less proficiency but with sufficient enjoyment to remain physically active beyond the school gates, in their young adulthood and beyond. In so doing, according to this logic, and providing there are no forces that promote the pursuit of external goods such as fame and fortune and in so doing undermine, through uncontrolled aggression, stress-induced injury, drug abuse or cheating, the 'true' character of games and sport, they would access the goods internal to sport as a social practice and become better people as a result.

If this logic of the dominant id^2 of physical education was realised in this way, physical education would be a form of cultural transmission that not only preserves what some consider to be the valuable cultural heritage of games and sports, but would also provide the possibility for cultural renewal since mass participation in pursuit of goods defined in part by the standards of excellence inherent in games and sports would in MacIntyre's words systematically extend human powers. If physical educators should be held to account for anything in relation to the perpetuation of the id^2 of physical education-as-sport-techniques, it is that they have had too much faith in this logic. Transposed to the school as an institution, their faith in the id^2 of physical education-as-sport-techniques has been misplaced.

Moreover, it is only recently, in the past ten to twenty years that there have been calls for a more reflective, socially-critical approach to physical education that would expose the reproduction of social inequality and injustice (see Macdonald et al., 2002 for an overview). Advocates for a 'critical pedagogy' in physical education argue that it is possible, through processes of reflection, critique, de-bunking and de-mystification (McKay and Pearson, 1984; Kirk, 2000c) for individuals and communities to come to understand, contest and change unequal and unjust practices, to be emancipated from oppressive practices and so to engage in cultural renewal. While critical pedagogy is now common-place in the research literature and is taught in some physical education teacher education courses and in senior high school examination versions of physical education (eg. Senior Physical

Education in Queensland), it arguably has had little effect on the dominance of the id^2 of physical education-as-sport-techniques. This research has successfully exposed the reproductive effects of this id^2 of physical education, but it has for the most part failed to understand the reasons why physical education has these effects, sometimes mistaking the 'effects' (eg. the reproduction of hegemonic masculinity, class-based disadvantage) as 'causes' in themselves.

The writings of critical pedagogues raise the question about what kind of id^2 of physical education could contribute to cultural transmission, reproduction and renewal if the id^2 of physical education-as-sport-techniques is unable in its current institutional forms to do so. Critical pedagogy has, valuably, not only exposed some of the unwanted and arguably unintended reproductive effects of the id^2 of physical education-as-sport-techniques, but it has also revealed pressing problems that this id^2 of physical education cannot recognise. For example, there would appear to be good reasons to educate young people about the social construction of bodies and about some of the more oppressive aspects of this process, such as for example the articulation of exercise = slenderness = health when this is presented as a necessary rather than a contingent set of relationships. Moreover, how might physical education provide opportunities for students to reflect upon and become aware of the social construction of knowledge in physical education, what counts as the valid acquisition and realisation of the subject, and how what counts is always produced, if not determined, by sectional interests? In other words, is it possible to imagine an id^2 of physical education that could foster a level of reflection and awareness in its students so that they themselves could imagine possible, better, futures that preserve and transmit the valued physical cultural heritage of society, acknowledging the work it inevitably does as a relay of the sectional interests of its authors, and in so doing transmit, critique and renew those values?

Conclusion

I have argued in this chapter that the exploration of the relationships between physical education and four issues of physical culture, transfer of learning, excellence and ability, and cultural transmission and renewal provides insights into the bigger picture in which the dominant id^2 of physical education is socially constructed. I have suggested, on the basis of this exploration, that versions of school physical education such as the multi-activity programme informed by the id^2 of physical education-as-sport-techniques are misaligned with contemporary physical culture, through a forward-looking recognition of the growing cultural relevance and salience of games and sport but a backward-looking and archaic notion of games and sport and of pedagogy. This situation has resulted in difficulties for any meaningful transfer of learning between school physical education and life beyond the school since the practice of sport-techniques is a form of knowledge specifically suited to the school as an institution and the highly valued 'culture of acquisition'. These difficulties of transfer in part explain physical educators' ineffectiveness in developing a majority of young people's skills and their apparent failure to achieve the aspiration of universal lifelong participation that is an intrinsic part of the logic of the id^2 of physical education-as-sport-techniques. Difficulties of transfer of learning also explain in part why physical educators, motivated by child-centred and egalitarian ideals such as sport-for-all find it difficult to articulate explicitly the standards of excellence inherent in games and sport, and so to define ability in physical education. As an unintended consequence of this difficulty, they thereby permit, as Evans (2004) argues, inequitable implicit definitions of ability to become manifest in practice. Since the acquisition of prerequisite skills is rarely achieved in the manner required by the logic of the id^2 of physical education-as-sport-techniques, young people are by and large unable to access the goods internal to games and sports thereby preventing the transmission and renewal of valued cultural practices.

In undertaking this relational analysis, we are better able to see the real source of the part physical education plays in reproducing social inequity and injustice and reproducing privilege, and to see that this outcome runs in direct contradiction to the child-centred and egalitarian values of many teachers. The real source is the industrial age school as an institution and the limits its sets on all school subjects to achieve their aspirations (Chanan and Gilchrist, 1974; Lawson, 2009). For physical education, the various institutional practices of mass compulsory secondary schooling identified in Chapter 5 including timetabling, the division of labour and responsibility among staff, the high status afforded to decontextualised, abstract and thus 'generalisable' knowledge and physical educators' collective desire to be treated as a school subject just like any other, all worked against its relationship to physical culture, its aspirations for transfer of learning, its willingness and capacity to reconcile issues around excellence and ability, and its contradictory role in cultural transmission. The id^2 of physical education-as-sport-techniques, in short, produces forms of school knowledge arguably shaped more by a residue of the institutionalised practices of schools concerned with the social regulation of children's bodies than by the practices of games and sports as these take place outside schools.

The fact that the id^2 of physical education-as-sport-techniques has been resistant to reform is remarkable at one level, given the relentless waves of innovation that have broken over education systems in Britain and elsewhere during the past 30 years as governments have increasingly taken on the micromanagement of the provision they fund. At another level, it is perhaps physical education's very success at becoming just like any other subject that explains why its practitioners cling to its currently dominant form so tenaciously. As a matter of historical fact, the good opinion of others in the academy has always mattered very much to physical education as a community. Achieving a place in the core curriculum of schools was a hard-fought struggle during the 1970s to the 1990s,[13] with the outcome never certain. But this achievement has ironically come at a cost. Physical education is expected by the school community to fulfil particular expectations: to display symbolically in its practices the authority of the school; in many schools, to produce sports teams that bring credit to the school; and to provide pupils with opportunities 'to let off steam' so that they are able to continue with the 'real work' of the school. These are powerful expectations.

So what futures can we anticipate for this most institutionalised of school subjects, whose basic configuration has remained more or less in tact since the 1950s? Can it continue to resist change and hold back the relentless waves of reform? Can the id^2 of physical education-as-sport-techniques meet the ambitious goals of governments? Can current practitioners of the id^2 of physical education-as-sport-techniques reform themselves to achieve the worthy vision of their predecessors, in which physical educators prepare all young people to be skilful lifelong participants in sport, exercise and active leisure? Can a new, yet to be imagined id^2 of physical education emerge, with a better alignment of school physical education and physical culture in a digital age? Or will its past finally catch up with it, so that its cultural obsolescence, inadequate preparation of its teachers, reproduction of social inequalities and its failure to achieve its core aspirations finally lead to its demise?

7 Physical education futures?

> We regard substantial change within the subject as a matter of necessity if it
> is to have educational worth in the 21st century. ... There is not only *one*
> possible future for physical education.
>
> (Penney and Chandler, 2000: 85)

In our discussion of futures talk in Chapter 3, Stier, Kleinman and Milchrist
(1994) offered three possible futures for physical education. Stier suggested
that physical education was basically doing a good job and that any problems
that did exist required only minor periodic adjustments. Milchrist disagreed
and argued that while physical education was worth retaining in schools, it
was seriously enough flawed to require a radical overhaul. Kleinman, offering
the least optimistic future for physical education, agreed with Milchrist's
assessment that there were serious problems but proposed that the subject
was beyond rescue and indeed deserved to become extinct. I plan to use these
three possible future scenarios for physical education to structure this final
chapter in order to provide answers to the questions posed at the conclusion
of the previous chapter and elsewhere in this book. I will do so in relation to
the specific configuration of physical education that I have identified as the
id^2 of physical education-as-sport-techniques. It is of this id^2 of physical
education, in the light of the preceding analyses in Chapters 4, 5 and 6 in
particular, that we will ask whether the future is 'more of the same', 'radical
reform', or 'extinction'.

In this context I will also raise the possibility of a future shift in the id^2 of
physical education of the proportions of the previous shift: from an id^2 of physical education-as-gymnastics to an id^2 of physical education-as-sport-techniques.
In so doing, we will seek to remind ourselves of the conditions under which
this previous shift took place, dated in Britain somewhere between the two
world wars, with the new id^2 of physical education manifest and emerging in
the 1950s. This task requires that we enter into the territory of Bernstein's
(2000) primary field of knowledge production, and consider the possibility
of a future that is at this moment unknown to us and so as yet unimagined.
In other words, we will seek to move beyond what Massengale (2000: 106)
described as 'trend extrapolation', where 'things will be exactly like they were

in the past, or ... things will change in the same way as they changed in the past, or ... what has been observed in the past will continue into the future, in the same direction, and at the same rate of speed'. We can be sure, can we not, that whatever future lies in store for physical education, 'things' are unlikely to follow the same course; history is unlikely to repeat itself?

Through all of this I will seek to address the contribution physical educators might themselves make to physical education futures. Penney and Chandler (2000: 85) are in the Milchrist camp insofar as they see 'substantial change as a matter of necessity if (physical education) is to have educational worth in the 21st century'. While I think it is unlikely that some sections of the community of physical educators would agree with Penney and Chandler on that point, I suspect they would strongly endorse their next comment that 'it is for all within the profession to address and debate what the futures should be and to ensure that policy and curriculum developments then reflect the visions established, and facilitate their realization' (p. 85). Is this a possibility, given Houlihan's (2002) insightful analysis of the 'crowded policy spaces' of educational reform in which physical educators' voices have in the past been silenced or ignored by more powerful lobbies? And Bernstein's (2000) concern that during the 1980s and 1990s in Britain the official recontextualising field (ORF) of government and its agents was progressively diminishing the influence of all other agents and alternative voices in the recontextualising process? Will 'the profession' be permitted to act like a profession, with at least some rights to self-determination and self-regulation? History in this case is not on physical educators' side, and so we need to consider what it would take for physical educators themselves to be included in, never mind central to, the radical reform of their subject.

Important to the possibility of physical educators taking an active and coordinated part in the construction of physical education futures is the kinds of individual recruited to physical education teacher education courses and the nature of these courses. As we saw in Chapter 4, the fate of school physical education and physical education teacher education is interdependent. Indeed, I suggested in Chapter 5 that one of the perverse reasons why the id^2 of physical education-as-sport-techniques has endured is because it is suited to teachers' lack of in-depth knowledge of games and sport relative to their pre-1970s predecessors. Given this interdependency of school and university programmes, in the course of this chapter I will consider the implications of each of the scenarios for physical education teacher education. On the basis of the analysis carried out so far in this study, what are physical education futures?

Future One: More of the same

In this 'more of the same' scenario, the id^2 of physical education-as-sport-techniques continues to legitimate multi-activity, sport-based programmes (Flintoff, 2008: 408), with molecularised teaching of techniques informed by the 'hegemony of biomechanics' (Rovegno, 1995). Politicians and policy makers are unaware of the deep problems within the subject that I have, in this study, suggested exist. Indeed, evaluations of initiatives associated with the DCMS/DCSF (2008) *Physical Education and Sport Strategy for Young People* suggest that the restructuring of schools into partnerships are extending opportunities, for instance, for extra-curricular experiences for young people (Quick et al., 2008; Loughborough Partnership, 2006), although we should also note that these evaluations are being carried out by government organisations within the ORF or by agents co-opted by the ORF. These politicians and policy makers treat with disdain the dissenting voices of, for example, feminists, sociologists and critical pedagogues from within Bernstein's pedagogic recontextualising field (PRF), who complain interminably in jargon-ridden prose, as the politicians and their agents see it, about the reproduction of social inequalities. Physical education in schools takes in its stride attempts to reform the subject through exercises such as, in England and Wales, the National Curriculum (Curtner-Smith, 1999; Smith et al., 2007). Even radical reforms of the whole school curriculum are absorbed and adjustments made in order that the core practices of the id^2 of physical education-as-sport-techniques can continue intact, such as was the case with the creation of Key Learning Areas in 1990s Australia (Penney and Kirk, 1996).

Meanwhile, some argue that any problems that physical education might be held accountable for, such as an (alleged) rise in the incidence of childhood obesity, can be resolved only if we have *more* of the same kind of physical education, *more* curriculum time, *more* facilities and *more* teachers. Responsibility for such problems is therefore displaced, and accountability evaded. Furthermore, some physical educators argue, only minor adjustments are required in order to keep physical education on track to face any new challenges that might emerge. They add that degree-qualified teachers are evidence of progress in the field and of the acceptance of physical education within the academy. Significantly, lobbyists for a 'more of the same' future skilfully make use of politicians' and policy makers' own expectations of multi-activity, sport-based physical education, many of them formed by their own experience of the private and grammar schools in which the games ethic has a natural home, to reinforce their view that even if they (the private and grammar-school educated politicians) personally were 'rabbits', they could still appreciate games and sports as a force for good.[1]

This, I believe, is the most likely future for physical education in the short to middle term. There are a number of reasons why this first scenario is a strong possibility. Despite overwhelming evidence of its failure to realise its core aspirations, there remain strong supporters for the id^2 of physical education-as-sport-techniques both inside and outside the subject. We met some in Chapter 4, where we saw that there are many academics in physical education pedagogy who believe that skill acquisition is the central task of physical education, even in the face of evidence they themselves have generated that shows this goal is rarely achieved, and that pupils' learning is not in fact the first priority of physical education teachers. We saw in Chapters 5 and 6 that the aspiration for universal lifelong participation is deeply held within the physical education community, as it is elsewhere. The logic of the id^2 of physical education-as-sport-techniques is compelling for supporters. With its roots in a commitment to child-centred pedagogy and an egalitarianism that sees games and sport as a means of dissolving class barriers and contributing to the real possibility if not the fact of lifelong participation, it is compelling enough for Green et al. (2005) to argue that the multi-activity, sport-based curriculum is actually working and indeed is the best way to provide for young people who come to school with a range of different dispositions and abilities. In Britain, as we have already noted, government has invested heavily in physical education and school sport as a means of reducing the incidence of obesity, improving the prospects of national sports performers, and combating antisocial behaviour among youth. While other governments in Britain since the late 1950s have held similar expectations for physical education, this time, in the first decade of the twenty-first century, they are backed-up with considerable public funds and the anticipation of a successful Olympic Games for Britain in 2012.

But beyond the support for the id^2 of physical education-as-sport-techniques from academics and politicians, there are two further factors that are decisive in ensuring that the 'more of the same' future is likely to prevail in the short to middle term. These are teachers and schools. There is no evidence to suggest that teachers would be willing to engage in a radical reform of their subject and, indeed, there is considerable evidence to the contrary from the literature on curriculum innovation that they would be likely to resist change of a radical nature (e.g. Curtner-Smith, 1999). In Chapter 3, we noted Locke's (1992) insightful comment that the possibilities for change in physical education initiated by physical educators depends on the kinds of person attracted to become physical education teachers. In Chapter 4, Lawson (1988) equally insightfully commented that the cycle of occupational socialisation creates and sustains inter-generational reproduction of like attracting like, and that this process in turn leads teachers to engage in 'acts of curriculum maintenance'.

Given the way that schools continue to be structured according to the logic of the industrial age (Lawson, 2009), physical education teachers can understandably see little to be gained from disrupting the status quo. After all, in Britain if not universally (Hardman and Marshall, 2000), the subject has secured its place in the 'core curriculum'. Its teachers are degree qualified and enjoy parity of esteem with their academic colleagues, in legislation if not always in fact. The subject is by and large popular with a slight majority of pupils, though not always for the reasons teachers might prefer. It serves the useful purpose in schools of providing a 'balanced' education, though the reality of this is more often expressed as providing opportunities for pupils to have a break from academic work. It is unlikely, then, that teachers will volunteer to engage in any radical reform that might undermine the considerable gains their subject appears to have made since the Second

World War. While the institutional imperatives of mass compulsory school-ing remain unchanged, physical educators may believe they would be wise to remain firmly within the parameters of the id^2 of physical education-as-sport-techniques. The risks associated with radical reform may be too high.

If this is the most likely future scenario, is it possible that more time, more resources and more teachers could make programmes informed by the id^2 of physical education-as-sport-techniques work, as recent and current governments in Britain would seem to believe, so that it realises the forward-looking aspirations for genuine skill development of young people and the real possibility that there could be universal lifelong participation? Could this happen? In addition to an explicit and concerted effort on the part of the entire physical education community, it would require a number of other factors to be taken into account. For one thing, as we noted in Chapters 4 and 5, it is unlikely that the current form of physical education teacher education can, without considerable changes to university courses, equip teachers with the subject-matter knowledge they need to develop the skills of cohorts of mixed-ability and differently-motivated and experienced pupils. For another, as we saw in Chapter 6, physical educators would need to come to terms with the standards of excellence built into their games and sports and reconcile their egalitarian educational mission with the sectional inter-ests that permeate these activities and that currently disadvantage the many children who come to school without the physical capital needed to succeed. And they would also need to be sure that the aspiration for lifelong partici-pation can indeed be achieved by teaching children the skills of games and sports, given the rapid speed with which physical culture is changing in a digital age.

In other words, even with more time and more resources, I suggest the odds are against the id^2 of physical education-as-sport-techniques overcoming the problems I have outlined in this book to achieve its own aspirations, never mind the British government's present challenging agenda. So the 'more of the same' scenario suggests that the id^2 of physical education-as-sport-techniques will persist for a time, but sooner or later events will create the need for change, change that physical educators are unlikely to be prepared for or to be consulted on. The short-term gain for physical education could lead to long-term pain.

Future Two: Radical reform

A longer-term future for physical education would seem then to require radical reform. This was the view of many of the contributors to futures talk in Chapter 3. Larry Locke, with characteristic and compelling eloquence, put it like this.

My assumption is that if the dominant model is not broken, at the very least there are a lot of schools in which what is done in the name of physical education is not working well. Further, what goes wrong (disturbing levels of student alienation, program marginality in school curriculum, deep and destructive role conflicts within those who teach) involves the kinds of problems that can't be repaired simply by improving existing forms of content or instruction. The level of change required is so substantial it would have to be called replacement, not repair. For me, the conclusion is unavoidable. If physical education is to have a significant presence in the secondary schools of the 21st century, it is better to chuck the dominant model (and thereby most school programs) and start over from scratch.

(Locke, 1992: 362)

To start over from scratch is more easily said than done, of course, since any future form of physical education will surely carry forward the residue of the present and the past, as we saw in Chapter 5, but Locke's point is taken and is strongly supported by this study. As my closing comments in the final part of the previous section try to make clear, nothing short of the replacement of the id^2 of physical education-as-sport-techniques would seem to be radical enough to reform physical education.

But what form might a new id^2 of physical education take? What is the likelihood of events coming together to create the conditions for a shift in the id^2 of physical education? In order to answer these questions, we need to enter the realm of the yet to be imagined and to consider two issues. The first issue is to consider some of the main conditions that prevailed around the time of the shift from the id^2 of physical education-as-gymnastics to the id^2 of physical education-as-sport-techniques in light of recent, current and possible future events. We must, of course, undertake this first task with Massengale's cautionary words in mind concerning trend extrapolation: no physical education future will be born out of the same combination of events in the past. The second issue is to consider how a new id^2 of physical education would relate to the four issues discussed in Chapter 6 and whether any of the futures proposed by the writers we met in Chapter 3 could meet the challenges these relational issues pose.

Can the past repeat?

Two world wars and an economic depression between them set a backdrop of social instability during the first half of the twentieth century that would have contributed something to the conditions that prevailed at the time of the shift from gymnastics to sport-techniques. As I noted in *Defining Physical Education* (Kirk, 1992a), social reconstruction was a preoccupation of the immediate post-Second World War period in British society, in which social consensus and political convergence were key themes in what was widely held to be a 'conflict-free' society. Clearly there is no immediate parallel with contemporary society in Britain, notwithstanding armed conflicts in other parts of the world in which the British military are involved, and periodic economic downturns. If broader, international events in the 1930s and 1940s had any direct bearing at all on hastening the demise of the id^2 of physical education-as-gymnastics, it may have been the new association with fascist politics of drilling in mass youth groups. But far more easily discernible are two events much closer to physical education itself. In Britain, these were the invention of compulsory mass secondary schooling in the early to mid-1940s and the consequent influx of substantial numbers of men into physical education teaching.

Without compulsory secondary education, physical educators would not have been needed in larger numbers. Nor would they have faced older and more physically mature adolescents who could no longer, as they had in elementary schools, be treated as androgynous. Until the late 1940s, as we saw in Chapter 5, physical education was a community populated mainly by women from the middle and upper-middle classes. The first colleges for specialist male teachers did not open until the early 1930s and were some 40 or so years behind the first colleges for women. As new wings were attached to the larger teacher training colleges to accommodate the demand for more physical education teachers, the women gymnasts, distracted at the time by their civil war, were soon outnumbered. While not universally recognised by physical educators at the time, there were still enough who understood that the days of Swedish gymnastics were numbered. The men argued that educational gymnastics, the only apparently viable alternative, may have been appropriate for primary school-age children, but that it did not suit the pubescent and post-pubescent pupils in the secondary schools. In England, all of the men trained before the war in the new specialist colleges either already possessed a two-year teacher's certificate or had a three-year university degree, to which, in both cases, they added a specialist third year.^{2} This meant that many would have had experience of sport at college or university, and some would also have attended private schools or grammar schools and experienced sport there. McIntosh (1968) reminds us too that there was already momentum behind the wider concept of physical recreation that included games and sports, evidenced in the 1937 Physical Training and Recreation Act in Britain and a similar National Fitness Act passed four years later in Australia.

These were the decisive factors that brought about the shift in the id^2 of physical education in the mid-twentieth century although, as we noted in Chapter 5, the replacement of gymnastics with sport-techniques was the culmination of a process that had been under way from at least the 1920s or earlier. Again, there seem to be few parallels with these events then and the current situation. There is little agitation for change from the majority within the physical education community. While there is always friction and fractious exchange, there is no civil war of the proportions of the Swedish versus educational gymnasts or of the subsequent struggle between the men and the women. Even though there is a push towards mass further and higher education in Britain, where this has been achieved elsewhere (e.g. the USA), it has not impacted on physical education in any way resembling the effects of compulsory mass secondary education from the 1940s.

There is on the horizon only one possibility at the moment for the influx of a new group into the territory currently occupied by physical educators paralleling the influx of men in the 1950s, and this is the emerging community of degree-qualified sports coaches. Perhaps their best chance for insurgence is in the primary school, where few physical education specialists exist but where there is growing recognition of a need for specialist teaching (Kirk, 2005). Even if this was to happen, though, such a development might only further consolidate and entrench the id^2 of physical education-as-sport-techniques, particularly if coaches were to be employed in large numbers in primary schools where they could take on the task of introducing sport-techniques. Most new degree courses in sports coaching focus on no more than three sports, and so this would limit the range of skills coaches could provide. Nevertheless, sub-degree qualified coaches are already working on a part-time basis in many primary schools in England, typically employed to provide short introductory units in specific sport sports such as 'tag rugby' and 'quick cricket'. If this trend was to accelerate, the challenge for secondary school physical educators would then be to move beyond the interminable introductory lessons in sport-techniques and facilitate the mastery of playing games and sports, a task to which they may be ill suited given the current situation in physical education teacher education and the constraints of the school timetable, discussed in Chapters 4 and 5.

The arrival of sports coaches from outside the education system and the physical education community is one of the few possible parallels with the influx of large numbers of male teachers in the 1940s and 1950s, and it may be possible for the id^2 of physical education-as-sport-techniques to absorb such a development and perhaps become further entrenched because of it. It would seem then, if there is to be a shift in the id^2 of physical education, it will have to come from outside the community of physical educators and possibly outside the education system. The prospects of this for the moment seem remote, and so we can only speculate on the kinds of event that might trigger such a move towards radical reform, and the id^2 of physical education that might result. For instance, with so much financial investment in the Physical Education and Sport Strategy for Young People (DCMS/DCSF, 2008) and the high expectations for British success at the 2012 Olympics, it is possible that physical educators may be held accountable for disappointing sports results in 2012 and beyond, a continuing trend towards obesity, and serious delinquent behaviour from a broad cross-section of young people.

A new id^2 of physical education and the bigger picture

If there was a convergence of events that triggered a shift in the id^2 of physical education, the new id^2 would need to meet the challenges presented by the four relational issues discussed in Chapter 6. A strong alignment between school physical education and physical culture would be required, a somewhat daunting task given the speed with which the practices of sport, in particular, change, at least at the elite level. As we saw in Chapter 3, Fernandez-Balboa recognised that future forms of physical education could not resist the embrace of the many new technologies of digital society. Indeed, there is evidence that physical educators are already using digital images of student performances, sometimes employing ready-made systems such as Dartfish, to assist learning through feedback and analysis. While the increasing permeation of all school subjects by digital technologies seems inevitable, this does not, nevertheless, constitute a substantive alignment of physical education and physical cultural practices, nor does it threaten necessarily the hegemony of the id^2 of physical education-as-sport-techniques.

The discussion in Chapter 6 suggested that the relationship between school physical education and physical culture is of crucial importance, since it is in terms of the nature of the alignment of school knowledge and culture that the other three issues of transfer, excellence and renewal are determined. In Bernstein's (2000) terms, the 'instructional discourse' (ID) of school knowledge, in our case school physical education, is embedded in the 'regulative discourse' (RD) of the primary field of knowledge production, which in the case of this study is physical culture. It is this embedding of ID within RD that generates in Bernstein's theory 'pedagogic discourse' or, in our case, the id^2 of physical education. If the two are misaligned, as I have argued, the multi-activity curriculum and globalised and commercialised physical culture are, then, the result is an incoherent id^2 of physical education with inevitable consequences for the transfer of learning, standards of excellence, and cultural transmission and renewal. We might ask, given this need for the tight alignment of school physical education with physical culture, whether there are any resources available to us currently in terms of ideas of physical education, either in Chapter 3's futures talk or elsewhere, that have the potential for a better alignment than is provided by ideas of physical education such as the sport-based, multi-activity curriculum.

Arguably, the idea of physical education that is best aligned with the sport dimension of physical culture is the pedagogical model Sport Education (Siedentop, 1994). I have written elsewhere (e.g. Kirk and Macdonald, 1998; Kirk and Kinchin, 2003) that Lave and Wenger's (1991) theory of situated learning helps us to see how the alignment between Sport Education and sport could provide authentic and meaningful experiences for young people, where Sport Education facilitates their learning trajectories from 'novitiate' to 'expert' or (in Lave and Wenger's terms) from peripheral to fuller membership of the community of practice of sport through 'legitimate peripheral participation'. Transfer of learning can then be seen to be direct and explicit. At the same time, Penney et al. (2002) have recognised that Sport Education offers a selective version of sport that is in a number of respects at odds with the dominant, powerful and pervasive form of elite professional sport. While

I believe this is correct, in Chapter 6 I have argued that we cannot 'read off' the whole of sport as a practice from elite, high performance sport. Moreover, I suggest that Siedentop's (2002b) application of MacIntyre's (1985) virtue ethics to theorise this alignment between Sport Education and sport, and my development of this position (Kirk, 2002b), goes some way towards addressing Penney et al.'s concerns. Standards of excellence and associated definitions of ability and the transmission of valued social practices are built into Sport Education as a pedagogical model, while the possibilities for critique and renewal have been explored by Kinchin and O'Sullivan (2003) through their 'cultural studies approach', through Hastie and Buchanan's (2000) integration of Sport Education with Hellison's (1995) personal and social responsibility model to create 'empowering sport', and Ennis's (1999) 'Sport for Peace'.

Next to Sport Education as a specific idea of physical education, there are few other pedagogical models or proposals for radical reform that are as well theorised and researched (Kinchin, 2006; Wallhead and O'Sullivan, 2005). Nevertheless, the relationship of health-related exercise (HRE) to the exercise dimension of physical cultural seems self-evident. Surprisingly to some observers, physical education teachers have remained ambivalent about HRE (Kirk, 2006b), an ambivalence made clearly evident in the weak position of HRE as a thematic element of the NCPE. This ambivalence is all the more peculiar given some of the good examples that exist of holistic forms of HRE (e.g. Harris, 2005; Whitehead and Fox, 1983). The fact or fiction of an obesity crisis notwithstanding (Gard and Wright, 2006), HRE would appear to have obvious cultural relevance at this time and thus could align well with the exercise dimension of physical culture. Apart from the practical challenges of implementing HRE in schools (Kirk, 2006b), some of which could be relatively easily met with the use of new technologies, a weakness of some current models of HRE is that they tend either to be grounded in a mainly functionalist, biological perspective or, where they do include a more 'holistic' approach to include students' emotions and attitudes, in psychological theories focused on the individual. The biology and the motivation of individuals are clearly important subject matter for HRE. However, there would also appear to be a strong case for a critical concern for the social construction of the body through the media and by the health and fitness industries themselves (Oliver and Lalik, 2001; Evans et al., 2004). The construction of such a comprehensive pedagogical model addresses the challenge of physical cultural relevance and transfer of learning, though it would need to deal with Evans's (2004) concerns about the physical capital young people bring to school physical education which in turn requires HRE to embrace an appropriately broad definition of 'health' to include the beliefs and practices of all sections of the community served by state-funded schools.

In Chapter 6, we saw Fairclough et al.'s (2002) claim that some physical activities are more likely to be pursued by adults than others, which they named 'lifetime activities'. One category of lifetime activities that aligns directly with active leisure is outdoor adventure activities (OAA). OAA embraces a wide range of active leisure pursuits including walking, cycling, sailing and skiing, and has a well-developed pedagogy that includes personal and team challenges, a respect for and preservation of the environment, and spirituality (Hubball and West, 2008; Quay, 2003). Interestingly, OAA cannot easily be fitted into the school timetable, since it obviously needs to be practised away from the school and requires more substantial chunks of time than a timetable normally accommodates. It may be that these characteristics have prevented this pedagogical model being routinised and molecularised within the id^2 of physical education-as-sport-techniques, though this may also account for the fact that it remains a marginal aspect of most school physical education programmes. Indeed, in this respect, it might be argued that, like Sport Education which challenges timetabling and unit design conventions, OAA sits outside the id^2 of physical education-as-sport-techniques. Again, OAA aligns directly with the active leisure dimension of physical culture, and has clear potential for transfer of learning into adulthood as a category of lifetime activities. Because of the element of risk in many OAAs, standards of excellence and ability are relatively clearly defined, while the strong focus on personal and collective challenge and the care of the outdoors connect strongly to cultural transmission and renewal.

Other dimensions of physical culture, such as dance and the meditative and martial arts, could also meet the challenges presented by the four relational issues. While dance remains one of the six categories of activity in the current National Curriculum in England and Wales, its full potential to align with physical culture, transfer learning, identify standards of excellence and transmit and renew culture is seriously limited within the id^2 of physical education-as-sport-techniques. The risk of molecularisation is as real for dance as it is for sport. It is significant that the dance community has sought to distance itself from physical education, with the development of specific forms of the subject in the senior secondary schools, and the education of specialist dance teachers (Gard, 2001). The risk of molecularisation is just as real for the meditative and martial arts, given their important spiritual focus. These arts consist of techniques of the body that have their cultural roots in countries such as Japan, Korea and India, but nevertheless there are advocates who have stressed the educational benefits of their inclusion in physical education in Western countries such as Britain (Brown and Johnson, 2000). The globalisation of physical culture in some respects makes it more likely now than even 20 or 30 years ago that the meditative and martial arts could have a strong cultural resonance outside their countries of origin. It is interesting to note that where the martial arts, for instance, do appear in physical education programmes, they most often take the form of 'self-defence' or are practised as sports.

In Chapter 3, some of the futures talk centred on the likelihood of the commercialisation and outsourcing of physical education, with both Hoffman (1987) and Tinning (1992) 'dreaming impossible dreams' that, in Tinning's case in particular, actually have a foundation in reality. We also noted what appears to be an increasing trend in the growth of businesses that offer a range of physical activity services and equipment to schools, families and communities. In Tinning's case, the reality was Tri-skills, a company formed in 1991 in South Australia to offer a skills-based programme to government and private primary schools. The significant point in this example is that the form of physical education provided by Tri-skills did not challenge the id^2 of physical education-as-sport-techniques and, indeed, was entirely consistent with it. So the trend towards commercialisation and outsourcing, predicted by some of the writers in Chapter 3, may be a reality and may continue, but it does not in itself offer radical reform of physical education.

'Several fields out of one': A proliferation of id^{2}s of physical education

If the conditions were right for radical reform, we can perhaps catch a glimpse of one possible future from this discussion which calls into question the dominance of a single id^2 of physical education. In discussing the challenges facing the field in higher education, Lawson (2007: 239) has suggested that the desire to resist fragmentation and to retain unity is perhaps misplaced. Instead, he suggests, it may be time to acknowledge that we are in a position to construct 'several fields out of one'. Considered in relation to schools, it could be that Sport Education, HRE and OAA and indeed dance and the meditative and martial arts could exist as stand-alone programmes, in much the manner of the spoof futuristic newspaper report below.

The Times, 27 June 2013

New Scheme for Sport and Exercise in Schools

The Prime Minister's Office announced today that Lord Coe had agreed the new schemes for sport and exercise in schools. This follows the decision late last year to abolish the National Curriculum. In place of physical education, all pupils aged 5–14 will from September participate in a minimum of 3 hours of exercise per week. They will be required to meet stringent fitness targets set by the new Office for Health Standards. The franchise for this service has been won by Lifestyle and Weight Management Group Ltd, the multi-national research and development company. A spokesperson for LWMG commented that 'Obviously we are delighted with this decision. LWMG's pioneering work in the field of childhood obesity over the past 15 years makes the Group the obvious candidate to manage this franchise.' The collapse of the National Health Service in March coupled with ongoing reports of high Body/Mass Index scores and critical levels of obesity among the British population were identified by LWMG as decisive factors in shaping the new coalition Government's decision.

Prime Minister Coe is also said to be keen to ensure England's third world cup win next year following the victories of 1966 and 2010, and to build on Britain's historic record medal haul from the London Olympics. Sports Minister Sir David Beckham has been in close consultation with the two lead bodies in youth sport, the Youth Sport Trust and Sports Coach UK, who have recommended that the multi-skills Talent Development Program first introduced in 2003 be further extended. An additional 800 school/club sports coaches will be recruited to work with the existing 9000 coaches. It is hoped that it may be possible to recruit some of these additional coaches by retraining former, now redundant, physical education teachers.

All children aged 5–7 will undergo intensive multi-skills training prior to selection for the Talent Development Program for 8–16 year olds. This initiative, Minister Beckham said, will further consolidate the Government's recently announced investment in the development of a network of residential sports colleges for 12–16 year olds. The first college opened last year in Loughborough, and further colleges will open in Bath, Leeds, Liverpool, London and Glasgow later this year.

(Kirk, 2006a: 15)

In this example, two of the major dimensions of physical culture as it is configured currently have clear and tight alignment with forms of school knowledge. Even with this tight alignment, the scenario has aspects which would not necessarily be well received in the physical education community and elsewhere. The point of including these scenarios is to suggest that even though some kinds of physical education could form the future, their possibility does not necessarily make them benign or desirable. The example suggests two future possibilities, proliferation and unification.

The first possibility is a proliferation of id^2s of physical education, so that there is an id^2 of physical education-as-sport, an id^2 of physical education-as-exercise, the id^2 of physical education-as-active-leisure, and so on. In this future scenario, where there are 'several fields out of one', each of the major dimensions of physical culture is tightly aligned to a form of school practice to construct a coherent id^2 of physical education. In the case of the id^2 of physical education-as-sport, Sport Education could be one school version of this configuration of knowledge, and no doubt other models would also be possible. The same point applies for the other id^2s.

We can see, too, implications for the education of teachers/coaches/ instructors for each of these id^2s of physical education. The current generalist programmes of physical education teacher education could not develop the depth of subject-matter knowledge each of these id^2s of physical education would require, from which, as Hoffman (1987: 128) suggested in Chapter 3, physical education teachers are currently 'specialists in generalism'. In this first possible future, they would need to be, instead, specialists in sport, specialists in exercise, and specialists in various aspects of active leisure. This scenario has the strength, then, of strong alignment with elements of physical culture, but it requires the intentional fragmentation of the subject as it currently exists.

A second possibility is unification through conceptualising pedagogical models such as Sport Education and HRE as the id^2 of physical education-as-physical-culture. This scenario would still, in all likelihood, require specialisation by teachers, but it has the advantage of suggesting some degree of unity of the field. Its obvious disadvantage is the abstract character of the notion of physical culture compared to its constituent parts of, for example, sport, exercise and active leisure, and the risk to meaningfulness and coherence for pupils, their parents and the broader public. At the same time, it may be possible that an id^2 of physical education-as-physical-culture could come close to producing versions of school physical education that are thematic, along the lines proposed in Chapter 3 by Penney and Chandler (2000), among others.

For either of these future scenarios to improve on the currently dominant id^2 of physical education-as-sport-techniques, the institutional form of the school itself must change. Lawson (2009: 94) has suggested that 'PE is an industrial-age invention developed specifically for industrial age schools'. As such, he argues that we require new 'design criteria' for reconstructing the subject. He notes five 'foundational premises' for these new criteria. First, new physical education programmes must take forms that fit the new institutional forms of the school, in particular with community-school designs (Lawson, 2008). Lawson describes physical education in a community-school configuration as follows.

> PE in this community school configuration was not limited to the regular school day. Community school programs enabled offerings during out-of-school time, and some linked the regular day classes with play opportunities unconstrained by class time. Most importantly, the conditions needed for genuine play – true choices, opportunities to experience flow, engaging in activities for their intrinsic benefits, learning without reference to grades and tests – could be achieved in extra-school contexts in ways that regular school programs rarely approximated. All of these features-as-possibilities were important to me because I had rejected the long standing assumption that PE should be designed and conducted in conformity with other school subjects. This traditional assumption, in my view, was flawed. It denied PE's uniqueness and actually robbed it of its most important contributions to young people and school improvement.
>
> (Lawson, 2009: 88)

Second, then, physical education must end its quest to be treated just like other school subjects, and recognise and celebrate the characteristics that make it a unique, different and valuable source of educational experience.

Third, Lawson suggests that we need to be more astute in recognising and taking into account the powerful forces in society that offer competing and often harmful lifestyles to young people, a point which reinforces the importance of alignment with valued aspects of physical culture that we wish to transmit and renew. Fourth, physical education programmes must take a life-course development perspective, confirming the significance of strong transfer of learning. And fifth, Lawson argues that we must recognise the power of physical education programmes both as stand-alone and combined social interventions that involve collaboration with other helping professions to address urgent social problems.

The application of these five principles to construct new design criteria needs to proceed in tandem with the reconstruction of the school as an institution if an id^2 of physical education is to be radically reformed. The renewal and transformation of the school is a task that physical educators by themselves cannot undertake. But it is an essential condition for radical reform. Without change to the school, to its time and place boundedness, its abstract and generalised knowledge, its distance from the 'real life' of the communities it is supposed to serve, there is a third possibility, which is extinction.

Future Three: Extinction

I suggest that while 'more of the same' is the most likely future scenario in the short term, 'extinction' is the least likely. However, without 'radical reform', it is the most likely longer-term scenario. This will be the case no matter which reforms are attempted unless there is a reconstruction of the school as an institution or, at the very least, a repositioning of physical education within the school. Industrial-age schools were created to serve purposes that are now for the most part defunct. They create conditions that support and sustain versions of school subjects that molecularise knowledge and, furthermore, hold these up as high status. They disconnect knowledge from students' lived experiences of life beyond the school. Once we understand the power of the institutional imperatives of the school for social regulation in particular and the part played by practices that work on the bodies of students in which both the id^2s of physical education-as-gymnastics and of sport-techniques have been strongly implicated, then we begin to better understand why many innovative ideas have had little actual effect on changing the practices associated with the dominant id^2 of physical education.

For example, despite widespread interest from teachers and researchers from the early 1980s to the present, Sport Education remains a 'novel' idea in specialist physical education settings. This is because it challenges some core assumptions of unitisation and timetabling and of the role of teachers who support the id^2 of physical education-as-sport-techniques. Sport Education requires units of lessons to be recast as sport 'seasons', and for the season to run for at least 12 lessons or more so that it can incorporate a pre-season, a period of practice, round-robin league competitions, and a festive climax such as play-offs and finals. Lessons need to be long enough for meaningful practice and competition to take place. Pupils take responsibility for much of the coaching, practice organisation, equipment, team organisation and refereeing, and also, in some cases, sit on a sports panel which makes rules and deals with their breaches. Implemented in primary schools, there is also the opportunity for cross-curricular work in the maintenance of team portfolios, designing team uniforms, keeping statistics, writing news reports of matches, and planning practice and competition strategies (MacPhail et al., 2004). Typical objections to these 'unconventional' features of Sport Education are that it is not possible to maintain pupil interest over this period or that pupils can't be trusted to fulfil all the roles for running their teams, practices and matches – concerns that studies show can be overcome (Kinchin, 2006). But to work, Sport Education requires changes to unitisation, the timetable, and to teachers' and pupils' roles.

In senior high schools in Britain, though perhaps not yet in Australia, high-stakes examination versions of 'physical education' require very little learning in and through actual physical activity, focusing almost exclusively instead on the 'about' dimension of academic study. It would be appropriate and accurate to describe these subjects as Sport, Exercise and Active Leisure, or even Kinesiology or Physical Culture. In this sense, physical education as a means of learning in and through physical activity is already 'extinct'. Here, 'physical education' has been so successful at becoming a school subject just like other subjects that the characteristics that make it unique, different and valuable have all but disappeared. Foreshadowing this possibility almost 30 years ago, educational sociologist David Hargreaves (1982: 6), in a 'private' conversation with physical educators in the *Bulletin of Physical Education*, clearly foresaw this danger. He said that physical education's 'non-academic character is the very source of its importance in the provision of a balanced education for all. PE teachers should revel and rejoice in their standing and reject the strategy of striving for a pale imitation of academic subjects'.

Physical educators who advocate 'more of the same' may be able to sustain their belief and to maintain the illusion that the id^2 of physical education-as-sport-techniques will eventually achieve is core aspirations. But as financial pressures mount, it must surely only be a matter of time before governments begin to look closely at the high costs of teachers' salaries, teacher education programmes, and facilities and equipment. In Britain, where skilful manipulation of political processes has led to large-scale investment in physical education, we should anticipate that with this investment will come closer scrutiny of the outcomes of school programmes. Could these programmes withstand the intense interest generated by student attainment target (SATs) testing that is required of literacy, numeracy and science? How well prepared would the physical education community be if such intensive, detailed testing was mooted? Advocacy of 'more of the same' is a high-risk strategy, particularly if the higher levels of funding in physical education result in higher levels of real accountability. For example, Bailey et al. (2008) suggest that:

> Avoiding the issue of accountability also enables the PESS [physical education and school sport] profession to avoid making the dramatic changes to curriculum and pedagogy that some claims would warrant. Claims made about health outcomes provide an interesting example. If physical educators want to have an impact on enhancing young people's physical activity levels in order to improve their health, then it could be argued that some current practices should be discontinued because they do not appear to 'work' for many young people. Instead, if physical educators were serious about promoting physical activity for health then nutrition and physical literacy would surely be central to their strategies. They would also need to work closely with families and the wider school, education and health communities. It seems likely that radical changes to pedagogy would be required too – particularly if PESS is to meet the daunting challenges embedded in the rhetoric of meeting the individual needs of each child.
>
> (Bailey et al., 2008: 16)

If held accountable for the core aspirations of the id^2 of physical education-as-sport-techniques, physical educators would, as Bailey et al. suggest, be forced into radical reform, a prospect which may, perversely, encourage support for the status quo.

One of the strongest forces propelling physical education towards extinction is the form of physical education teacher education that has emerged along with the academicisation of higher education, physical activity programmes since the 1970s. The consequent reduction and marginalisation of the experience of practical physical activity has produced teachers better suited to teaching senior high school examination versions of physical education than the core programmes for younger pupils. There is, as we learned in Chapters 4 and 5, deep ambivalence within the physical education community about the kinds of practical expertise in games and sports that physical educators require, which in turn feeds the problematic status of excellence and ability Evans (2004) noted exists in schools. Despite the appearance in many countries of standards for teaching and for teacher education, and of rigorous and detailed inspection regimes intended to maintain them, such standards do not replace the subject-matter knowledge teachers of physical education need to teach practical versions of the subject. The general and amorphous nature of the multi-activity curriculum and its ongoing expansion since the mid-1950s merely exacerbates the problem. If teachers were, as Hoffman (1987) maintained in the mid-1980s, 'specialists in generalism', there is little evidence to suggest this situation has changed.

The sub-discipline model of sport and exercise science or kinesiology would appear to be well entrenched in universities and is thriving in many parts of the world. The field in its several manifestations, as sport and exercises sciences, sports therapy, and sport and leisure studies, is popular with students. Students entering the field typically required high scores from senior high school examinations. Popular courses are everywhere oversubscribed and are thus of considerable value to universities in economically difficult times, where competition among universities for students is high. National reviews of the quality of research such as the Research Assessment Exercise (RAE) in Britain have further institutionalised an amorphous physical activity field in the academy under the heading of 'Sport-related Studies'.

Yet, as we saw in Chapter 4, the very momentum and success of this new academic field that emerged from physical education teacher education in the post-Second World War period contains the seeds of its own extinction. Specialisation and fragmentation appear to be hard-wired tendencies of the field, creating the constant danger of the dissolution of departments and the transfer of their staff to other units in the university, or to the insurgence of other fields into the territory of sport and exercise. Beyond the North American debates we encountered in Chapter 4, there is little evidence to suggest that sport and exercise academics have any taste for the social epistemological work that is required to provide touchstones that could counter the processes of specialisation and fragmentation. At the same time, as Lawson (2007) suggests, perhaps fragmentation isn't such a bad thing if it permits the construction of new fields out of one.

In this context of the juggernaut-like progress of the physical activity field in higher education, there are few signs that physical educators have the desire to tackle large-scale reform to produce programmes that will better prepare teachers for schools. In some respects, given the incoherence of the id^2 of physical education-as-sport-techniques, this is unsurprising, and the 'specialist in generalism' is the product. Versions of physical education tightly aligned with dimensions of physical culture such as Sport Education, HRE and OAA hold clear implications for more focused and more specialist forms of teacher education. But they too would require a different kind of knowledge base from that offered by the academic, sub-discipline model. However we consider the issue, the radical reform of school physical education rests on a parallel reform of teacher education. The fate of each is so closely intertwined that this process must unfold in tandem. Failure here is the surest indicator that extinction is a longer-term future scenario for physical education.

Conclusion

More of the same, radical reform and extinction are the three futures scenarios we have considered in this chapter, with the first being judged most likely in the short to middle term and the last in the longer term. The difficulty for radical reform is that it requires change not just to school programmes, but also to university programmes of physical education teacher education and to the school as an institution or, at the very least, to how physical education is positioned in it. This is a momentous task and one fraught with risk. For instance, many physical educators will no doubt consider their place in the government school system to be secure following more than five decades of hard work to make their subject become just like any other subject. Why would they as a community risk that security for reforms that could undermine their status, pay and conditions? It seems unlikely then that reform will be led by physical educators in schools and in other roles that support the id^2 of physical education-as-sport-techniques.

We also considered the possibility of history repeating itself so that a combination of events could provoke a shift in the id^2 of physical education in a fashion similar to the move from gymnastics to sport-techniques. We can say with some conviction that some of the key events of the period leading up to that shift, such as two world wars and an economic depression, we would never want to see again. Closer to physical education and within the period of social turmoil created by war and depression, the invention of compulsory mass secondary schools and the influx of large numbers of men into what had been mainly a profession of women are unlikely to be paralleled now or in the future. That said, there is the possibility of other groups, such as degree-qualified sports coaches, viewing schools as a suitable territory for them to occupy. But such an event in itself might not necessarily disturb, and indeed might only more firmly entrench, the id^2 of physical education-as-sport-techniques.

The 'more of the same' scenario is seductive. Even if its supporters accept that the id^2 of physical education-as-sport-techniques cannot achieve its own aspirations to provide young people with the skills to play games and sports now and for a lifetime, these are worthy aspirations. One can appreciate why they may believe that more resources, teachers and time just might make a difference. The emotional pull of the id^2 of physical education-as-sport-techniques and this logic is strong. It is a hard scenario to give up. But that is what must be done if some kind of physical education is to have a future in compulsory mass schooling. If this is so, then we must, however reluctantly, embrace radical reform. But where will the impetus for this come from and what needs to be done? A brief answer to this question forms part of the next chapter which is the conclusion to this study of physical education futures.

8 Securing the conditions for radical reform

> The need for significant reforms and, indeed, transformations begin with due recognition that today's schools are industrial age institutions. PE has been developed, organized and conducted to conform to this industrial age logic. Both PE and schools are out-of-step with today's global societal realities, needs and opportunities. Both need to be reformed and even transformed.
>
> (Lawson, 2009: 93)

While Lawson produced this insight from his own programme of study, conducted quite separately from mine, his statement nevertheless forms an appropriate conclusion to this book. Indeed, the fact that his programme is centred primarily on the USA provides support for my position, stated in Chapter 1, that differences between forms of physical education in countries and regions are less significant than their similarities. While the situation in the USA differs from Britain in a plethora of local detail, at the level of temporal analysis that the id^2 of physical education as a conceptual tool permits, physical education in both countries (and elsewhere) is facing the same or similar broad challenges. These challenges have their roots in physical education's past, and have shaped a form of physical education that is, as Lawson suggests, more suited to an industrial rather than a digital age. Physical education is, I have claimed, the most institutionalised of school subjects. Furthermore, the id^2 of physical education-as-sport-techniques, with its molecularisation and abstraction of subject matter, its child-centred and egalitarian philosophy and its aspiration for universal lifelong physical activity, is a powerful and obdurate but incoherent construction of school knowledge relating to obsolete forms of physical culture, with consequent problems for transfer of learning, standards of excellence and cultural transmission and renewal.

I suggested in Chapter 7 that of the three futures scenarios I sketched, the more likely short- to middle-term possibility was 'more of the same', while in the longer term it was 'extinction'. This is because the most likely scenario to guarantee a longer-term future, 'radical reform', is risky and complex. But while this may be the case, and while the challenges facing physical education may seem intractable and insurmountable, we must nevertheless consider what is required to be done in order to make radical reform more rather than less likely as a possible future. Having completed our first task, which as Larry Locke noted in Chapter 4 was to properly understand the problem, we now have a responsibility to sketch, albeit briefly, what it would take to produce solutions.

Lawson (2009), as we noted in Chapter 7, proposed five fundamental principles that should underpin the construction of new design criteria for physical education, suited to a new, future configuration of the school, specifically, in his terms, the community school. We might add to these five principles a sixth, which is that whatever forms school physical education take, they must be as tightly aligned as possible with the major dimensions of physical culture that we value and wish to transmit and renew. It is physical culture, as a non-pedagogic form of knowledge, that provides school physical education with its substance but also with its relevance, its currency and its legitimacy. This will be no easy task since, as we have noted, dimensions of physical culture such as sport have been transforming rapidly in a digital age. We also noted that forms of physical education represent selections from physical culture and aspects of physical culture that we collectively as a society believe are worth preserving and transmitting to new generations. This process of selection, as we saw in Chapters 6 and 7, is no neutral act. It is a profoundly political act which, in a social democracy, should be widely debated and critically scrutinised. Physical educators should properly be party to such discussions. Often, however, in Britain at least, as we noted through Houlihan's (2000) and Penney and Evans's (1999) work, they have been either excluded, under-represented or ignored. Other sectional interests have often secured a larger share for themselves of the 'crowded policy spaces' surrounding physical education. At the same time, the physical education community has its own sectional interests which, I argued in Chapter 7, are likely to work against radical reform and towards the status quo. I have warned that such a role will, in the longer term, work against the best interests of both the physical education community and the young people it seeks to serve. In this complex scenario for change, how can we begin to secure the conditions that might lead to radical reform, to a shift in the id^2 of physical education, to the application of the six principles for new design criteria?

I suggest that universities should play a particular and crucial role in securing the conditions for radical reform. In making this statement, I am aware that I am bringing yet another set of interests into a complex mix of views, values and interests. However, I suggest it is only universities that provide the spaces for the critical intellectual work required to inform our judgements about public education, pedagogy and the curriculum. It is in universities that the complex range of views, values and interests can be considered and brought together, options weighed and different scenarios for the future considered against sometimes complementary and sometimes conflicting local and global priorities.

In making these statements, I am working with a particular view of universities developed by Ernest Boyer (1990) in *Scholarship Reconsidered*. Boyer noted with concern a general drift towards convergence within the higher education sector in the USA, towards a narrowly defined concept of research associated with what he called 'discovery'. Boyer argued instead for a broader concept of scholarship which included discovery, and also 'integration', 'application' and 'teaching', with each of these having parity of esteem across the sector. Building on this broader concept of scholarship, Boyer's plea was for universities to diversify their missions rather than converge on just one, with the inevitable 'league-table' mentality that goes with convergence. In other words, since universities have different histories, different resource bases, and serve different local and global communities, there should be a rich diversity of missions, some focused primarily on the scholarship of teaching and of application, while others concern themselves with the scholarship of integration and of discovery.

Particularly noteworthy in Boyer's argument is his restatement of the importance of scholarship as a broad category of academic work which encompasses narrower notions of 'research'. This broader category is essential to the work of universities since it is this characteristic more than any other that marks them out as distinctive educational institutions. The practice of scholarship is one of the common features of an otherwise differentiated and diverse higher educational sector. This notion of scholarship sits well alongside the distinction Lawson (2009) draws between 'search' and 're-search'. He argues that 'search' is a form of scholarship that precedes research, the latter being a more recent invention and more narrowly focused. Indeed, he claims that, historically, research replaced a broader notion of scholarship in the physical activity field in higher education in the 1960s. He notes that while this was a remarkable achievement for a field new to the academy, it has nevertheless produced a convergent form of academic work among university faculty who, as a result, are often ill-equipped to recognise and address serious challenges to the field and to universities in a digital age.

A broadly conceived notion of scholarship, which includes specific forms of search and research, is the central component of the university's contribution to securing the conditions for the radical reform of public education. I suggest that this notion of scholarship can be characterised by C.W. Mills's (1959) idea of 'the sociological imagination', in which historical, anthropological and socially critical knowledge is of central concern in order to gain analytical distance from the immediate and pressing circumstances of people's lives and to literally see 'the bigger picture'. Seeing the bigger picture, I suggested in Chapter 2 and elsewhere in this book, is one of the key uses of a notion like the id^2 of physical education. Universities are uniquely placed to practise this notion of scholarship based on historical sensitivity, anthropological insight and critical awareness in the service of local and global communities.

History in particular is of vital importance in assisting all members of the physical education community to see beyond what Australian journalist Philip Adams once called 'the lurid present'. It is not possible to conceive of physical education futures if we are trapped in the here and now and pre-occupied with the immediate present. It is significant, I suggest, that the teaching of histories of physical education has gradually disappeared from physical education teacher education courses over the last 30 years (Phillips and Roper, 2006). If history is taught at all, it tends to be the history of specific sports rather than of physical education. While histories of sports are valuable, they are no substitute for physical educators' understanding of the roots of their field. This is significant because without sensitivity to the past, physical educators cannot appreciate how their subject came to be the way it is now. Without this knowledge, it is hard to imagine futures that are likely to become fact rather than remain fiction. Moreover, they cannot be prepared collectively to meet new challenges that will inevitably come along. The absence of history from physical education teacher education courses and, indeed, from the field in higher education more broadly, is one telling sign that the physical education community will be unlikely to make a sub-stantial contribution to radical reform, and perhaps why physical educators have been excluded, under-represented or ignored in policy debates.

One of the key means of securing the conditions of radical reform, then, is to embark on the education or re-education of physical educators in the various histories and her-stories (Carli, 2004; Fletcher, 1984) of the subject. Physical education teacher education courses must reinstate historical study as an urgent priority, not in the form of 'disinterested antiquarianism' in which teachers dust off curios for their students' entertainment, but where the past is shown to be alive in the present (Kirk, 1992c; Kirk, 2000c). While history has not featured in the plans for new forms of continuing profes-sional development (CPD) of physical educators, this proposal would be entirely consistent with Armour and Duncombe's (2004) arguments for radical reform which will move teachers away from a fragmented grab bag of experiences of coaching sports skills that has made up the majority of tea-cher CPD since the 1970s. Without this historical sensitivity to their subject, physical educators can only fight for the reality they know through personal experience of the recent past and the here and now, and to engage in 'acts of curriculum maintenance' that safeguard the status quo.

Not all universities will be able or will want to engage in this task of working towards securing the conditions for radical reform in physical edu-cation. Consistent with Boyer's call for a broader and more diverse concept of scholarship, some will wish to shape their mission to engage only in the scholarship of discovery or in the scholarship of teaching. Some universities with a particular commitment to school physical education, pedagogy, and physical education teacher education, in which the service mission Hellison (1987) dreamed of in Chapter 4 is strong and valued by university leaders, will take on a specialised role in relation to this task. They should not, however, have to go it alone. As one of what Lawson (1998) describes as the 'helping professions', physical education academics need to work in partnership with other helping professions and with other agencies, such as sports and cultural organisations, that have a stake in supporting particular communities. The formation of strong partnerships between universities with differing expertise is vital too. Not only would such partnerships strengthen work towards securing the conditions for radical reform by bringing complementary expertise to bear on the issues, but it is also in the interests of universities whose primary mission lies elsewhere to assist in increasing the possibility of sustainable physical education futures. As Bressan (1979) pointed out in her 'suicide or murder' scenarios in Chapter 3, the longer-term futures of units of kinesiology or sport and exercise sciences are threatened if school physical education fails.

We need, then, to apply a broader range of scholarship of the highest standard to the task of securing the conditions for radical reform in physical education, drawing on evidence from a scholarship of discovery, imagining new possibilities through a scholarship of integration, testing these ideas through a scholarship of application, and transmitting them through a scholarship of teaching. Universities that are shaping missions that seek as a primary function to serve local and global communities will be the seedbeds for curriculum reform of physical education teacher education, where new courses need to reinstate the importance of expertise in practical knowledge of physical activities, whether this is of sport, exercise, active leisure, dance or the meditative and martial arts. If the workplace for these teachers is the community-school, then such courses will also benefit from being constructed in universities that already work 'beyond boundaries' (Lee, 2003), that see the school as an integrative concept rather than a building contained by four walls. We need particular institutions to take a lead, but we also need the formation of strong partnerships with a broad range of groups who have an interest in physical education futures.

It hardly needs to be said, given the conclusions reached in this book, that all of this requires urgent action. There already exists an international community of critical pedagogues in physical education, with some formally established links through national educational research associations as well as many institutional-level relationships, which can provide the networks required to mobilise action globally as well as locally and to provide the basis for the formation of alliances and partnerships to take forward specific projects. They work, though, in what Basil Bernstein (2000) described as the pedagogic recontextualising field (PRF), along with other educators and scholars, independent charities and foundations, in contrast to the official recontextualising field (ORF), consisting of government agencies and co-opted organisations. The ways in which work gets done in the recontextualising field is of central importance to the construction of the school curriculum, since it is here that selection of aspects of regulative discourse, in this study, physical culture, takes place. It is, then, a highly charged political field.

Eminent sociologist of education Michael Apple (2002: 613) suggested that the existence of a PRF means that the state can never monopolise the curriculum production process, and that it provides the relative autonomy necessary for schools 'to create a new social order'. Bernstein expressed concern, however, that 'today, the state is attempting to weaken the PRF through its ORF, and thus attempting to reduce relative autonomy over the construction of pedagogic discourse and over its social contexts' (Bernstein, 2000: 33).

This is a very real concern in Britain as government has sought over a period of at least 20 years to manage in an increasingly more direct and interventive manner the provision that it funds. The National Curriculum in England and Wales is one outcome of that process, while the continual setting of standards and the ubiquitous inspection regimes are examples of its micro-management. The diminishing influence of a PRF in physical education and the growing dominance of the ORF increase the level of challenge for universities, their networks and their partners, to be involved in the process of securing the conditions for radical reform, particularly when key organisations with strong sectional interests in physical culture are co-opted into the ORF (Penney and Evans, 1999).

Nonetheless, I believe that universities are best placed, through scholarship of the highest standard, to generate the good ideas that will be vital to securing physical education futures. They are also best placed to conduct the research that will provide the evidence of what works and to what effect, a matter of urgent priority since much of what is claimed for physical education cannot be supported by robust evidence. Universities are organisations that are rooted in local communities but that also, with appropriate vision and character, transcend boundaries to address the challenges of globalisation. Consequently, they present themselves as ideal hubs for the organisation of networks and partnerships. Since they are educational institutions first and foremost, they are not only repositories of expertise that has been tried and tested by peer review. They also possess the pedagogical resources to communicate this expertise. As daunting as the prospect may seem, as key members of the PRF, universities need to begin to organise themselves to secure the conditions for radical reform in physical education. Without coordinated and concerted action on their behalf, locally and globally, beyond boundaries, I see little possibility of moving past industrial-age physical education until it is too late to secure a long-term future for physical education. Indeed, as Larry Locke suggested in 1998, it may already be too late.

Notes

Chapter 1

1 I explain this concept and its use in this study in Chapter 2. Suffice it here to understand that 'the idea of the idea of physical education', adapted from the work of Rothblatt (1997), is a means of identifying and naming the dominant configurations of the field without committing the error of essentialism. As I will argue in Chapter 2, it is a device for a *social* epistemological study of fields of knowledge and their changing shape and substance over time.

2 Puhse's and Gerber's (2005) collection of accounts of physical education from 35 countries provides an excellent source of these similarities and differences. The analysis in this study draws mainly on Britain and Australia since I am most familiar with physical education in these countries. While I will seek to make connections to other countries and regions as appropriate, it is for the reader to determine to what extent my account of physical education resembles the versions in their own local context.

3 I leave outdoor and adventurous activities out of this account for the moment since they rarely form a regular part of timetabled physical-education classes, and discuss them as a form of active leisure in Chapter 7.

4 Indeed, to *only* play the game without teaching sport-techniques is considered a grave offence in physical education. This is a deeply held conviction, and often unarticulated, though when it is it often takes the form of the accusation that such and such a teacher merely 'rolls out the ball'.

5 If they *did* we might more accurately talk of 'Sport education', and give due credit to Daryl Siedentop (1994) and his colleagues who helped us to see that physical educators have not done sport very well at all.

6 See Kirk (2000a) for an account of this process in Australia and Kirk (1992a) for an account in Britain. We consider this issue in detail in Chapter 4.

Chapter 2

1 See Chanan and Gilchrist (1974) for a helpful and still-current discussion of these issues in the context of mass compulsory schooling.

2 In Chapter 3 we will see that a number of researchers have quite clearly understood that it is the id^2 in physical education that is resistant to change, though they have not necessarily characterised the issue in these terms.

3 In Chapter 6, for the sake of a more complete account, I add to these three dimensions of physical culture: dance, and meditative and martial arts.

Chapter 3

1 Roberta Park (1998), Cathy Ennis (2006) and Hal Lawson (2007) are some exceptions.

2 At the same time we should note Massengale's (2000: 106) words of caution that 'trend extrapolation is absolutely the weakest form of futures research currently available'.

3 Based on the Conant Report of 1963, see Rikli (2006). A similar process was unfolding in Australia. In 1966, the Martin Report recommended that Australian universities should cease to offer sub-degree courses, a recommendation that was enacted as law in 1970. At this time, all physical education courses in Australian universities were two- or three-year diplomas (see Kirk, 2000a). For a summary of legislation in Britain that had a similar effect, see Connell (1983).

4 Confusingly, in this USA literature, *inter*disciplinarity is sometimes referred to as *cross*-disciplinarity, which is contrasted with the currently dominant sub-discipline model which is of course *multi*disciplinary, but which is itself sometimes referred to as *inter*disciplinary.

5 See, for example, the collection of Academy Papers (1998) in *Quest* concerned with 'Meeting the challenges of the 21st century in higher education'.

Chapter 4

1 The key principle underpinning these assumptions is 'generalisation before specialisation'. In Chapter 5, we will investigate the historical source of this principle and its residual influence within the id^2 of physical education-as-sport-techniques.

2 Note that they were not questioning the central place in physical education that games and sport had attained. While they confined their work to games, they nevertheless questioned the central place of skill learning in physical education and so challenged the hegemony of the molecular approach. At least one of their co-workers (Almond, 1997) did seize the opportunity provided by TGfU's critique of the molecular approach to offer an alternative approach to physical education more broadly.

Chapter 5

1 Histories of physical education are available for Britain (for example, McIntosh, 1968; Smith, 1974), France (Gleyse, 1995; Klein, 2003), Sweden (Carli, 2004; Lundvall and Meckbach, 2003), Spain (Martinez Alverez, 2004), Belgium (Lenoir et al., 2007) and the USA (Freeman, 1977; Park, 1998; Ennis, 2006). The chapters in Puhse and Gerber (2005) also include brief historical sections for most of the 35 countries.

2 Willee (1955: 37); Randall (1967: 31–32). McIntosh (1968) argued that there were 'two traditions' of physical education emerging in England during the 19th century, one from the public (private) schools for boys serving the wealthy minority of English society, and a second in the government-provided elementary schools for the masses. The former was 'games', the latter 'physical training'. He goes on to claim that in the first 50 years of the 20th century these two traditions began to 'fuse'. We need to approach with caution the idea that the games-playing tradition was thought of as a form of 'physical education' in the 19th and early 20th centuries. As I argue in *Defining Physical Education*, this idea was a social construct of the 1940s and 1950s in Britain as male specialist physical education educators sought to justify a sport-based form of physical education in the new compulsory secondary schools for the masses.

3 He noted that both were called systems in Britain when, in his view, Swedish gymnastics was the system and *Turnen* the sport. At the risk of complicating matters further, in the USA, *Turnen* was known as gymnastics and Swedish gymnastics was called callisthenics.

4 'The disciplinary value of drill was everywhere recognised, for it seemed the only way of assembling large numbers of children in restricted spaces, and of moving them safely from one part of a school to another. ... In the early years of the schools, particularly when compulsory attendance was enforced by the

prosecution of recalcitrant parents, the free use of corporal punishment and a rigid code of external discipline seemed the only possible means of quelling ill-disciplined and even riotous children' (Smith, 1974: 92).

5 Willee (1955: 3), for example, argued that 'staffs in teacher training colleges in England have been urging the 'new' methods since before the 1914–18 war'.

6 'The wider the claims became the more sceptical and antagonistic were the men specialists. The emotional atmosphere became tense and rational discussion of the potentialities and limitations of Modern Dance became almost impossible.' Although McIntosh (1968: 261) was writing as a historian, we need to recall that he lived through this period and experienced this atmosphere at first hand.

7 For detail, see Kirk (1992a), particularly pp. 65–69 and the footnotes on pp. 80–81. McIntosh (1968: 253–54) noted wider policy directions that required physical education teacher education to follow the same pattern as other subject areas. This meant that the days of the specialist colleges, mostly for women, were numbered, since they were required to offer training on a broader educational basis than they could supply.

8 'Objective' in the sense intended by Willee here refers to the child having an objective for an activity, for example, to pretend to fly like an aeroplane. In this sense of objectivity, an activity has meaning for the child. The 'subjective' exercises of Swedish gymnastics, in contrast, are the arbitrary invention of the syllabus, and as such are likely to be less meaningful to the child.

9 See, for example, Randall (1961) and my account in *Defining Physical Education*, pp. 70–74.

10 These dates of his tenure in this post are important because they span the transitional years of the shift from the id^2 of physical education-as-gymnastics to the id^2 of physical education-as-sport-techniques. He was also involved with the development of circuit training with G.T. Adamson, an individualised method of fitness development initially devised for male students at the University of Leeds.

11 See Rovegno and Dolly (2006: 245–46) for a contemporary account of learning from this perspective.

12 'The curriculum in the Colleges of PE is ever-widening. This is something that I rejoice to be able to report, and my only comment is "high time, too!". We are British people – for which I can find no cause for apology – and we are a games-playing nation. It has always puzzled me, for instance, that gymnastics should be regarded as being synonymous with Physical Education. Gymnastics is a part – a very valuable part – of a vast subject, and in some countries it may have been looked on as being the main fraction of the whole. No longer is that so here. However good a system may be, the folly of adopting it in its entirety and foisting it upon people, unadapted to peculiar needs, is at last recognised. What may delight the Germans or the Danes, and what suits their national characteristics, does not necessarily make a similar appeal here. Now we are recognising this!' (Hugh Brown, Principal, Scottish School of Physical Education, Reported in *Physical Education*, 1958, 50: 92)

13 Again, I acknowledge that dates vary here even within countries as well as between them. For example, the University of Birmingham in England offered the first (non-teacher education) degree in Physical Education from the late 1940s. The University of Sydney also had a degree in Physical Education approved in 1948, though it was never made available. BEd degrees were available in Britain from the late 1960s. Degree-level study was available in the USA much earlier still.

Chapter 6

1 See further developments by Griginov (2004), Jirasek (2003) and Broninowski and Muszkieta (2001) who have drawn on the rich traditions of physical culture in Eastern European countries.

2 Mauss's use of the word *habitus* and its etymological relationships to French words such as *habile* (skilful or adroit), *habiller* (to dress or wear), *habitation* (a dwelling or home), *habiter* (to live in) and *habitude* (habit) conveys powerfully how he intends his notion of techniques of the body to be understood. These techniques are performed more or less skilfully, but habitually and routinely, apparently unconsciously. Their performance is individualised to the extent that they express something of a person's identity, whether this be in relation to their nationality, social class, occupation, religion, gender, and age or generation. The *habitus* thus expresses a notion of the body as a dwelling place, something that is lived in. Likewise, the body can be 'dressed' by or 'wear' these techniques in so far as they provide a layer or source of information, both when the body is in action or repose, since, as Mauss points out, there are different ways of relaxing and sleeping as well as moving.

3 I have argued elsewhere (Kirk, 2006b) that it may be in the self-interests of some obesity researchers and health educators, for example, to suggest that this relationship is necessary rather than contingent. See also Gard and Wright (2006) and Gard and Kirk (2007).

4 I argue in Chapter 7 that this process must be the topic of future research programmes if we are to understand the full complexity of the social construction of school and university knowledge and other programmes (for example, community based) of educational intent.

5 There is a large sociological and historical literature that outlines these changes in physical culture; see Coakley and Dunning (2000); Phillips and Roper (2006).

6 This was the well-known slogan of the Sports Council during the 1960s.

7 Bereiter (1990) has expressed a similar idea with his notion of the 'schoolwork module', which we have applied to attempting to account for high school students' apparent inability to make sense of a practice in a TGfU basketball unit (see Kirk et al., 2000).

8 According to the *European Physical Education Review*'s own rankings, updated monthly, the paper appeared as one of the journal's most cited, indicating the strength of interest in this aspiration.

9 Heads of physical education.

10 Curiously, they include basketball as a 'new' activity. Whitehead and Hendry (1976) claimed that basketball was already well established as an indoor activity by the late 1960s.

11 See, more recently, the special issue of *Sport, Education and Society*, 11: 3, 2006, edited by Dawn Penney and lisahunter.

12 We saw in Chapter 4 another way of making this point, this time in higher education, in Siedentop's (2002a) and Locke's criticism of Franklin Henry's mistaken analogy for physical education as a field based in sub-disciplines of knowledge. They point out that the equivalent in mathematics would be students studying (for example) the sociology, history and philosophy of mathematics rather than mathematics itself, or the biomechanics and physiology of dance rather than dance itself.

13 For example, in Scotland in the mid-1970s with the Munn Report, in England at the end of the 1980s with the National Curriculum, and in Australia in the early 1990s with the National Statements and Profiles.

Chapter 7

1 See, for example, Kirk (2004) and the involvement of prime ministers and other politicians in Britain recently.

2 This contrasts with the Scottish School of Physical Education where students entered specialist training immediately from school and completed first a two-year certificate then later a three-year diploma, a process that more closely resembled the training arrangements in the colleges for women (Fletcher, 1984; Webb, 1999).

Bibliography

Academy Papers (1998) 'No. 31: Meeting the challenges of the 21st century in higher education', *Quest*, 50: 2.

Almond, L. (ed.) (1997) *Physical Education in Schools*, 2nd edn, London: Kogan Page.

Apple, M.W. (1979) *Ideology and Curriculum*, London: Routledge and Kegan Paul.

——(2002) 'Does education have independent power? Bernstein and the question of relative autonomy', *British Journal of Sociology of Education*, 23, 4: 607–16.

Armour, K.M. and Duncombe, R. (2004) 'Teachers' continuing professional development in primary physical education: lessons from present and past to inform the future', *Physical Education and Sport Pedagogy*, 9: 3–22.

Australian Sports Commission (1997) *Game Sense: Developing Thinking Players*, Belconnen: ASC.

Bailey, R., Armour, K., Kirk, D., Jess, M., Pickup, I. and Sandford, R. (2008) 'The educational benefits claimed for physical education and school sport: an academic review', *Research Papers in Education*, http://dx.doi.org/10.1080/02671520701809817.

Becher, T. and Trowler, P.R. (2001) *Academic Tribes and Territories*, 2nd edn, Buckingham: SRHE and Open University Press.

Benn, T.C. (2005) '"Race" and physical education, sport and dance', in K.M. Green and K. Hardman (eds) *Physical Education: Essential Issues*, 197–219, London: Sage.

Bereiter, C. (1990) 'Aspects of an educational learning theory', *Review of Educational Research*, 60: 603–24.

Bernstein, B. (1971) 'On the classification and framing of educational knowledge', in M.F.D. Young (ed.) *Knowledge and Control: New Directions for the Sociology of Education*, 47–69, London: Collier-Macmillan.

——(2000) *Pedagogy, Symbolic Control and Identity: Theory, Research, Critique*, London: Rowman and Littlefield Publishers.

Blakemore, C.L., Gill Hilton, H., Gresh, J., Harrison, J.M. and Pellett, T.L. (1992) 'Comparison of students taught basketball skills using mastery and nonmastery learning methods', *Journal of Teaching in Physical Education*, 11: 235–47.

Board of Education (1909) *Syllabus of Physical Exercises for Schools*, London: HMSO.

——(1933) *Syllabus of Physical Training for Schools*, London: HMSO.

Boyce B.A., Coker, C.A. and Bunker, L.K. (2006) 'Implications for variability of practice from pedagogy and motor learning perspectives: finding a common ground', *Quest*, 58: 330–43.

Boyer, E.L. (1990) *Scholarship Reconsidered: Priorities of the Professoriate*, New York: Jossey-Bass.

Bressan, E.S. (1979) '2001: The profession is dead – was it murder or suicide?', *Quest*, 31: 77–82.

Broninowski, M. and Muszkieta, R. (2001) *Dilemmas of Modern Physical Education in Teaching Children and Youth*, Poznan: Akademia Wychowania Fizycznego.

Brown, D. (1999) 'Complicity and reproduction in teaching physical education', *Sport, Education and Society*, 4: 143–59.

Brown, D. and Evans, J. (2004) 'Reproducing gender? Intergenerational links and the male PE teacher as a cultural conduit in teaching physical education', *Journal of Teaching in Physical Education*, 23: 48–70.

Brown, D. and Johnson, A. (2000) 'The social practice of self-defence martial arts: applications for physical education', *Quest*, 52: 246–59.

Brown, H.C. (1958) 'The training of the man teacher of physical education', *Physical Education*, 50: 91–94.

Brownell, C.L. and Hagman, E.P. (1951) *Physical Education: Foundations and Principles*, New York: McGraw-Hill.

Bryson, L. (1990) 'Challenges to make hegemony in sport', in M.A. Messner and D.F. Sabo (eds) *Sport, Men and the Gender Order: Critical Feminist Perspectives*, 1–15, Champaign, IL: Human Kinetics.

Bunker, D. and Thorpe, R. (1982) 'A model for the teaching of games in the secondary school', *Bulletin of Physical Education*, 10: 9–16.

Carli, B. (2004) *The Making and Breaking of a Female Culture: The History of Swedish Physical Education in 'a Different Voice'*, Goteborg: Acta Universitatis Gothogurgensis.

Carnegie Physical Training College (1937) *Syllabus*, Leeds: Author.

——(1955) *Syllabus*, Leeds: Author.

Chanan, G. and Gilchrist, L. (1974) *What School Is For*, London: Methuen.

Charles, J.M. (2005) 'Changes and challenges: A 20/20 vision of 2020', *Quest*, 57: 267–86.

Clark, J.E. (2008) 'Kinesiology in the 21st century: A preface', *Quest*, 60: 1–2.

Coakley, J. and Dunning, E. (eds) (2000) *Handbook of Sports Studies*, London: Sage.

Connell, L. (1983) *Carnegie: A History of Carnegie College and School of Physical Education 1933–1976*, Leeds: Leeds University Printing Service.

Connell, R.W. (1983) *Which Way Is Up? Essays on Class, Sex and Culture*, Sydney: Allen and Unwin.

Cothran, D.J. (2001) 'Curricular change in physical education: Success stories from the front line', *Sport, Education and Society*, 6: 67–79.

Côté, J. and Hay, J. (2002) 'Children's involvement in sport: A developmental perspective', in J.M. Silva and D. Stevens (eds) *Psychological Foundations of Sport*, 484–502, Moston: Merrill.

Crum, B. (2001) 'The "idola" of sport pedagogy researchers', *Quest*, 53: 184–91.

Curtner-Smith, M.D. (1999) 'The more things change the more they stay the same: Factors influencing teachers' interpretations and delivery of National Curriculum Physical Education', *Sport, Education and Society*, 4: 75–97.

Dening, G. (1993) *Mr Bligh's Bad Language: Passion, Power and Theatre on the Bounty*, Cambridge University Press.

Department of Culture, Media and Sport (2009) *Taking Part: England's Survey of Culture, Leisure and Sport: Headline Findings from the Child Survey 2007*, www.culture.gov.uk/reference_library/publications/5481.aspx, accessed 22 January 2009.

DCMS/DCSF (2008) *Physical Education and Sport Strategy for Young People*. London: Author.

Dodds, P., and Locke, L. (1984) 'Is physical education in American schools worth saving? Evidence, alternatives, judgment', in N.L. Struna (ed.) *National Association of Physical Education in Higher Education Proceedings, Vol. V,* 76–90, Champaign, IL: Human Kinetics.

Eagleton, T. (1991) *Ideology: An Introduction,* New York: Verso.

Education Department of Victoria (1946) *Physical Education for Victorian Schools,* Melbourne: Wilke.

Ennis, C. D. (1999) 'Creating a culturally relevant curriculum for disengaged girls', *Sport, Education and Society,* 4: 31–50.

——(2006) 'Curriculum: forming and reshaping the vision of physical education in a high need, low demand world of schools', *Quest,* 58: 41–59.

Evans, J. (ed.) (1986) *Physical Education, Sport and Schooling,* Lewes: Falmer.

Evans, J. (2004) 'Making a difference? Education and "ability" in physical education', *European Physical Education Review,* 10: 95–108.

Evans, J. and Davies, B. (2008) 'The poverty of theory: Class configurations in the discourse of Physical Education and Health (PEH)', *Physical Education and Sport Pedagogy,* 13: 199–214.

Evans, J, Davies, B. and Wright, J. (eds) (2004) *Body Knowledge and Control: Studies in the Sociology of Physical Education and Health,* London: Routledge.

Evans, J. and Penney, D. (2008) 'Levels on the playing field: The social construction of physical "ability" in the physical education curriculum', *Physical Education and Sport Pedagogy,* 13: 31–47.

Fairclough, S., Stratton, G. and Baldwin, G. (2002) 'The contribution of secondary school physical education to lifetime physical activity', *European Physical Education Review,* 8: 69–84.

Fernandez-Balboa, J-M. (2003) 'Physical education in the digital (postmodern) era', in A. Laker (ed.) *The Future of Physical Education: Building a New Pedagogy,* 137–52, London: Routledge.

Fitzgerald, H. (ed.) (2009) *Disability and Youth Sport* London: Routledge.

Fletcher, S. (1984) *Women First: The Female Tradition in English Physical Education 1880–1980,* London: Althone.

Flintoff, A. (2008) 'Targeting Mr Average: Participation, gender equity and school sport partnerships', *Sport, Education and Society,* 13: 393–411.

Flintoff, A. and Scraton, S. (2001) 'Stepping into active leisure? Young women's perceptions of active lifestyles and their experiences of school physical education', *Sport, Education and Society,* 6: 5–22.

Floud, J., Halsey, A. and Martin, F. (1956) *Social Class and Educational Opportunity,* London: Heinneman.

Foucault, M. (1977) *Discipline and Punish: The Birth of the Prison,* New York: Allen and Unwin.

Freeman, W.H. (1977) *Physical Education in a Changing Society,* Boston: Houghton Mifflin.

French, K.E., Rink, J.E., Rikard, L., Mays, A., Lynn, S. and Werner, P. (1991) 'The effects of practice progressions on learning two volleyball skills', *Journal of Teaching in Physical Education,* 10: 261–74.

Friere, P. (1973) *Pedagogy of the Oppressed,* New York: Seabury Press.

Gard, M. (2001) 'Dancing around the "problem" of boys and dance', *Discourse: Studies in the Cultural Politics of Education,* 22: 213–25.

Gard, M. and Wright, J. (2006) *The Obesity Crisis,* London: Routledge.

Gard, M. and Kirk, D. (2007) 'Obesity discourse and the crisis of faith in disciplinary technology', *Utbildning & Demokrati*, 16: 17–36.

Giroux, H.A. (1981) *Ideology, Culture and the Process of Schooling*, Lewes: Falmer.

Gleyse, J. (1995) *Archeologie de l'Education Physique au XXe Siecle en France*, Paris: PUF.

Goodson, I.F. (1985) 'Towards curriculum history', in I.F. Goodson (ed.) *Social Histories of the Secondary Curriculum: Subjects for Study*, 1–8, Lewes: Falmer.

——(1987) *School Subjects and Curriculum Change*, Lewes: Falmer.

——(1997) *The Changing Curriculum: Studies in Social Construction*, New York: Peter Lang.

Gramsci, A. (1971) *Selections from the Prison Notebooks*, London: Lawrence and Wishart.

Green, K. (1998) 'Philosophies, ideologies and the practice of physical education', *Sport, Education and Society*, 3: 125–43.

——(2000) 'Exploring the everyday "philosophies" of physical education teachers from a sociological perspective', *Sport, Education and Society*, 5: 109–29.

——(2002) 'Physical education teachers in their figurations: A sociological analysis of everyday "philosophies"', *Sport, Education and Society*, 7: 65–83.

——(2008) *Understanding Physical Education*, London: Sage.

Green, K., Smith, A. and Roberts, K. (2005) 'Young people and lifelong participation in physical education: A sociological perspective on contemporary physical education programmes in England and Wales', *Leisure Studies*, 24: 27–43.

Grehaigne, J-F., Richard, J-F. and Griffin, L.L. (2005) *Teaching and Learning Team Sports and Games*, London: RoutledgeFalmer.

Griffin, L.L., Brooker, R. and Patton, K. (2005) 'Working towards legitimacy: Two decades of Teaching Games for Understanding', *Physical Education and Sport Pedagogy*, 10: 213–23.

Griffin, L.L., Oslin, J.L. and Mitchell, S.A. (1995) 'An analysis of two instructional approaches to teaching net games', *Research Quarterly for Exercise and Sport*, 66: 65–66.

Griginov, V. (2004) 'Eastern European sport: Nomen', *The International Journal of the History of Sport*, 21: 690–709.

Hall, S. (1985) 'Signification, representation, ideology: Althusser and the post-structuralist debates', *Critical Studies in Mass Communication*, 2: 91–114.

Hardman, K. and Marshall, J.J. (2000) *Worldwide Survey of the State and Status of School Physical Education Final Report*, Manchester: University of Manchester.

Hargreaves, D.H. (1982) 'Ten proposals for the future of physical education', *Bulletin of Physical Education*, 18: 5–10.

Hargreaves, Jennifer (1997) *Sporting Females: Critical Issues in the History and Sociology of Women's Sports*, London: Routledge.

Hargreaves, John (1986) *Sport, Power and Culture*, Cambridge: Polity.

Harris, J. (2005) 'Health-related exercise and physical education', in K. Green and K. Hardman (eds) *Physical Education: Essential Issues*, 78–97, London: Sage.

Hastie, P. (2003) 'Sport Education', in A. Laker (ed.) *The Future of Physical Education: Building a New Pedagogy*, 121–36, London: Routledge.

Hastie, P. and Buchanan, A.M. (2000) 'Teaching responsibility through Sport Education: Prospects for a coalition', *Research Quarterly for Exercise and Sport*, 71: 25–35.

Hellison, D. (1987) 'Dreaming the possible dream: the rise and triumph of physical education', in J.A. Massengale (ed.) *Trends toward the Future in Physical Education*, 137–52, Champaign, IL: Human Kinetics.

——(1992) 'If Sargent could see us now: Values and program survival in higher education', *Quest*, 44: 398–411.

——(1995) *Teaching Responsibility through Physical Activity*, Champaign, IL: Human Kinetics.

Hendry, L.B. (1976) 'Survival in a marginal role: The professional identity of the physical education teacher', in N. Whitehead and L.B. Hendry (eds) *Teaching Physical Education in England*, 89–102, London: Lepus.

Henry, F.M. (1964) 'Physical education: An academic discipline', *Journal of Health, Physical Education and Recreation*, 35: 32–33.

Hirst, P.H. (1974) *Knowledge and the Curriculum*, London: Routledge and Kegan Paul.

Hoffman, S.J. (1971) 'Traditional methodology: Prospects for change', *Quest*, 23: 51–57.

Hoffman, S.J. (1987) 'Dreaming the impossible dream: the decline and fall of physical education', in J.A. Massengale (ed.) *Trends Toward the Future in Physical Education*, 121–136, Champaign, IL: Human Kinetics.

Holt, J.E., Ward, P. and Wallhead, T.L. (2006) 'The transfer of learning from play practices to game play in young adult soccer players', *Physical Education and Sport Pedagogy*, 11: 101–18.

Holt, N.L., Strean, W.B. and Bengoechea, E.G. (2002) 'Expanding the Teaching Games for Understanding model: New avenues for future research and practice', *Journal of Teaching in Physical Education*, 21: 162–76.

Houlihan, B. (2002) 'Sporting excellence, school and sports development: The politics of crowded policy spaces', *European Physical Education Review*, 6: 171–94.

Hubball, H. and West, D. (2008) 'Silence and authentic reflection strategies: Holistic learning in an outdoor education program', *Physical and Health Education Journal*, 74: 12–14.

Jewett, A., Bain, L.L. and Ennis, C.D. (1995) *The Curriculum Process in Physical Education*, 2nd edn, Dubuque: Brown.

Jirasek, I. (2003) 'Philosophy of sport, or philosophy of physical culture? An experience from the Czech Republic: Philosophical kinanthropology', *Sport, Education and Society*, 8: 105–17.

Kay, T. (2000) 'Sporting excellence: A family affair?', *European Physical Education Review*, 6: 151–69.

Kinchin, G.D. (2006) 'Sport Education: A view of the research', in D. Kirk, D. Macdonald and M. O'Sullivan (eds) *The Handbook of Physical Education*, 596–609, London: Sage.

Kinchin, G.D. and O'Sullivan, M. (2003) 'Incidences of student support for and resistance to a curricular innovation in high school physical education', *Journal of Teaching in Physical Education*, 22: 245–60.

Kirk, D. (1988) *Physical Education and Curriculum Study: A Critical Introduction*, London: Croom Helm.

——(1992a) *Defining Physical Education: The Social Construction of a School Subject in Postwar Britain*, London: Falmer.

——(1992b) 'Physical education, discourse and ideology: Bringing the hidden curriculum into view', *Quest*, 44: 35–56.

——(1992c) 'Curriculum history in physical education: A source of struggle and a force for change', in A.C. Sparkes (ed.) *Researching into Physical Education and Sport: Exploring Alternative Visions*, 210–30, Lewes: Falmer.

——(1993) *The Body, Schooling and Culture*, Geelong: Deakin University Press.

——(1998a) *Schooling Bodies: School Practice and Public Discourse 1880–1950*, London: Leicester University Press.

——(1998b) 'Educational reform, physical culture and the crisis of legitimation in physical education', *Discourse: Studies in the Cultural Politics of Education*, 19: 101–12.

——(1999) 'Physical culture, physical education and relational analysis', *Sport, Education and Society*, 4: 63–73.

——(2000a) 'The reconfiguration of the physical activity field in Australian higher education, 1970–86', *Sporting Traditions: Journal of the Australian Society for Sports History*, 16: 17–38.

——(2000b) 'Gender associations: Sport, state schools and Australian culture', *The International Journal of Sport History*, 17: 49–64.

——(2000c) 'A task-based approach to critical pedagogy in sport and physical education', in R. Jones and K.M. Armour (eds) *Sociology of Sport: Theory and Practice*, 201–19, Harlow: Pearson.

——(2002a) 'Quality physical education through partnerships: A response to Karel J van Deventer', Paper presented to the 12th Commonwealth International Sport Conference, Manchester, July.

——(2002b) 'Junior sport as a moral practice', *Journal of Teaching in Physical Education*, 21: 402–8.

——(2003) 'Student learning and the social construction of gender', in S.J. Silverman and C.D. Ennis (eds) *Student Learning in Physical Education*, 67–82, Champaign, IL: Human Kinetics.

——(2004) 'Framing quality physical education: The elite sport model or Sport Education?', *Physical Education and Sport Pedagogy*, 9: 185–95.

——(2005) 'Physical education, youth sport and lifelong participation: The importance of early learning experiences', *European Physical Education Review*, 11: 239–55.

——(2006a) 'The idea of physical education and its discontents', Inaugural Lecture, Leeds Metropolitan University, June, www.leedsmet.ac.uk/carnegie/inaugural_lecture_2006.pdf.

——(2006b) 'The "obesity crisis" and school physical education', *Sport, Education and Society*, 11: 121–33.

Kirk, D., Brooker, R. and Braiuka, S. (2000) 'Teaching games for understanding: a situated perspective on student learning', Paper presented to the American Educational Research Association Annual Meeting, New Orleans, April.

Kirk, D., Carlson, T., O'Connor, A., Burke, P., Davis, K. and Glover S. (1997) 'The economic impact on families of children's participation in junior sport', *The Australian Journal of Science and Medicine in Sport*, 29: 27–33.

Kirk, D. and Colquhoun, D. (1989) 'Healthism and physical education', *British Journal of Sociology of Education*, 10: 417–34.

Kirk, D. and Kinchin, G. (2003) 'Situated learning as a theoretical framework for sport education', *European Physical Education Review*, 9: 221–35.

Kirk, D. and Macdonald, D. (1998) 'Situated learning in physical education', *Journal of Teaching in Physical Education*, 17: 376–87.

Kirk, D. and Macdonald, D. (2001) 'The social construction of PETE in higher education: towards a research agenda', *Quest*, 53: 440–56.

Kliebard, H.M. (1986) *The Struggle for the American Curriculum*, New York: Routledge.

Klein, G. (2003) *Une affair de discipline: l'education physique en France et en Europe (1970–2000)*, Paris: Editions Revue E.P.S..

Knapp, B. (1963) *Skill in Sport*, London: Routledge and Kegan Paul.

Krahenbuhl, G.S. (1998) 'Higher education in the 21st century: The role of kinesiology and physical education', *Quest*, 50: 108–15.

Kretchmar, R.S. (1990) 'Commentary: Riding the juggernaut', *Quest*, 42: 330–34.

Laker, A. (2003) 'The future of physical education: Is this the "new pedagogy"?', in A. Laker (ed.) *The Future of Physical Education: Building a New Pedagogy*, 153–70, London: Routledge.

Laker, A. (ed.) (2003) *The Future of Physical Education: Building a New Pedagogy*, London: Routledge.

Langley, D.J. (1995) 'Student cognition in the instructional setting', *Journal of Teaching in Physical Education*, 15: 25–40.

Lave, J. (1988) *Cognition in Practice: Mind, Mathematics and Culture in Everyday Life*, Cambridge: Cambridge University Press.

Lave, J. (1997) 'The culture of acquisition and the practice of understanding', in D. Kirshner and J.A. Whitson (eds) *Situated Cognition: Social, Semiotic and Psychological Perspectives*, 17–36, Mahwah, NJ: Erlbaum.

Lave, J. and Wenger, E. (1991) *Situated Learning: Legitimate Peripheral Participation*, New York: Cambridge University Press.

Lawson, H.A. (1983) 'Toward a model of teacher socialization in physical education: The subjective warrant, recruitment, and teacher education', *Journal of Teaching in Physical Education*, 2: 3–16.

——(1984) 'Problem setting for physical education and sport', *Quest*, 36: 48–60.

——(1988) 'Occupational socialization, cultural studies and the physical education curriculum', *Journal of Teaching in Physical Education*, 7: 265–88.

——(1991) 'Specialization and fragmentation among faculty as endemic features of academic life', *Quest*, 43: 280–95.

——(1997) 'Children in crisis, the helping professions, and the social responsibilities of universities', *Quest*, 49: 8–33.

——(1998) 'Here today, gone tomorrow? A framework for analyzing the development, transformation, and disappearance of helping fields', *Quest*, 50: 225–37.

——(2007) 'Renewing the core curriculum', *Quest*, 59: 219–43.

——(2008) 'Crossing borders and changing boundaries to develop innovations that improve outcomes', The Cagigal Lecture, AIESEP World Congress, Sapporo.

——(2009) 'Paradigms, exemplars and social change', *Sport, Education and Society*, 14: 77–100.

Lawson, H. and Morford, W.R. (1979) 'The crossdisciplinary nature of kinesiology and sport studies: Distinctions, implications, and advantages', *Quest*, 31: 222–31.

Lawton, D. (1983) *Curriculum Studies and Educational Planning*, London: Hodder and Stoughton Educational.

Lawton, J. (1989) 'Comparison of two teaching methods in games', *Bulletin of Physical Education*, 25: 35–38.

Lee, A.M. and Solmon, M.A. (1992) 'Cognitive conceptions of teaching and learning motor skills', *Quest*, 44: 57–71.

Lee, S. (2003) 'Beyond boundaries: Bradford to Brown to Botham', Inaugural Lecture, Leeds Metropolitan University, www.leedsmet.ac.uk/the_news/nov03/r19nov.pdf.

Lenoir, M., Tolleneer, J. and Laporte, W. (eds) (2007) *100 Jaar Opleiding Lichamelijke Opvoeding en Bewegingwetenschappen aan de Universiteit Gent*, Gent: Academic Press.

Locke, L.F. (1990) 'Conjuring kinesiology and other political parlor tricks', *Quest*, 42, 323–29.

——(1992) 'Changing secondary school physical education', *Quest*, 44: 361–72.

——(1998) 'Advice, stories and myths: The reactions of a cliff jumper', *Quest*, 50: 238–48.

Loughborough Partnership (2006) *School Sport Partnerships: Annual Monitoring and Evaluation Report for 2005*, Loughborough: Institute of Youth Sport.

Lounsbery, M. and Coker, C. (2008) 'Developing skill-analysis competency in physical education teachers', *Quest*, 60: 255–67.

Lundvall, S. and Meckbach, J. (2003) *Movement in Motion: The Subject of Gymnastics in the Physical Education Teacher-Training Programme of the Royal Central Institute of Gymnastics/Stockholm College of Physical Education and Sport during the Years 1944–1992*, Stockholm: HLS Forlag.

Macdonald, D. (1995) 'The role of proletarianization in physical education teacher attrition', *Research Quarterly for Exercise and Sport*, 66: 129–41.

Macdonald, D. and Kirk, D. (1996) 'Private lives, public lives: Surveillance, identity and self in the work of beginning physical education teachers', *Sport, Education and Society*, 1: 59–75.

Macdonald, D., Kirk, D. and Braiuka, S. (1999) 'The social construction of the physical activity field at the school/university interface', *European Physical Education Review*, 5: 31–51.

MacIntyre, A. (1985) *After Virtue: A Study in Moral Theory*, 2nd edn, London: Duckworth.

MacPhail, A., Kirk, D. and Kinchin, G. (2004) 'Sport Education: Promoting team affiliation through physical education', *Journal of Teaching in Physical Education*, 23: 106–22.

Maguire, J. (2004) 'Challenging the sports-industrial complex: Human sciences, advocacy and service', *European Physical Education Review*, 10: 299–321.

Major, E. (1966) 'The development of physical education in England during the present century with special reference to gymnastics', *Carnegie Old Students Association Conference Papers*, 1: 1–9.

Mangan, J.A. (1981) *Athleticism in Victorian and Edwardian Public Schools*, Cambridge: Cambridge University Press.

Martinez Alvarez, L. (2004) 'Una approximacion historica a las politicos educativas de la educacion fisica en Espana', in F.E. Caparroz and N.F. de Andrade Filho (eds) *Educacao Fisica Escolar*, 71–92, Vitoria: UFES, LESEF.

Massengale, J.A. (ed.) (1987) *Trends Toward the Future in Physical Education*, Champaign, IL: Human Kinetics.

Massengale, J.A. (2000) 'Doing PE at the new university', *Quest*, 52: 102–9.

Mauss, M. (1973) 'Techniques of the body', *Economy and Society*, 2: 70–87.

McCrone, K.E. (1988) *Sport and the Physical Emancipation of English Women*, London: Routledge.

McIntosh, P.C. (1968) *PE in England since 1800*, 2nd edn, London: Bell.

McKay, J. (1991) *No Pain, No Gain: Sport in Australian Society*, Sydney: Prentice Hall.

McKay, J. and Pearson, K. (1984) 'Objectives, strategies and ethics in teaching introductory courses in sociology of sport', *Quest*, 36: 261–72.

McKenzie, T.L., Alcaraz, J.E. and Sallis, J.F. (1994) 'Assessing children's liking for activity units in an elementary school physical education curriculum', *Journal of Teaching in Physical Education*, 13: 206–15.

McKenzie, T.L., Alcaraz, J.E., Sallis, J.F. and Faucette, F.N. (1998) 'Effects of a physical education program on children's manipulative skills', *Journal of Teaching in Physical Education*, 17: 327–41.

McMorris, T. (1998) 'Teaching games for understanding: Its contribution to the knowledge of skill acquisition from a motor learning perspective', *European Journal of Physical Education*, 3: 65–74.

Mills, C.W. (1959) *The Sociological Imagination*, New York: Oxford University Press.

Miller, J., Vine, K. and Larkin, D. (2007) 'The relationship of product and process performance of the two-handed sidearm strike', *Physical Education and Sports Pedagogy*, 12: 61–75.

Ministry of Education (1952) *Moving and Growing*, London: HMSO.

Morgan, R.E. (1973) *Concerns and Values in Physical Education*, London: Bell.

Morgan, R.E. and Adamson, G.T. (1961) *Circuit Training*, 2nd edn, London: Bell.

Morgan, W.J. (2006) 'Philosophy and physical education', in D. Kirk, D. Macdonald and M. O'Sullivan (eds) *The Handbook of Physical Education*, 97–108, London: Sage.

Mosston, M. and Ashworth, S. (1994) *Teaching Physical Education*, 4th edn, New York: Macmillan.

Munrow, A.D. (1963) *Pure and Applied Gymnastics*, 2nd edn, London: Bell.

National Professional Development Program Health and Physical Education Project (1997) *Reviewing the Curriculum in Health and Physical Education Key Learning Area: A Model for Professional Development using the Health and Physical Education Statement and Profile for Australian Schools*, Canberra: DEETYA.

Newell, K.M. (1990) 'Physical education in higher education: Chaos out of order', *Quest*, 42: 227–42.

Oberteuffer, D. (1951) *Physical Education: A Textbook of Principles for Professional Students*, New York: Harper and Brothers.

O'Donovan, T.M. and Kirk, D. (2008) 'Reconceptualizing student motivation in physical education: An examination of what resources are valued by pre-adolescent girls in contemporary society', *European Physical Education Review*, 14: 1–22.

O'Keeffe, S.L., Harrison, A.J. and Smyth, P.J. (2007) 'Transfer or specificity? An applied investigation into the relationship between fundamental overarm throwing and related sport skills', *Physical Education and Sport Pedagogy*, 12: 89–102.

Oliver, K.L. and Lalik, R. (2001) 'The body as curriculum: Learning with adolescent girls', *Journal of Curriculum Studies*, 33: 303–33.

Oslin, J. and Mitchell, S. (2006) 'Game-centred approaches to teaching physical education', in D. Kirk, D. Macdonald and M. O'Sullivan (eds) *The Handbook of Physical Education*, 627–51, London: Sage.

Oslin, J.L., Mitchell, S.A. and Griffin, L.L. (1998) 'The Game Performance Assessment Instrument (GPAI): Development and preliminary validation', *Journal of Teaching in Physical Education*, 17: 231–43.

O'Sullivan, M. and Dyson, B. (1994) 'Rules, routines, and expectations of 11 high school physical education teachers', *Journal of Teaching in Physical Education*, 13: 361–74.

O'Sullivan, M., Siedentop, D., and Tannehill, D. (1994) 'Breaking out: Codependency of high school physical education', *Journal of Teaching in Physical Education*, 13: 421–28.

Park, R.J. (1998) 'Critical issues for the future: A house divided', *Quest*, 50: 213–24.

Parker, J. (1995) 'Secondary teachers' views of effective teaching in physical education', *Journal of Teaching in Physical Education*, 14: 127–39.

Peddiwell, J.A. (1937) *The Saber-Tooth Curriculum*, New York: McGraw-Hill.

Penney, D. and Chandler, T. (2000) 'Physical education: What future(s)?', *Sport, Education and Society*, 5: 71–87.

Penney, D., Clark, G. and Kinchin, G. (2002) 'Developing physical education as a "connective specialism": Is Sport Education the answer?', *Sport, Education and Society*, 7: 55–64.

Penney, D. and Evans, J. (1999) *Politics, Policy and Practice in Physical Education*, London: Spon.

Penney, D. and Kirk, D. (1996) 'National curriculum developments in Australia and Britain: A comparative analysis', *Journal of Comparative Physical Education and Sport*, 18: 30–38.

Peters, R.S. (1966) *Ethics and Education*, London: Allen and Unwin.

Phillips, M.G. and Roper, A.P. (2006) 'History of physical education', in D. Kirk, D. Macdonald and M. O'Sullivan (eds) *Handbook of Physical Education*, 123–40, London: Sage.

Proctor, N. (1984) 'Problems facing physical education after the Great Debate', *Physical Education Review*, 7: 4–11.

Puhse, E. and Gerber, M. (eds) (2005) *International Comparison of Physical Education: Concepts, Problems, Prospects*, Oxford: Meyer.

Qualifications Curriculum Authority (1999) *Terminology in Physical Education*, London: Author.

——(2007) *Physical Education: Programme of Study for Key Stage 3 and Attainment Targets*, http://curriculum.qca.org.uk/uploads/QCA-07-3342-p_PE_KS3_tcm8-407.pdf?return=/key-stages-3-and-4/subjects/physical-education/keystage3/index.aspx%3Freturn%3D/key-stages-3-and-4/subjects/physical-education/index.aspx, accessed 11 March 2009.

Quay, J. (2003) 'Experience and participation: Relating theories of learning', *Journal of Experiential Education*, 26: 105–12.

Quick, S., Dalziel, D., Thornton, A. and Rayner, S. (2008) *School Sport Survey 2007/08*, London: Department of Children, Schools and Families.

Randall, Majorie (1961) *Basic Movement: A New Approach to Gymnastics*, London: Bell.

Randall, Martin (1967) *Modern Ideas on Physical Education*, 3rd edn, London: Bell.

Rikard, G.L. and Banville, D. (2006) 'High school student attitudes about physical education', *Sport, Education and Society*, 11: 385–400.

Rikli, R.E. (2006) 'Kinesiology – a "homeless" field: Addressing organization and leadership needs', *Quest*, 58: 288–309.

Rink, J.E. (1993) *Teaching Physical Education for Learning*, 2nd edn, St. Louis: Mosby-Yearbook.

Rink, J.E., French, K. and Tjeerdsma, B. (1996) 'Foundations for the learning and instruction of sport and games', *Journal of Teaching in Physical Education*, 15: 399–417.

Rink, J.E., French, K.E., Wemer, P.H., Lynn, S. and Mays, A. (1991) 'The influences of content development on the effectiveness of instruction', *Journal of Teaching in Physical Education*, 11: 139–49.

Roberts, K. (1996) 'Young people, schools, sport and government policies', *Sport, Education and Society*, 1: 47–58.

Rothblatt, S. (1997) *The Modern University and Its Discontents: The Fate of Newman's Legacies in Britain and America*, Cambridge: Cambridge University Press.

Rovegno, I. (1995) 'Theoretical perspectives on knowledge and learning and a student teacher's pedagogical content knowledge of dividing and sequencing subject matter', *Journal of Teaching in Physical Education*, 14: 283–304.

Rovegno, I. and Dolly, J.P. (2006) 'Constructivist perspectives on learning', in D. Kirk, D. Macdonald and M. O'Sullivan (eds) *Handbook of Physical Education*, 242–61, London: Sage.

Rubenstein, D. and Simon, B. (1966) *The Evolution of the Comprehensive School 1922–1966*, London: Routledge and Kegan Paul.

Rugby Football Union in England (2000) *National Coaching Development*, Twickenham: Author.

Ryle, G. (1990) *The Concept of Mind*, Harmondsworth: Penguin.

Sage, G. (2003) 'Foreword', in A. Laker (ed.) *The Future of Physical Education: Building a New Pedagogy*, x–xiv, London: Routledge.

Sanders, S. and McCrum, D. (1999) '"Peaks of excellence, valleys of despair": What is the future of physical education?', *Teaching Elementary Physical Education*, January: 3–4.

Schempp, P.G. (1985) 'Becoming a better teacher: An analysis of the student Teaching experience', *Journal of Teaching in Physical Education*, 4: 158–66

Scottish Education Department (1972) *Physical Education in the Secondary School: Curriculum Paper 12*, Edinburgh: HMSO.

Scottish Education Department/Consultative Committee on the Curriculum (1977) *The Structure of the Curriculum in Years 3 and 4 of Scottish Secondary Schools*, Edinburgh: HMSO.

Siedentop, D. (1981) 'Teaching research: The interventionist view', *Journal of Teaching in Physical Education*, 1: 42–50.

——(1990) 'Commentary: The world according to Newell', *Quest*, 42: 315–22.

——(ed.) (1994) *Sport Education: Quality PE through Positive Sport Experiences*, Champaign, IL: Human Kinetics.

——(1998) 'Regaining the public trust: Complex social problems meet specialised academic disciplines', *Quest*, 50: 170–78.

——(2002a) 'Content knowledge for physical education', *Journal of Teaching in Physical Education*, 21: 368–77.

——(2002b) 'Junior sport and the evolution of sport cultures', *Journal of Teaching in Physical Education*, 21: 392–401.

Siedentop, D. and Locke, L. (1997) 'Making a difference for physical education: What professors and practitioners must build together', *Journal of Physical Education, Recreation and Dance*, 68: 25–33.

Skilbeck, M. (1984) *School-Based Curriculum Development*, London: Harper and Row.

Smith, A. and Parr, M. (2007) 'Young people's views on the nature and purposes of physical education: A sociological analysis', *Sport, Education and Society* 12: 37–58.

Smith, A., Thurston, M., Lamb, K. and Green, K. (2007) 'Young people's participation in National Curriculum Physical Education: A study of 15–16 year olds in North-West England and North-East Wales', *European Physical Education Review*, 13: 165–94.

Smith, W.D. (1974) *Stretching their Bodies: The History of Physical Education*, London: David and Charles.

Spirduso, W.W. (1990) 'Commentary: The Newell epic: A case for academic sanity', *Quest*, 42:297–304.

Sport England (2002) www.sportengland.org, accessed 17 January 2002, quoted at http://tlfe.org.uk/sport/activeschools.htm.

——(2009) *Active People Survey*, www.sportengland.org/index/get_resources/research/active_people.htm, accessed 22 January 2009.

Squire, M.E. (1945) 'Gymnastics and physical education I', *Journal of Physical Education*, 37: 101–4.

Steel, W.L. (1965) 'Twenty years on', *Carnegie Old Students Association Conference Papers*, 1: 19–25.

Stier, W.F., Kleinman, S., and Milchrist, P.A. (1994) 'The future of physical education – survival or extinction?', ERIC document ED 383 644, www.eric.ed.gov/ERICDocs/data/ericdocs2sql/content_storage_01/0000019b/80/13/fc/ba.pdf, accessed 16 March 2009.

Stroot, S.A., Faucette, N. and Schwager, S. (1993) 'In the beginning: The induction of physical educators', *Journal of Teaching in Physical Education*, 12: 375–85.

Struna, N.L. (1991) 'Further reactions to Newell: Chaos is wonderful!', *Quest*, 43: 230–35.

Techow, G. (1866) *Manual of Gymnastic Exercises for the use of Schools and at Home*, Melbourne: Author.

Theberge, N. (1985) 'Towards a feminist alternative to sport as a male preserve', *Quest*, 37: 193–202.

Thomas, J.R. (1998) 'Prominence within the university is essential; prominence within the academic field is nice', *Quest*, 50: 159–65.

Thorpe, R., Bunker, D. and Almond, L. (eds) (1986) *Rethinking Games Teaching*, Loughborough: Esmond.

Tinning, R. (1987) *Improving Teaching in Physical Education*, Geelong: Deakin University Press.

——(1988) 'Student teaching and the pedagogy of necessity', *Journal of Teaching in Physical Education*, 7: 82–89.

——(1992) 'Not so sweet dreams: physical education in the year 2001', *ACHPER National Journal*, 138: 24–26.

——(2000) 'Unsettling matters for physical education in higher education: implications of "new times"', *Quest*, 52: 32–48.

——(2001) 'The 2001 Senate inquiry: A non-preferred scenario for physical education', *ACHPER National Journal*, 48: 14–16.

——(2002) 'Towards a "modest" pedagogy: Reflections on the problematics of critical pedagogy', *Quest*, 54: 224–41.

Tinning, R. and Fitzclarence, L. (1992) 'Postmodern youth culture and the crisis in Australian secondary school physical education', Quest, 44: 287–303.

Tjeerdsma, B.L., Rink, J.E. and Graham, K.C. (1996) 'Student perceptions, values, and beliefs prior to, during, and after badminton instruction', *Journal of Teaching in Physical Education*, 15: 464–76.

Toffler, A. (1970) *Future Shock*, London: Pan.

Tousignant, M. and Siedentop, D. (1983) 'A qualitative analysis of task structures in required secondary physical education classes', *Journal of Teaching in Physical Education*, 2: 47–57.

Turner, A. (1996) 'Teachers' perceptions of technical and tactical models of instruction', *Research Quarterly for Exercise and Sport*, March Supplement, A–90.

Turner, A. and Martinek, T.J. (1992) 'A comparative analysis of two models for teaching games: Technique approach and game-centred (tactical focus) approach', *International Journal of Physical Education*, 29: 15–31.

Underwood, G.L. (1983) *The Physical Education Curriculum in the Secondary School: Planning and Implementation*, Lewes: Falmer.

Vertinsky, P. (1992) 'Reclaiming space, revisioning the body: The quest for gender-sensitive physical education', *Quest*, 44: 373–96.

Vincent-Moran, M. and Lafont, L. (2005) 'Learning-method choices and personal characteristics in solving a physical education problem', *Journal of Teaching in Physical Education*, 24: 226–42.

Wade, M.G. (1991) 'Further reactions to Newell: Unravelling the Larry and Darryl magical mystery tour', *Quest*, 43: 207–13.

Walkerdine, V. (1997) 'Redefining the subject in situated cognition theory', in D. Kirshner and J.A. Whitson (eds) *Situated Cognition: Social, Semiotic and Psychological Perspectives*, 57–70, New Jersey: Erlbaum.

Wallhead, T. and O'Sullivan, M. (2005) 'Sport Education: Physical education for the new millennium?', *Physical Education and Sport Pedagogy*, 10: 181–210.

Webb, I.M. (1999) *The Challenge of Change in Physical Education: Chelsea School 1989–1998*, London: Falmer.

White, J. (1973) *Towards a Compulsory Curriculum*, London: Routledge and Kegan Paul.

Whitehead, J. and Fox, K. (1983) 'Student-centred physical education', *Bulletin of Physical Education*, 19: 21–30.

Whitehead, N. and Hendry, L.B. (1976) *Teaching Physical Education in England*, London: Lepus.

Whitty, G. (1985) *Sociology and School Knowledge: Curriculum Theory, Research and Politics*, London: Routledge.

Williams, A. and Bedward, J. (2001) 'Gender, culture and the generation gap: Student and teacher perceptions of aspects of National Curriculum Physical Education', *Sport, Education and Society*, 6: 53–66.

Williams, E.A. (1985) 'Understanding constraints on innovation in physical education', *Journal of Curriculum Studies*, 17: 407–13.

Williams, E.A. and Bedward, J. (1999) *Games for the Girls: The Impact of Recent Policy on the Provision of Physical Education and Sporting Opportunities for Female Adolescents*, Winchester: Winchester King Alfred's College.

Willee, A.W. (1955) *Small Apparatus for Primary School Physical Education*, Melbourne: Melbourne University Press.

Wilmore, J.H. (1998) 'Building strong academic programs for our future', *Quest*, 50: 103–7.

Wilson, J. (2003) 'The concept of education revisited', *Journal of Philosophy of Education*, 37: 101–8.

Wolfenden Report (1960) *Sport and the Community*, London: Central Council for Physical Recreation.

Wright, J. (1997) 'The construction of gendered contexts in single-sex and co-educational physical education lessons', *Sport, Education and Society*, 2: 55–72.

Young, M.F.D. (ed.) (1971) *Knowledge and Control: New Directions for the Sociology of Education*, London: Collier-Macmillan.

Young, M.F.D. (1998) *The Curriculum of the Future: From the 'New Sociology of Education' to a Critical Theory of Learning*, London: Falmer.

Index